## Praise for FastSOA

"You might think you know what SOA is and how to build SOA-based systems, b
you the tools you need to do it right."

—Jim Melton, Jim Melton, Oracle Corp., Editor of the SQL standard, Co-chair of the W3C XML Query Working Group, Author of Querying XML

"In FastSOA Frank Cohen puts attention to actual performance and scalability issues caused by the unsuitable tools traditionally used to build SOA. He proposes using the right tools that are specifically designed for XML messaging - a core concept of SOA. FastSOA is an elegant architecture aimed to improve scalability, governance and performance of SOA by using native XML technologies like XQuery instead of objects and other common but unnatural data representations. FastSOA goes beyond architecture by answering common SOA performance issues and proposing tools to test and evaluate SOA system scalability and performance."

—William Martinez Pomares, Software Architect, Group Avantica

"If it is possible for a technical book to present an intimate side to one engineer's experiences getting SOA applications to deliver good performance, then this book is it."

—Ilya Sterin, Software Engineer at Nextrials, Author of XML and Perl

"FastSOA is a great book with lots of meat on the bones and practical real-world XML and SOA knowledge. Much of what passes for SOA right now is simply block diagrams and vague exhortations to get the architecture right. Frank Cohen gives a practical guide to what software developers, architects, and CIOs have to do to deliver highly scalable, well performing, and easy to maintain services."

—Jeff Barr, Amazon.com, Web Services Evangelist

"Anyone considering an SOA should definitely study Chapter 5. It not only shows how to construct the middle-tier FastSOA, it also backs up the impressive performance-improvement claims with data based on real-world tests."

—Douglas K. Barry, Barry & Associates, Inc., Author of Web Services and Service-Oriented Architectures: The Savvy Manager's Guide

"Frank Cohen is both a keen observer and a key participant as the software industry struggles to understand what the words 'Enterprise SOA' really mean. FastSOA is an excellent guide to the current technologies (and how to route around their pitfalls and shortcomings)."

—William Grosso, Software Development Forum, Board Member; Author of Java Enterprise Best Practices and Java RMI

"Current SOA implementations suffer from poor performance and scalability. Frank's book introduces FastSOA, a new and exciting approach which can eliminate these problems. A must read for anyone considering SOA."

—P. Simon Tuffs, D. Phil., Software Architect of OneJar and SOAPStone

# FastSOA

# FastSOA

Frank Cohen

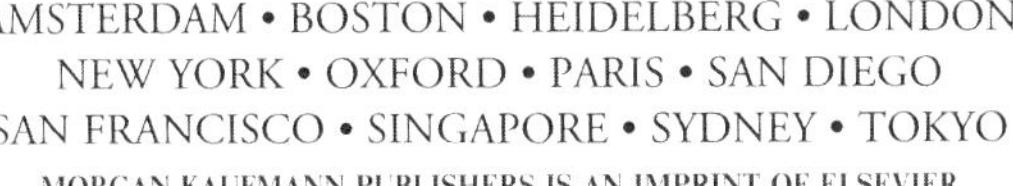

| | |
|---|---|
| *Publisher* | Diane Cerra |
| *Publishing Services Manager* | George Morrison |
| *Editorial Assistant* | Asma Palmeiro |
| *Cover Design* | Frank Cohen |
| *Composition* | Multiscience Press, Inc. |
| *Copyeditor* | Andrew Therriault |
| *Proofreader* | Katherine Antonsen |
| *Indexer* | Steve Rath |
| *Interior printer* | Maple-Vail Book Manufacturing Group |
| *Cover printer* | Phoenix Color |

Morgan Kaufmann Publishers is an imprint of Elsevier.
500 Sansome Street, Suite 400, San Francisco, CA 94111

∞ This book is printed on acid-free paper.



Library of Congress Cataloging-in-Publication Data
Application submitted

ISBN 13: 978-0-12-369513-0
ISBN 10: 0-12-369513-9

For information on all Morgan Kaufmann publications,
visit our Web site at www.mkp.com or www.books.elsevier.com

Printed in the United States of America
06 07 08 09 10 5 4 3 2 1

*Our lips draw close and I feel the spark of my love for you, darling Lorette.*

# Contents

# Introduction

## Where SOA Meets The Real World

For many enterprises, business, and institutions Service Oriented Architecture (SOA) is an excellent technology choice to rapidly deliver new business processes and improve IT efficiency. With the right tools, methodology, and skills SOA delivers reusable composite software applications to interact with your existing data sources. Choosing the wrong tools, choosing methodology that leaves you not being able to quantify success, and hiring people with missing skills makes it much more likely that your SOA will never achieve success.

This book goes beyond what passes for SOA today – simple block diagrams and vague exhortations – to get the architecture *right* by showing guidelines, detailed solutions and instruction to get an IT team to SOA success. This book teaches practical real-world experiences, methods, and tools to help you deliver excellent SOA performance, scalability, and reliability in a short period of time.

Software tools vendors often make a presumption that their tools are appropriate for building SOA. Sometimes that turns out not to be the case. For instance, many software developers ask me if their existing Java development tools, relational database, and application server can build well performing SOA? For very simple SOA designs the answer is "yes." In the real world where SOA environments use big, complex, and changing messages, protocols, and designs the answer is "no." This book shows how to detect scalability and performance problems in SOA and gives you the FastSOA architecture as a solution.

I coined the name FastSOA as an architectural design pattern to achieve good scalability and performance in SOA and XML environments. FastSOA uses new standards-based native XML database and XML Query (XQuery) technology to provide scalability and flexibility in SOA environments. Used in conjunction with the scalability and performance testing tools and methodology I present in this book you will be well equipped to achieve rapid development of SOA software code that performs well, is scalable, and is inexpensive to maintain.

Frank Cohen

2006

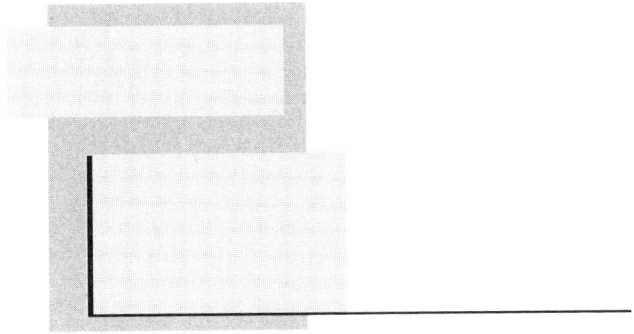

# Acknowledgments

I wrote this book from experiences at Raining Data, a software publishing company of the TigerLogic XML data management system (XDMS.) Raining Data reminds me of my time at Sun Microsystems in that the engineers, salespeople, administrators, and management are visionary, smart, energetic, and experienced professionals. This book is the culmination of many ideas, projects, and findings from Raining Data's efforts.

This book would not have been possible without my lovely wife, Lorette, who supported me on all those sleepless nights. My children, Jack and Madeline, missed many nights and weekends with me as I disappeared into the manuscript.

Many people provided their ideas, feedback, comments and suggestions to better this book. In particular I would like to highlight the following individuals for their contributions. Jeff Dexter for showing me what XQuery was really all about. Eric Soirot for helping me to understand the inside of a multi-dimensional, hierarchical database. Danny Hyun and Kelli Rotstan for their ideas on profiling performance problems. Robert Smik for being my first XQuery teacher. Premal Parikh, Murty Gurajada, Ash Parikh, and Ajay Ramachandran for their combined design effort on composite data services. Ilesh Garish, Steve Graves, Toni Guttman for their feedback. Carlton Baab, Robert Albo, John Bramley, Brian Cheek, Varun Gupta, Abi Kariguddaiah, Scott Lesko for their ideas, support, and encouragement.

William Martinez Pomares and Simon Tuffs made instrumental contributions in developing the test design and implementations covered in this book. They went down several rabbit holes trying to find problems and uncover alternatives, including understanding at the JAX-RPC level why encoded XML data was taking so long to process.

Darin MacBeath of Elsevier found the problems with SOAP RPC scalability that are highlighted in this book. To my knowledge Darin's designs for a next generation content publishing engine that uses SOAP as a means to publish APIs was the first SOAP-based Web Service in production.

For helping me deliver this book: Dianne Cerra (publisher), Asma Palmeiro (assistant editor), Alan Rose (production), Tim Donar (page composition.) The technical editors provided excellent feedback: Doug Barry, Jim Melton, Greg Wdowiak, Ronald Bourret, Simon Tuffs, William Martinez Pomarez, Sam Ramji, and Carl Ververs.

Thanks to Jason Hunter, Michael Kay, and Michael Dyck for helping me to understand native XML tools. Thanks go to Tim Bray, Jeff Barr, and Adam Bosworth for their efforts to evangelize *simple* to the software developer community.

Finally, thank you to you for your interest in this book. Buying this book helps put food on my families' table and keeps me going to improve my tools, techniques and methods. I appreciate your interest and hope the experience is rewarding for you personally and professionally.

## You are about to hear from me, I would like to hear from you.

Please write or email me at fcohen@rainingdata.com and tell me what you thought about this book, and about testing and building scalable SOA applications in general. Let me know your contact information (including email address) and I will keep you informed about my current and future work, new products and services, and new books and articles.

Also from Frank Cohen:

- Java Testing and Design: From Unit Tests To Automated Web Tests, Prentice Hall, 2004
- Java Web Services Unleashed, SAMS Publishing, 2002, Contributing Author
- Java P2P Unleashed, SAMS Publishing, 2002, Editor and Contributing Author

For a full listing of publications, articles and various ramblings point your browser to http://docs.pushtotest.com and http://www.xquerynow.com.

# Chapter 1

# The Problem with Service-Oriented Architecture

*Enterprises*, organizations, and institutions want their existing datacenters, their existing software developers, and their existing information systems operations managers to work cooperatively on composite applications. A composite application is stitched together by using many small and very well focused services to solve a business problem. Imagine the efficiency, low costs, and fast time-to-market speed if composite applications were a reality?

Business managers love the idea of Service-Oriented Architecture (SOA). They widely believe SOA will get them to composite applications immediately. By 2006, many businesses quickly and widely adopted SOA as their strategy for building new information systems.

Enterprises, organizations, and institutions adopted SOA even though there is no standards body, such as the World Wide Web Consortium (W3C), OASIS, or others, to formalize SOA into a recommended specification. SOA has no core group of thought-leaders to tell software architects, developers, and operations managers the best practices to build functional, scalable, and maintainable SOA.

Instead, in the world of SOA, you find people like me. I am a practitioner. Businesses and institutions hire me to apply my deep technical knowledge and software testing experience to learn the scalability and performance profile of their information systems. In 2001, I began to look deeply into the impact Extensible Markup

Language (XML) was having on scalability and performance. At first I looked at distributed systems that used XML to make remote procedure calls. Then I looked at SOAP-based Web Services. These experiences led me to look at SOA scalability and performance built using application server, enterprise service bus (ESB), and business integration (BI) tools. Across all of these technologies I found a consistent theme:

```
At the intersection of XML and SOA are significant scalability
and performance problems that are found using my test
methodology and solved by using native XML technology,
including XQuery and native XML databases.
```

The scalability and performance problems in XML-based SOA designs are significant enough that I've seen entire projects canceled because of them. For instance, when General Motors asked me to write their Web Services Performance Benchmark, I found that a modern and expensive multiprocessor server that could easily serve 80 Web pages per second could only serve 1.5 to 2 XML transactions per second. Scalability and performance indexes like that shown in Figure 1-1 can kill a project.

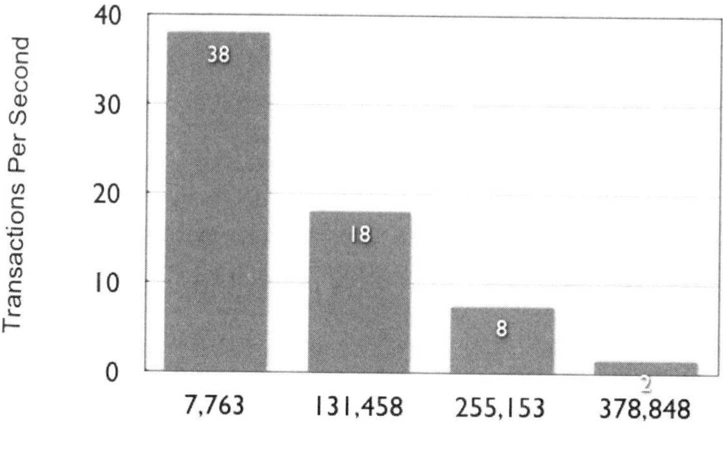


***Figure 1-1*** *As the XML message size and complexity grow the throughput, measured in transactions per second (TPS) at the service consumer, reveals a scalability and performance problem.*

I followed a path most Java developers will take. I fell in love with XML. I investigated the impact on performance and scalability that my choice of XML parsers, SOAP binding proxy generators, XML encoding styles, object-relational XML mapping techniques, databases, and architectures had on the resulting services. I found a solution to the SOA problem through the use of native XML technology.

I coined the name FastSOA for an architectural design pattern created to achieve the following goals:

1. Good scalability and performance in SOA and XML environments
2. Rapid development of software code
3. Flexible and easy maintenance of software code as the environments and needs change

The FastSOA architecture and software development patterns I present in this book are a way to mitigate and solve XML scalability and performance problems in your environment.

To understand FastSOA, I begin by explaining my view of the driving forces behind the rapid adoption of SOA in the business, software development, and software tools communities. I demonstrate the benefits of adopting SOA. I show the building blocks of SOA and the pitfalls of using existing tools and technology to implement SOA applications. I end this chapter with an introduction to the FastSOA architecture and patterns you may use in your own environment.

## 1.1 What Drives a Business to SOA?

In the late 1990s, Sun Microsystems was well along the way to adopting Web-based e-commerce technology for Sun's internal and customer-facing information systems. Sun wanted to get new distributions of Java, Solaris, and other software titles to customers quickly. Slow Internet connections were still prevalent and 100-megabyte downloads were not practical to customers. Compact disc (CD) distribution through the mail cost Sun a fortune in fulfillment costs. Sun's financial managers asked customers to pay $10 to $20 to receive a CD in the mail. This required Sun to take orders through an on-line store, process credit card payments, and integrate with manufacturing systems to fulfill the CD orders.

One of the Information Technology (IT) engineers at Sun wrote a credit card processing service for the CD fulfillment on-line store. The service uses HTTP transport protocols and an XML encoded form to process a credit card charge. The engineer later changed jobs and began working in the Java group. He wrote an application that let users order a subscription to a service to receive quarterly update CDs in the mail. The subscription service took a credit card as payment. The engineer coded the new application to use the on-line store credit card processing service from his old group.

A few years went by. The engineer moved on to another job with another company. Internet connection speeds improved and Sun decided to stop offering the CD fulfillment service. Sun took down the fulfillment service and the credit card processing service. Consequently, the Java subscription service stopped taking orders. From this experience it was apparent to many people that Sun had problems:

- No manager could tell you which services depended on other services. There was no map to show the choreography and interdependencies of services.
- No manager, software developer, or operations executive could forecast his or her computer hardware and network bandwidth needs to serve a given population of users at a defined quality of service.
- No software division could answer the question, "Who will answer the phone when the service stops working?" There was no governance plan for the services.
- No division's financial manager could tell Sun's executive management how to forecast the costs of engineering a new service.
- No engineering manager could determine the skills needed by a software developer to maintain an existing service. Each change to the system—no matter how minute—required a developer to go back into the code.
- Sun could not determine if a newly planned service already existed.

Sound familiar? IT managers contend with these problems every day. In my experience helping software architects, developers, and IT managers, I found that these issues are universally suffered at General Motors, the U.S. Navy, Lockheed Martin, BEA Systems, the

European Union, and others. These are the issues that SOA is meant to solve.

Sun experienced these issues while deploying a customer-facing e-commerce system. Indeed, most businesses, institution, and organizations face the same issues when delivering supply-side vendor integration, customer service and support systems, financial analysis services for management, manufacturing and operations controls, market and customer trend analysis functions, and communication (email newsletter, phone, email, and Web) services. Take your pick. The issues are the same. The developers and architects who build these systems, the operations managers who run them, and the CIOs who manage their maintenance over time of these systems are looking for something in common. They all need methodology, procedures, and software to accomplish enterprise system integration projects.

By the early 2000s, IT groups tried to use Enterprise Application Integration (EAI) and Extract, Transform, and Load (ETL) tools and techniques to reduce integration and development costs and shorten the time it takes to build applications. These tools provide data synchronization between a system of record and a system to which you are copying the data. Applications communicate through the system of record whenever they need data.

EAI works well for very large enterprises, where economies of scale come into play for thousands of applications. Many enterprises, institutions, and organizations, however, find that EAI requires cooperation among the departments and organizations within the enterprise and that this cooperation is usually not present unless a strong central leader emerges to mandate EAI use. The tightly controlled, top-down approach works well in only a few organizations in the world.

While many consider the EAI approach to be dead, it is still useful in many environments. Managers propose systems integration projects today instead of EAI projects, even though they may use EAI tools in the project. With an open mind to EAI alternatives, many managers began to consider SOA to be a good choice for system integration efforts.

SOA emerged as a popular architectural choice with CIOs, software developers, and software architects because SOA works well in environments lacking centralized control and planning. The general feedback I get from the software development community is that SOA is reminiscent of the early days of the Web. Enthusiasm abounds and experimentation is frequent. Many developers are learning what works in an SOA environment as they share their knowledge in on-line communities, sharing example code, and participating in open-source projects. Figure 1-2 shows the convergence of excitement, experiments, and protocols around SOA.

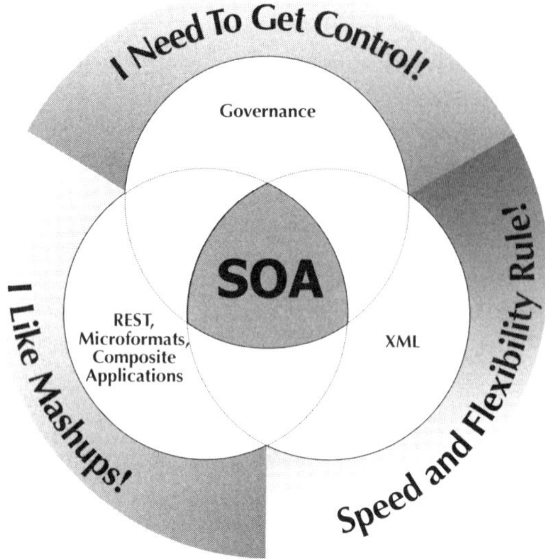


*Figure 1-2 SOA allows software developers, architects, and IT executives to come together to deliver the next generation of software applications.*

CIOs, software architects, and developers have individual needs and goals for building the next generation of software applications. They also have a lot of excitement. Consider the following.

### 1.1.1 Software Developers Like Mashups

Mashups are integrations of data available on the Web. For instance, I wrote an application that integrates a map-generating service with a donut shop locator service. Never again will I be far from a donut as I travel on business.

Mashups are possible because many services on the Web support important connectivity and data encoding techniques. For instance, the Representational State Transfer (REST) lets me use HTTP protocols with XML data to make complex requests to Web services and receive the response in XML format that is easily parsed by my application. Additionally, a body of emerging standards known as microformats[1] embed XML data tags into Web page content, making the Web even more of a data source for my mashups. For instance, a calendar microformat enables Web page authors to embed special tags around dates that appear on a Web page for a conference schedule that I may easily use from within an application. While my mashup application delivers dubious business value, it taught me the skills needed to build composite applications.

Composite applications are the end-products of SOA. They deliver the business value a company derives from its SOA. Whether the composite application is designed for internal teams, customers, partners, or vendors, a composite application represents how organizations map business needs and processes to underlying information assets using SOA. Figure 1-3 illustrates a business that uses composite applications in an SOA environment to deliver business process automation.

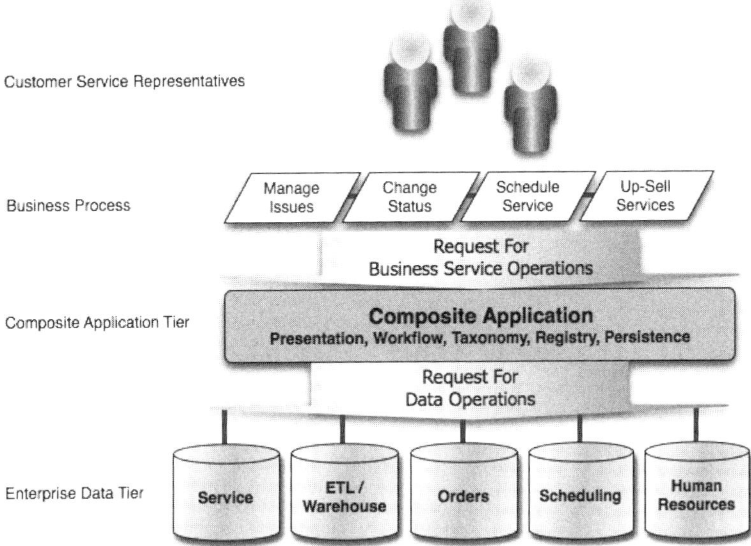


***Figure 1-3*** *Composite applications deliver the business processes users must follow while interoperating with the underlying data tier, without requiring changes in data tier.*

Composite applications create value by delivering new views, transformations, and persistent queriable stores of data connected through a business process workflow to a presentation interface

1 http://www.microformats.org.

such as a Web browser or service interface. For instance, in Figure 1-3, a business operates a customer service desk to implement a set of business processes. When a customer calls the help desk, a representative manages the customer issues and updates the customer status. If the customer issue requires a technician to visit the customer's premises, the representative schedules a service call. Finally, the representative offers new products and services based on the customer's current subscriptions. The application to implement this business process must interoperate with several independent systems and develop a common view of the customer's data for the representative. Composite application techniques are well suited for this scenario for three reasons.

First, a composite application does not require any of the enterprise data tier providers to make changes to their databases. In an EAI or ETL approach, the applications would copy and synchronize data with the system of record. Composite applications get only the data they need at the time the user operates the composite application. The composite application uses the transaction capabilities of the databases to commit or rollback changes.

Second, once a composite application exists, it may be treated as a database itself. The component approach makes enterprises and organizations more nimble and easier to build, orchestrate, and assemble new business processes and their corresponding composite application.

Finally, as organizations respond to change, the composite applications deliver a way to store and reuse all data, including the metadata about the database and application itself. Composite applications enforce a Web service reuse policy to facilitate rapid response to change.

SOA answers software developer excitement over mashups and consequently a business or organization's need for agility through composite applications. Next, I look at software architects and SOA.

### 1.1.2 Architects Need a Flexible and Fast Data Model

Software architects are in a difficult situation when building applications. They know they can greatly improve business productivity and save their organization time and effort to build and maintain systems by making good decisions on the tools, techniques, and approaches they use to build the system. Yet innovation moves so rapidly that they are seldom able to accurately predict the future to ensure that their decisions today will not prevent the business from missing a business goal in the future because the IT architecture lacks the needed flexibility.

In my experience working with software architects, their first composite application experience leads them to a reevaluation of the roll of data in their designs. Composite applications work with data from multiple data sources and in multiple data formats and schemas. Software architects need to find tools and technology that makes working with data easy and fast. XML attracts them.

XML is more than a data markup language; XML is a data model. Think of an XML document as a linear phrasing of a tree structure. At every node in the tree there is a set of data. The tree structure and the data sets together form the information content of an XML document. Almost everything will follow naturally from that. For instance, native XML databases add queriable collections of XML documents and a database of collections to the data model using the XML query language (XQuery.)

In my opinion, the XML data model makes it easier to represent real-world things than the relational data model. Hierarchies of data come in nature and in a business or organization's need to model data. Additionally, native XML databases store collections of XML documents, where the schema of one stored document may be different from the next stored document. In the real world, where software architects work with multiple departments, customers, vendors, and partners, the XML data model provides flexibility in the way you store data that often protects you from going back into the software code to make a change to a system.

### 1.1.3 CIOs Need Control

CIOs are in a difficult position too. CIOs are often unable to control the software used in their data centers, yet they are judged by the performance of this software. For instance, a survey of CIOs attending the Gartner Application Integration conference in 2006 revealed that a third of the conference attendee survey respondents already had AJAX in their production environments. New technology like AJAX seeps into datacenters.

SOA benefits CIOs by enabling faster delivery of business processes and reduced software maintenance costs over time. SOA facilitates CIO measurement of SOA value to a business as a function of up-time, cost to implement, cost to maintain, number of users, user satisfaction, and the hardware and network connectivity costs to operate. Taken together, these measurements of SOA value cause a CIO to make a judgment on the real business need to create and operate each service. For instance, in the light of SOA governance, the CIO considers the following options:

- The proposed new service may be redundant with an existing service.
- It may be that the business can live without the service for the time being.
- It may be better to buy an existing service than to build the service.
- It may be better to outsource development of the service.
- It may be too difficult to operate the service to achieve a sufficient level of user satisfaction.
- The service may not fit the business mission, or, worse, the service may be a distraction from achieving the mission goals.

Now that you understand the motivations and needs of software developers, architects, and CIOs, we will look at SOA from the enterprise perspective.

## 1.2 SOA Benefits in an Enterprise

The reason we love SOA is the promise of less integration effort and cost, greater efficiency of our development efforts, easier software maintenance, and better performance. In this section, I describe the topmost desired enterprise benefits of an SOA approach from my experiences working with enterprises on the road to SOA.

### 1.2.1 Make Existing Data More Useful

SOA takes a new approach to the role of data within an organization. SOA prefers data linking over data import. SOA assumes your organization already has applications that present data in a transactionally aware way. Many software architects and CIOs I work with have an attitude against data silos. SOA is much more loose. SOA

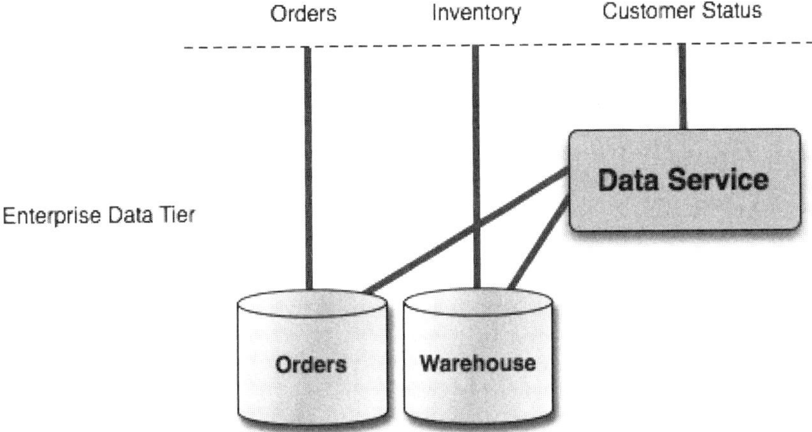


***Figure 1-4*** *Rather than extract the data, the SOA approach creates data services to link existing data in new and valuable composites.*

says, "What is wrong with silos if I can build a data service that can get to the data in each of the silos?"

SOA uses data federation to create new business value from existing data. For instance, in Figure 1-4, a business implements a data service to provide a single view of customer status by federating data from an orders database and the warehouse. The federated view becomes a single URL providing the new view of the data from two existing databases.

### 1.2.2 Software Maintenance Gets Easier

As the business faces changes—for example, when new partners, new customers, and new suppliers come on-board—then writing new composite applications and data services becomes a way for the business to respond quickly and with less effort. Figure 1-5 illustrates a business or organization that employs a data service when a composite application needs data that is not directly available from any of the enterprise data sources.

Each data service is highly focused to solve a business need. This makes it easier for the average software developer to understand the context of the data service and composite application, to make needed changes to the existing code, and to test the code for functional completeness.

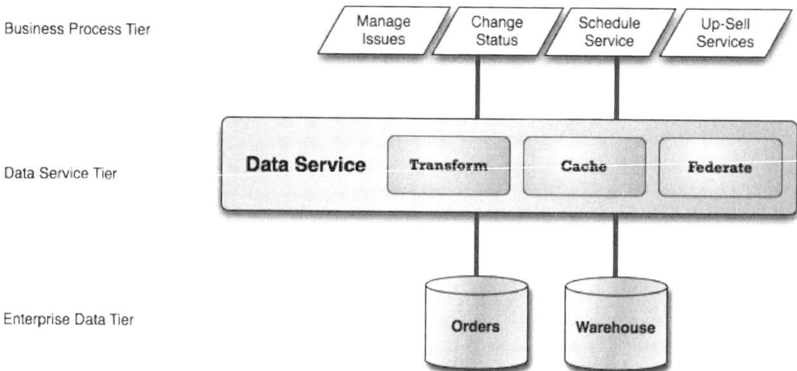


***Figure 1-5*** *Composite applications use data services for a flexible way to bridge an existing enterprise data store to what the business process needs.*

### 1.2.3 SOA Enables a Service Marketplace

The speed at which an enterprise and organization may respond to change is enhanced by the emergence of a service marketplace. Many times it is more appropriate to find an existing service that may be integrated into a composite application or data service from a service provider. This has given rise to service marketplaces from businesses such as Strike Iron, SalesForce.com, and others. These marketplaces have an advantage in that they make administration of contracts to service providers more streamlined and uniform, provide a registry to locate needed services, and help users share problems and solutions using the services.

Next, we will discuss the building blocks to create SOA.

### 1.2.4 SOA Building Blocks

Books on SOA appear to have slightly different definitions of SOA. Carl Ververs of ThoughtWorks defines SOA as follows:

> A service-oriented architecture (SOA) is the organizational and technical framework that enables an enterprise to deliver self-describing, platform-independent business functionality and make it available as building blocks of current and future applications.[2]

2 Read Carl Ververs' blog at http://carlaugustsimon.blogspot.com.

Experience with these systems makes Carl's definition ring true to me, because it does not include the words Java, .NET, Web Services, integration, warehouse, and a hundred other technology-specific words. Instead, Carl's definition focuses on how SOA delivers value to a business. SOA delivers value by making a business more rapid, agile, and less expensive.

SOA may remind you of other distributed system architectures, including Web Services. It took me a while to understand the difference between SOA and other architectures.

### 1.2.5 Contrasting SOA with Web Services

SOA is a component approach to building integrated systems. The Web Services vision is an architecture of discoverable, loosely coupled, finely grained software components that are accessible as always-on services.[3] SOA keeps the Web Service component idea, focuses on a composite application approach to business workflows, loses the discoverable service concept in exchange for more statically defined brokered service endpoints, and relies on a governance model that determines service choreography, business issues, troubleshooting, and quality of service levels. Table 1-1 may help you understand the differences between SOA and Web Services.

***Table 1-1*** *Contrasting Web Services with SOA*

| | SOA | Web Services |
|---|---|---|
| What is the nature of the architecture? | SOA automates business processes by building composite applications that use a set of data services. | Web Services use finely grained, loosely coupled, automatically discoverable services federated into a composite application. |
| How do I find a service? | Use a registry or repository, but more commonly a service consumer connects to a known endpoint (URL). | Use a UDDI registry at run-time. |
| What protocol do I use to access the service? | SOA gives a variety of options, including SOAP, Java Message Service (JMS), AJAX, REST, SMTP, FTP, CICS, and others. | SOAP |

3 Read http://www.pushtotest.com/Library for an explanation of the Web Service buzz-words.

***Table 1-1*** *Contrasting Web Services with SOA (continued)*

| | **SOA** | **Web Services** |
|---|---|---|
| How do I learn the service interface? | WSDL or anything else that works, including in the case of REST a Web page that describes the interface in an HTML/text Web page formatted document. | WSDL |
| Who manages and maintains the service? | Determined by a governance plan for the service. | If a service goes down, then the service consumer's dynamic discovery finds another service automatically. |
| Which language /platform must I use to build the service? | SOA uses service interfaces that are platform and language independent. | Web Services interfaces that are platform and language independent. |
| Who controls the standard? | SOA is not a standard, it is an IT industry theme. | The World Wide Web (W3C) Consortium manages the SOAP and WSDL standards. OASIS manages UDDI. |
| Which format must I use for messages? | Whatever works best for your application. However, most SOA applications I have seen use XML. | XML messages following the SOAP standard. |

### 1.2.6 Workflow and Documents for SOA Scalability

SOA implements business processes in composite applications using data it gets from one or more data sources. Understanding the best practices to implement composite applications and data services is key to building scalable and well-performing software.

Consider a business that runs a parts ordering center. Each new order requires a purchase order (PO) that has a unique PO number, the correct local tax code, and a manager's approval. Figure 1-6 shows the typical remote procedure call (RPC) approach to building the parts ordering application.

The RPC architecture in Figure 1-6 creates an application named Parts Order Center (POC). Within the POC code is the business process ("workflow") code that every PO needs to contact the Allocate New PO Number service to get a new and unique PO number, then contact the Apply Local Tax Code service to look up the tax

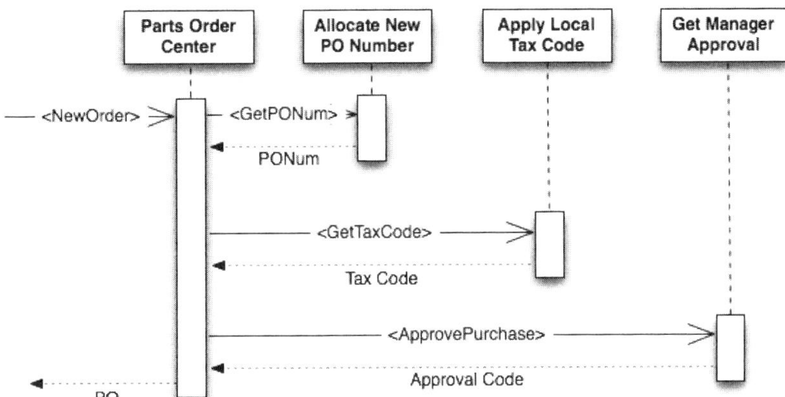


***Figure 1-6*** *A sequence diagram showing the Parts Order Center service using a remote procedure call (RPC) architecture. The service takes a request for a new order and returns a completed and approved purchase order (PO).*

code for the purchaser, and finally to contact the Get Manager Approval service to receive approval on the PO.

The above architecture stuffs all of the business logic of the POC into one big package and that package makes RPC requests to the supporting services. For instance, the Allocate New PO number service does not handle the actual PO. It simply receives a request and returns a new and unique PO number. Only when the POC needs to send the actual PO does it do so. For instance, the Get Manager Approval service requires the POC to send the completed PO as input to the service. Otherwise, the PO exists solely as an object in the POC.

This architecture requires the POC to know the sequence of events in the workflow. For instance, the Get Manager Approval service rejects any requests that do not have a valid PO number. Unfortunately, this means the software developer coding the POC needs to know how to implement workflow code to make requests to the services in the correct order. The software developer also needs to handle errors during the processing of the PO. For instance, what happens to the PO number when the manager rejects the order?

Last, consider that software developers need to recreate all this workflow and exception handling code each time the business needs a new service like the POC. That's a lot of work!

Now, let's consider the same POC built using SOA. Figure 1-7 illustrates this new architecture.

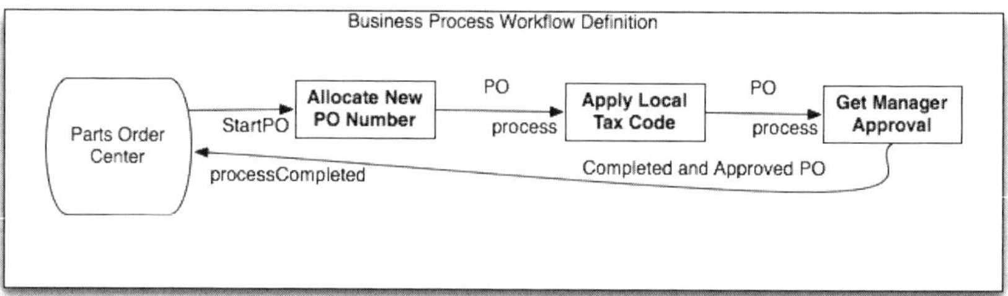


***Figure 1-7*** *The SOA approach to building the Parts Order Center implements a business process workflow to move a Purchase Order (PO) document through the correct order of services for completion and approval.*

The Purchase Order Center is a business process that creates a purchase order (PO), assigns the local tax code to the PO, and gets a manager's approval of the PO. The SOA approach defines the workflow from process to process, the document format for the PO that is exchanged, and the service interface for each process.

The following list shows today's popular ways to implement the SOA service:

- **Objects**—implement all of the services as objects in an object-oriented programming platform. The workflow starts with a call to the StartPO method of the AllocateNewPONumber class. This class initiates a new purchase order (PO) object and makes a call to the process method of the ApplyLocalTaxCode class. This calls modifies the PO object and makes a call to the process method of the GetManagerApproval class. Finally, this class calls the processComplete method of the Parts Order Center class.
- **Multiple Services + Remote Service Interfaces**—define the purchase order (PO) schema, define the service interface for each service, and implement the services on multiple systems. Each service calls the next service in the workflow and exchanges the PO document. The services move the PO document over a network through a set of service interfaces. This allows the services to be created on platforms and languages that are appropriate to each service, including services provided by a partner company and a service provider.
- **Workflow Container + Service Description**—define the purchase order schema, define the workflow in the work-

flow container's description language, write the code to implement each of the services, and let the container run the workflow. This approach reduces the amount of code you need to write since the container handles the choreography of one service calling the next service, exceptions, and rollbacks when the service needs to abort an operation. Workflow containers normally use XML too. The downside is that you need to learn the business process workflow definition language (BPWD) of the container and how to configure the workflow container environment.

The SOA approach has some interesting and beneficial aspects. Consider the following:

- Each service only needs to know about its function on the document it receives. The workflow container knows the order in which to call the next service in the workflow process. The workflow container coordinates the state and transfer of the document between the services in a scalable architecture. When put into a production environment, workflow containers scale up to dynamically routing flows between a group of servers—in a server, cluster of servers, or group of datacenters—that are able to operate the needed function.
- Like Web Services, the SOA architecture uses individual services that are expert at their own area of function. For instance, the Apply Local Tax Code service might come from a tax accounting business that offers the service. Why try to be a tax accounting business yourself? There is always someone else with more expertise who will offer your business his or her expertise through a service.
- The SOA approach makes it easy to create federations of services among disparate and loosely connected organizations while allowing each organization to maintain the autonomy of how it builds and designs services and their ownership.
- Each service used is responsible for its own data. SOA avoids the need to synchronize data between applications. The document follows an accepted definition and carries the needed data.

- Although there is no SOA standards body to develop and maintain an SOA standard, most SOA applications I have worked with use XML to exchange messages. XML is widely understood and used in the software development community that makes SOA a very interoperability-friendly choice of architectures.

I am a fan of the SOA approach because it enables building scalable and well-performing document-oriented workflows and service components under the management of a governance model that determines service choreography, business issues, troubleshooting, and quality of service levels. Before we go further into SOA, let's take a closer look at workflow containers.

### 1.2.7 The Problem with Workflow Containers

Workflow containers are analogous to application servers. Instead of running servlets, a workflow container runs business processes. The workflow container knows the order in which to call a set of services and the document that needs to be passed from service to service from a workflow description document.

While enterprises, institutions, and organizations were rallying toward SOA through the standards bodies,[4] the platform vendors (Sun, Microsoft, BEA, Oracle, and IBM) were heading away from each other on an agreement for a standard workflow container. While these groups and platform providers could come to agreement on SOAP and WSDL standards for message interfaces, they have not come to agreement on a standard way to express workflows.

At the time I wrote this book, the workflow container universe had fractured into these technologies and standards initiatives:

- Sun promotes its Java Business Integration (JBI) standard for Java developers. JBI provides a workflow description language, service components, and a Web Services-oriented construction set. Details can be found at http://java.sun.com.

4 For example, Java Community Process (JCP, http://www.jcp.org), the World Wide Web Consortium (W3C, http://www.w3c.org), the OASIS Group (OASIS, http://www.oasis-open.org), and the Liberty Alliance (Liberty, http://www.projectliberty.org).

- JBoss developed the JBoss Process Management (jBPM) system to deliver a Business Process Execution Language (BPEL)–like solution that adds a graphical workflow editor, Java programming interfaces, and a task manager to handle process wait-states. Details can be found at http://jbpm.org.
- Web Service Business Process Execution Language (WSBPEL, http://www.oasis-open.org) is a standard from OASIS that benefits businesses needing to implement workflow solutions by defining the syntax, context, and steps needed to build workflow solutions using Web Services.[5]

The above list is a very small taste of the many efforts to deliver a workflow container to software architects and developers. I have no good news to write about these efforts. For instance, while WSBPEL appears to be a periodically well-supported standard, it does little to address message mediation functionalities such as transformation, validation, and reliability. Chapters 4 and 5 will show the advantages of message mediation in the form of SOA service acceleration.

Eventually, one of the workflow container efforts will reach a stage of maturity where a large number of software architects and developers get behind it. The average developer needs a workflow container technology that includes the following:

- A task manager for long-running flows
- Clean Java integration, including easy application programming interfaces (APIs) with support for plain old Java objects (pojos) and Enterprise Java Beans
- A timer service for periodic workflows
- A message service
- A service provider interface (SPI) to any database and application server
- Easy deployment as a stand-alone application, Web application (WAR), or Enterprise Application Resource (EAR) file in an application server

5 A concise view of WSBPEL is found at http://www.javaworld.com/javaworld/jw-10-2005/jw-1031-webservices.html.

Additionally, a visually oriented programming environment to develop workflows helps developer productivity but is not required functionality. Chapter 8 describes these facets of a workflow container in much more depth and shows an XML approach to implementing a workflow container.

## 1.3 SOA Service Mediation

A major theme throughout this book is the need for you to adopt service mediation and aggregation patterns in your SOA designs. The possibilities for performance and scalability are huge. Service mediation also provides tremendous flexibility advantages. Chapters 4 and 5 show the FastSOA data binding patterns for SOA service acceleration and the mid-tier data transformation pattern. I will give a preview of these now.

### 1.3.1 Intermediaries and Transformation

Service interfaces are well known and understood in SOA designs. This makes it easier in SOA designs to write service intermediaries. A service intermediary is a proxy that adds value through caching, routing, transformation services in the context of the request, and response messages exchanged between the service and consumer.

For instance, SOA designs often overlook the potential for mid-tier service caching to accelerate SOA performance. Consider that most XML schemas in SOA designs define a time-to-live value for a response. Caching a service response and replaying the cached response the next time the service receives the same request is a valid and appropriate way to accelerate SOA service performance. Chapter 4 shows how to accomplish service acceleration through mid-tier caching. Figure 1-8 illustrates a service intermediary.

Service intermediation provides many benefits to an SOA design, including:

- Service acceleration through caching. Document schemas normally include a time-to-live value that can be used by a service intermediary to provide SOA caching.
- Off-line browsing of service data. Consumers may browse the most recent documents stored in the SOA mid-tier even if the service is not available.

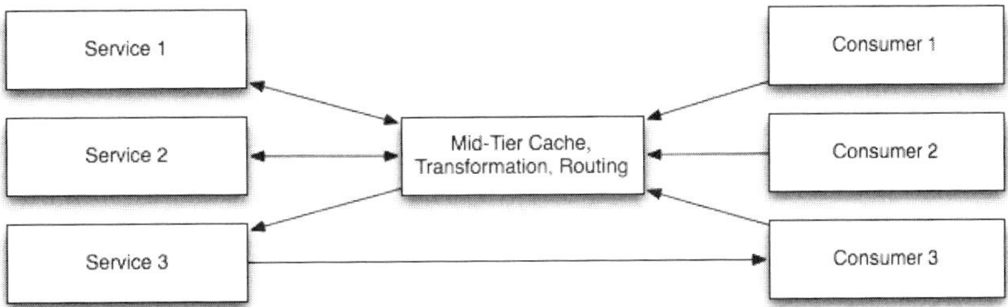


***Figure 1-8*** *Example of an intermediary providing mid-tier service acceleration through caching and data transformation to resolve incompatible document schema type, and intelligent routing of requests from a consumer to the appropriate service.*

- Reduced network bandwidth. Mid-tier data caching reduces the network bandwidth needed to service each and every round-trip request between consumer and service.
- Intelligent service discovery and routing. A service intermediary that understands the context of a request or response makes intelligent service routing decisions on the fly.
- Flexibility to handle multiple and often incompatible document schema types. A service intermediary that understands two incompatible document schema types transforms a response to the needed schema that the consumer understands in the mid-tier of a service request.
- Logging and analyzing message flows. Service intermediaries track message flows between consumers and services to understand and manage the service infrastructure. Additionally, a service intermediary provides a map of service and consumer interdependencies to help choreograph new services.
- Value-added functions without waiting in the IT development line. Service intermediaries understand the context of a message and can add their own value-added function to the request. This is useful when changes to a service will not happen within your schedule because IT is otherwise occupied with other projects.
- Security policy implementation. Service intermediaries implement security policies based on message exchanges between consumers and services. For instance, a service intermediary unobtrusively warns a network manager

when a consumer requests secure administrative directory documents.

This book shows you the patterns, designs, and techniques to implement service mediation in your SOA.

### 1.3.2 Aggregators, Orchestration, and Federation

Service aggregators provide federated service requests. The aggregator builds a composite document based on the responses from one or more services. The aggregator has a full programming environment available to build the composite response document, and several operations are possible. For instance, an aggregator that periodically makes the same request to a service provides a consumer with a history of the service's responses and shows trends underway. In another instance, an aggregator retrieves currency exchange responses from three services and assembles a composite document showing the differences in currency values. Figure 1-9 illustrates an aggregator pattern.

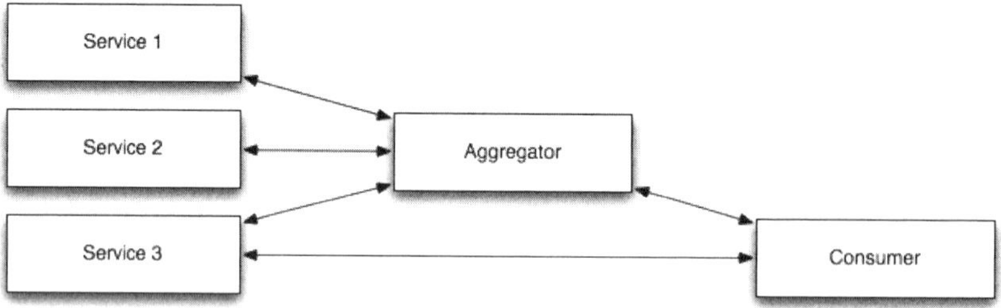


***Figure 1-9*** *Service aggregators combine documents received from multiple services to the consumer.*

Aggregators are useful in workflow designs because they make it easy to deliver reusable workflow code that implements a business process. The services remain more general and less application specific.

### 1.3.3 Security

SOA creates an entirely new set of security concerns, issues, and problems. Security controls and protection in Web and Web Services designs protects the resources of a defined endpoint from delivering data to a person who lacks sufficient credentials. Typically, businesses and institutions setup firewalls and use perimeter security protocols such as SSL to defend secure data.

Most SOA implementations I have seen are designed around an assertive security policy. A business often provides access to its SOA applications to business partners and other organizations. In an assertive security policy a request includes the consumer's security credential in the header of the request. The service (or any intermediary along the way) needs to accept the assertion that the request is from a valid consumer.

SOA security patterns and designs require resources managed in the SOA to be controlled as services, records, documents, and elements. SOA security is really about managing identity so that a business defines access control policies to manage the contents of the business architecture. Most of the SOA designs I have seen spend an inordinate amount of time getting SOA security policies coded, since the service resources are always changing and the business security policies change frequently too.

In this section, we covered service mediation and aggregation patterns in SOA designs. Next, we will discuss the role of data in SOA.

## 1.4 Can I Build SOA with My Existing Tools?

In the rush to achieve the benefits of SOA, business and organizations began bumping into the limitations of today's SOA development tools. Simply put:

```
Add XML to SOA and you get terrible performance.
```

The problem with SOA scalability and performance originates in XML's flexibility and data model. Most modern object-oriented platforms—for instance, Java and .NET—reached popular adoption in the software development community prior to XML's popular adoption. For instance, only now are efforts underway in the Java and .NET communities to incorporate XML as a native entity. At the 2006 JavaOne conference,[6] Mark Reinhold, chief engineer for Java SE at Sun Microsystems, presented his early thoughts on adding native XML support to Java. Separately, but more or less at the same time, Dr. Erik Meijer, architect in the SQL Server group at Microsoft, was working on the XML Language Integrated Query (Xlinq)[7] project to

6 Sun Microsystem's once-a-year conference for Java developers, architects, and tools vendors.

7 http://msdn.microsoft.com/VBasic/Future/XLinq%20Overview.doc.

add a common set of .NET definitions and methods for working with XML data. As a software developer, architect, or CIO, you should expect that XML is not yet well baked into these platforms.

The Domain Model[8] is a popular pattern to build Web applications and is being used by many developers to build SOA composite applications and data services. Figure 1-10 shows the Domain Model pattern architecture.

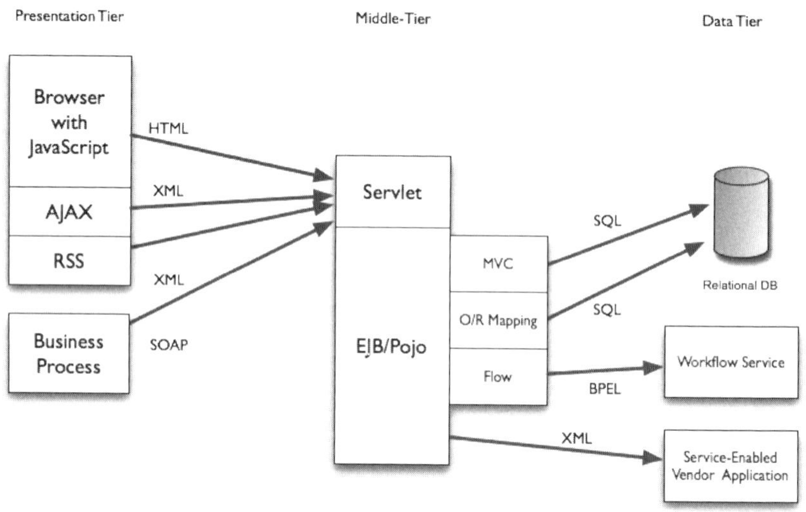


***Figure 1-10*** *The Domain Model pattern is a popular architecture in the Java community. It uses an application server and relational database.*

In the Domain Model, a Web browser makes a request to an application server hosting a set of objects that will query the database and respond to the user. Users operate a browser to submit requests and a servlet dispatches the request to an Enterprise Java Bean (EJB) or plain old Java object (pojo). The Bean or object parses the HTML form data or the content of the URL to understand the context of the request. A Model/View/Controller framework such as Tapestry or Struts helps the developer by separating business logic from presentation objects. The MVC controller objects use an object-relational mapping technology such as Hibernate or Spring to store and query needed data in a relational database. This architecture works well to

8 Chris Richardson explains the Domain Model pattern in his book *POJOs in Action.*

serve Web page requests, because the pattern is stable, well known, and scalable through a variety of techniques.

The Domain Model pattern is ready to implement SOA composite applications and data sources too. Figure 1-10 also shows a composite application servicing the needs of a business process by making a SOAP request to the middle-tier application server. The request contains XML content conforming to a schema that the SOAP service is willing to handle. The request goes through the same servlet-based interface. The servlet transforms the XML into an object and calls the EJB or object passing in the request data. The EJB or object uses an XML parser to understand the context of the request. MVC controller objects persist those request objects in a relational database through the object-relational mapping library.

The performance and scalability tests I conducted over the past five years show that the Web applications built with the Domain Model pattern deliver equivalent performance and scalability to XML-based applications when the following criteria are met:

- The XML content always uses the same message schema.
- The XML content follows a simple message schedule. Simple messages have five or less orders of hierarchy.
- The XML content is small. Small messages are less than 5 kilobytes long.

When the above criteria are met, you may expect your existing software development tools and operating environment to deliver performance and scalability commensurate with the message sizes and concurrent requests served in a Web application. However, XML's nature brings three issues that have an impact on SOA scalability and performance. In the following sections we will look at these issues. Chapters 3 and 4 cover this in more detail and present solutions.

### 1.4.1 There Is No Gatekeeper for XML Schemas

IT organizations are facing an explosion of XML data and schemas as a result of three trends. XML thought-leaders such as Tim Bray, Adam Bosworth, and Jeff Barr encourage software developers to create their own XML message schemas whenever existing message schema are not a close match. Second, industry associations and organizations are authoring, experimenting with, and investigating

XML schemas to embody business processes and workflow. For instance, the automotive industry organized an XML standard for common transactions between an auto dealership and a parts manufacturer. Finally, many of the existing schemas are upgraded and changed over time. Datacenters need to handle the explosion of XML data and schemas, the emergence of new schemas, and the schema evolution.

Experience shows a significant difference in developer productivity when using existing object-oriented tools and relational database technology over native XML technology. Application development tools that specialize in the Domain Model pattern deliver code-generating and deployment utility software to make it easy to go from an XML message schema or WSDL document to deployable code. The problem with SOA and these utilities is the one-way nature of the utilities. When a composite application or data service needs to interoperate with a new or updated XML schema, the utilities require a regeneration of the code. Regeneration often means that any customization to the previous generated code is lost.

Even with these utilities I find myself back in the code enough times to make me wonder if there is a more efficient alternative. Native XML technology is worthy of your investigation. For instance, I wrote a data service to handle incoming purchase orders expressed in an XML message. I wrote 680 lines of Java code to implement the service. I then wrote the same data service using native XML technology—XQuery and native XML database—in only 45 lines of code. (Chapter 7 teaches these native XML technologies.)

Additionally, as XML message schemas change over time, the native XML tools require fewer changes as compared with changes in the same services written in Java. There are less lines of code to maintain. Of course, your mileage may vary and there are functional differences, such as transactional capabilities, that are not as mature as those found in the Java platform.

Native XML approaches to composite applications and data services are appealing because of the greater developer productivity—less lines of code to write and maintain—and the easier maintenance for schema evolution and changes.

### 1.4.2 Your Choice of XML Tools Impacts Performance

XML comes in a variety of sizes and forms. A software developer's choice of XML tools and parsers impacts the scalability and performance of the SOA application. The topmost popular XML parsers in the Java space are XML binding compilers such as JAXB, streaming XML parsers such as StAX, and DOM tree parsers such as Xerces. Table 1-2 illustrates each parser's strengths and weaknesses.

***Table 1-2*** *Contrasting XML Parsers*

| **Technology** | **Plus** | **Minus** |
|---|---|---|
| XML Binding Compiler (JAXB) | Efficiently handles large and complex XML data by providing namespace-aware named elements so your application can jump right to the needed part of an XML tree. | Requires recompile of binding each time XML schema changes. No support for multiple schemas or schema evolution. |
| Streaming XML Parser (StAX) | Excellent performance for large XML documents by providing ability to skip unwanted elements. | Performance degrades with complex XML documents and large (>5 megabytes) messages. |
| Document Object Model (DOM, Xerces) | Acceptable performance when application needs to access/update most elements in an XML document. | Requires memory to load entire XML document into memory. Requires the most amount of coding. |

Native XML technology usually accounts for these XML sizes and forms. For instance, many XQuery implementations are built on streaming data processing engines. Many native XML databases provide indexes that are specially designed to handle the multidimensional queries through XML document collections for fast query speed. Chapter 4 describes XML parser performance and scalability issues in more detail.

### 1.4.3 Criteria for Applying Database Technology for SOA

While there is no SOA standard to recommend using XML, most SOA applications I see move XML documents from service to service. XML is already widely used to express documents, document formats, interoperability standards, and service orchestrations. There are even arguments put forward in the software development community to represent service governance in XML form and operated upon with XML query methods.[9]

As the world moves to become an XML environment, I am often asked to define criteria for when it makes sense to use native XML tools. The following are common questions about using relational databases in SOA environments.

- How difficult is it to get XML data into a relational database?
- How difficult is it to get relational data to a service or object that needs XML data?
- Can my database retrieve the XML data with lossless fidelity to the original XML data?
- Will my database deliver acceptable performance and scalability for operations on XML data stored in the database?
- Which database operations (queries, changes, complex joins) are most costly in terms of performance and required resources (CPUs, network, memory, storage)?

Here are criteria for applying relational and native XML database technology for SOA and XML data needs.

#### *Criterion 1: Relational data needs to be presented in XML form*

Data is already stored in a relational database and needs to be presented in XML form. For instance, a SOAP-enabled inventory management system that is built on a relational database needs to retrieve orders and present order information as an XML document.

Software developers and architects should investigate the following approaches to presenting relational data in XML form.

- **XML formatting operators**. Most relational databases now offer extensions to provide XML creation operators. For instance, the FOR XML (explicit) SQL extension introduced in Microsoft SQLServer 2000 allows the output of a SQL select statement to output XML data. While the FOR XML syntax is not the user-friendliest way to deal with the problem, it is a pragmatic one that works well for software developers familiar with SQL. FOR XML is typical of the XML output extensions for SQL in that it is expensive in

9 See http://radovanjanecek.net/blog/archives/000282.html.

terms of development time and during maintenance when coping with changes. Michael Rys, Microsoft's programmer manager for this type of technology, refers to it as the query from hell.[10] The SQLServer 2005 extensions make developing these types of applications a lot simpler, and although I can complain that these are proprietary and nonstandard, Microsoft customers seem to appreciate this a lot.

- **Mid-tier data mapping technology.** A quick search on Google for "mid-tier data mapping" shows products to create transformation engines that query a relational database through SQL and output XML data. These tools do not require changes to your existing database and provide easier maintenance as your need for various XML schemas change. Given that these mapping technologies know how to access your relational data and the XML schema you need in the output, I highly recommend you also consider using the mapping technology as a mid-tier persistence engine to cache views of the data and for service acceleration. Chapter 5 discusses this in depth.
- **n-Tier transformation**. Write a Java application that uses a JDBC driver to query relational data and an object-XML mapping library such as JAXB or XMLBeans to output XML data. The advantage to this approach is the huge number of software developers available with skills and experience to write and maintain this code. The downside comes from the loss of flexibility. Each time your XML schema needs change, your engineers will be back into the code.
- **Native XML technology**. Many XQuery engines now come with extensions that allow them to query a relational database through a JDBC or ODBC driver and output XML data. This approach is fast, easy, and efficient for the software developer. On the downside, introducing native XML technology is one more thing to be maintained in your datacenter.

The problem I have with SQL and XML is that all of the really good and cool stuff is found in individual implementations. I would love to have the XML creation functions in Microsoft SQLServer 2005 *and* the O/R XML field type in Oracle 10g. Unfortunately, nei-

---

10 http://sqljunkies.com/weblog/mrys/archive/2004/01/27/869.aspx.

ther product fully implements all of the other's XML handling features in its SQL database. I want pristine ANSI SQL code that does not use proprietary procedures and XML-centric syntax. Native XML technology seems to be a good place to continue hunting for a good solution.

### Criterion 2: XML data needs to be stored in a relational database

Much water has passed beneath the relational database XML capabilities bridge. Here is a sampling of the XML datatypes available in most common relational databases.

- **CLOB.** Store XML in character large object (CLOB) fields (also in VARCHAR2 fields.) CLOB fields allow easy inserts that perform fairly well depending on the size of the XML data being inserted. CLOB query performance is problematic, as the CLOB field types offer little help to the database engine and optimizer to deliver acceptable query performance for XML data.
- **XML CLOB.** Store XML in an XML CLOB datatype field. This is a specialized form of CLOB in which the database reads and stores as is the entire XML document in a CLOB object in the database. The XML CLOB datatype stores everything about the XML document verbatim, including the white space, processing instructions, and prolog. Depending on the implementation, the XML CLOB datatype offers functions for XPath querying capability, schema validation, XSL transformations, and often full text-style searching capabilities. Writing SQL commands to insert and query XML data requires specialized nonstandard XML commands, but these are not overly difficult to learn for the average software developer.
- **Object-Relational XML Type.** Store XML in an object-relational XML store. Unlike the verbatim storage technique of the CLOB datatype, object-relational storage breaks the XML document down into scalar values for storage in object attributes in a set of object-relational tables. As XML data is inserted into an object-relational datatype, the database shreds elements—that is, breaks them down into native object datatypes—in the XML data into objects and stores them in the table. The database reconstitutes the stored objects into XML data during query operations. The

object-relational XML datatype requires an XML schema to create the tables. The database uses the schema to create tables and master-detail relationship indexes to store the scalar values in the XML data. Once created, only XML data conforming to the schema may be stored.

Finally, consider a mid-tier data service built with native XML technology as an alternative to using relational XML datatypes. In the mid-tier a service receives the XML data, breaks it down into relational datatypes, and stores the data in relational tables. The XQuery needed to do this may then optimize the storage techniques, index techniques, and data loading techniques specifically for your data and database. This technique also takes into account differences in XML support that vary by relational database vendor and version of the database.

#### *Criterion 3: XML data needs to be stored in a relational database with lossless fidelity to the original XML data*

Many mandates to use XML schemas include requirements to provide the original XML data at some future point. For instance, energy companies use Energy Trading Standards Group (ETSG) XML documents to trade energy between producers. Australia mandates the ETSG documents be available to auditors in the original XML format.[11]

Relational database CLOB datatypes guarantee the order of characters in an XML document. The downside of CLOB is in poor query performance. Use caution with XML CLOB datatype, because certain relational database implementations do not follow hierarchical principles. Pay special attention to make certain the underlying persistence engine will guarantee that the result will be hierarchically accurate and canonically correct.

Native XML technology is a viable strategy to supplement relational database storage. The relational database holds the metadata for queries and the native XML database holds the original XML data for retrieval.

11 http://xml.coverpages.org/etsg.html.

#### *Criterion 4: Need to do ad hoc queries and complex joins on relational and XML data stored in a relational database*

Relational databases have a rich history of tools to provide ad hoc queries and complex joins. Many tools, both commercial and open-source, exist to query databases and provide mapping to object and XML datatypes. These are applicable to SOA environments for relational data. These tools typically do not allow the same rich features when querying XML data stored in a relational database, because the XML data model is too different for them.

The XQuery language supports iterators and other modern language constructs as part of the XQuery language standard specification. These constructs are necessary for complex joins, queries that go beyond a few levels of hierarchy, and inserting records that conform to multiple schemas. The same constructs are available in the SQL procedural languages delivered by the database vendors, but they are each different, not part of a standard, and offer a wide variation of performance and scalability.

#### *Criterion 5: Need to move XML documents between services, even if the data eventually ends up in a relational database*

Many SOA designs move relational data between services using XML. Usually, the relational database is the final destination along the stack of protocols and software components within an n-Tier SOA design. Once relational data is in XML form, using native XML technology is a scalable and maintainable way to move XML documents between services. There is no reason to think of native XML technology as an either-or proposition. For instance, some relational databases provide XQuery as an alternative to SQL. As you will learn in this book, many times the results of combining native XML technology with relational technology leads to better developer productivity and scalability and performance.

### 1.4.4 Flexibility or Performance

In SOA, environment relational database tools often require developers to make a painful choice between flexibility and performance. Some XML handling datatypes provide flexibility to support multiple schemas with good insert performance, while others provide no support for multiple schemas and provide good query performance.

For instance, tests I ran to compare insert speeds with a popular commercial database show the CLOB insert is 22 times faster than the XML CLOB. The difference in insert performance comes from XML CLOB's need to validate the XML data to be well formed. Developers building SOA composite applications and data services usually do not have the option of choosing the CLOB datatype because they need the XML query functions (XPath, transformations, searching) of XML CLOB to achieve satisfactory performance.

Insert operations using object-relational XML datatypes are slow as well. For instance, insert performance on a commercial relational database shows the CLOB datatype to be 11.7 times faster than the object-relational XML datatype. The difference comes from the check for well-formed XML data, parsing the document into local object types, and loading the values into object-relational tables. Of course, insert performance is not the entire story.

Object-relational XML datatype data access has an architectural advantage over XML CLOB datatype for better query performance. Query against an XML CLOB datatype and the database must read entire documents into memory, render them in a document object model (DOM), traverse the DOM to find the values, and build a result set. Object-relational XML datatype queries are transformed into path operations that access individual rows of the object tables and read only the necessary field values.

Chapters 3 and 4 show how combining native XML technology, XQuery, and native XML databases is an alternative that avoids the above two problems by adhering to standards efforts and providing scalable and well-performing solutions.

### 1.4.5 While You Can, You May Not Want To

The issues of managing through the XML schema explosion, the performance impact of XML parsing tools, and choice of flexibility versus performance make it possible to build SOA composite applications and data services using today's popular tools. But you might not want to! Our goal as software developers, architects, and CIOs should be to choose a good set of SOA tools to deliver good scalability and performance for a wide range of SOA applications and data services. Chapters 4 and 5 expand on these problems and propose the use of native XML technology as a solution.

Two problems emerge from using your existing relational database to build SOA applications:

1. None of the relational choices offers good performance in an SOA world filled with XML schemas that are constantly changing. For instance, even as your application benefits from good query performance in object-relational XML datatypes, when your XML schema changes over time, you will need to rework your application.
2. All of these choices require you to lock your application into a set of nonstandard functions.

It may seem from the previous section that SOA focuses on service interfaces and messaging. While it can be easy to focus on the technology, the real business value that comes from adopting SOA is in the information and knowledge the services deliver. We will discuss that next.

## 1.5 Data in the Service-Oriented Architecture

"Value is in the knowledge services convey, not in the method it takes to convey the message," Adam Bosworth of Google told a group of software developers at the Software Development Forum.[12] Chapter 2 shows what Bosworth and other software development thought-leaders are telling the software development community about SOA.

Bosworth's issue is reflected in industry and institutional emphasis on document definitions (schema) and workflow message exchange patterns. Many enterprises I have worked with began their SOA efforts by forming industry associations to define the document schemas they have in common.

For instance, the automotive industry used the Universal Business Language (UBL) to define a standard document schema for transactions between auto dealers and manufacturers called Business Object Documents (BOD).[13] UBL defines a common XML schema business documents for things such as purchase orders and invoices that are common to all businesses in an industry. General Motors (GM) uses Electronic Business using Extensible Markup Language (ebXML) to process BOD-formatted documents.[14] A dealership's parts department sends a GetPurchaseOrder BOD-formatted document to the

12 http://www.sdforum.org.
13 http://www.oasis-open.org/committees/tc_home.php?wg_abbrev=ubl.
14 http://www.ebxml.org.

GM parts distributor. The distributor sends an Acknowledgement BOD-formatted document in response and the Acknowledgement document contains the completed purchase order for the parts.

While the automotive industry has BODs and other document schemas, other industries have formed standards bodies to work out common document schemas for their industries. For instance, the U.S. healthcare industry has the Health Level 7 (HL7) standard for patient healthcare records,[15] and the supply-chain industry has the EPCGlobal standards group, which defined the Electronic Product Code (EPC) to support use of the Radio Frequency Identification (RFID) standard.[16] Finally, the U.S. Defense Information Systems Agency[17] (DISA) created the Net-Centric Enterprise Services (NCES) program to provide enterprise services in support of the Global Information Grid (GIG), the U.S. military version of the Internet.[18] NCES is a document-oriented SOA that uses XML schemas.

The great thing about these efforts to define document schemas is the impact they are having on software architects and developers. Enterprises and institutions are mandating document schemas and SOA. For instance, Wal-Mart met with its top 100 vendors in 2003 to tell them its plans to begin using RFID tags to track supplier shipments. The plan called for all pallets from its vendors to be equipped with RFID tags by 2005 and a year later to be able to track even cases of products received on the pallets. Wal-Mart gave its vendors a mandate to make it happen. Considering its size—Wal-Mart controls 17 percent of the worldwide retail market and receives more than 5 billion cases and pallets each year—the vendors took the mandate seriously.

Consider what a SOA for Wal-Mart must do to deliver business value. Each RFID tag emits an Electronic Product Code (EPC) containing a long number. RFID is by design an XML-oriented technology. Each EPC scan moving through the warehouse is an XML document, which needs to be stored, managed, and queried. Storing all that XML data using traditional relational data management solutions will not provide the SOA flexibility that Wal-Mart needs to understand its product trends and manage its supply chain. The scale is just too big.

---

15 http://www.hl7.org.
16 http://www.epcglobalinc.org.
17 http://www.disa.mil.
18 http://www.disa.mil/main/prodsol/cs_nces.html.

The Wal-Mart mandate made many software architects and developers wonder, "What is the role of data in an information system?"

In the pre-SOA world data was something to be siloed away into a database. It rarely moved, was often queried, and sometimes copied (or synchronized or replicated) to another silo. When new applications of the siloed data were needed, entire subindustries sprung up, such as data warehousing. Database architecture patterns are good at storing data, but they miss the value of having data available.

Many software architects and developers came to the conclusion that these document definitions are where the rubber meets the road in terms of SOA performance, scalability, reliability, and overall benefit. For instance, the GM-created BODs can represent an order for a windshield wiper that results in a BOD-formatted document that takes approximately 8,000 bytes of data with 800 elements, or an order for a GM Suburban truck that takes approximately 10,000,000 bytes of data with 9,000 elements. With this kind of variety in the size and complexity of documents, a new approach to data persistence is necessary to make data available within a SOA context.

As you will see in Chapters 3 and 4, the tools that previously created Web Services and remote procedure call (RPC) services are ill designed to work with document-oriented architectures such as SOA. The result is systems that are hard to build, slow to perform transactions, and offer performance that gets worse with increased use.

At a minimum I recommend you consider the following design guidelines that relate to data in SOA.

1. All data in SOA is a resource. Data is not tightly coupled to any specific application in an SOA. Instead, composite applications operate on data from one or more data services to deliver knowledge to a consumer.
2. All resources need to have a unique address within the SOA.
3. Data should be locally available but stored in a way that is globally accessible.
4. Data in an SOA is useful over the lifetime of the data, so the data's address needs to be consistent over time. In SOA there should be no "Where's my hat? Didn't I just put it down there?" scenarios.

5. The data from a service should be self-describing. The ultimate achievement would be a situation where a developer from another team or business began using the data in his or her application without having to go back to a manual or the original software developers. It should be apparent what the data is and how to use it.
6. Metadata (data about the data) should explain the structure of the data. Metadata needs to be published in a machine-readable form and be available through message exchange protocols.
7. Metadata should be created in a machine-readable form to facilitate automated transformation of data to resolve incompatible datatypes in service interfaces. You should expect that at some point an automated software "robot" or search engine spider will try to understand the semantic knowledge of your data.
8. Where industry standard document definitions (schemas) exist, your data should be returned in a standard schema. The whole goal here is to make it easier for the soft developer to rapidly develop interoperable systems.
9. Data definitions should support caching. For instance, a schema for frequently retrieved data should include a time-to-live value to assist mid-tier service caches in avoiding unnecessary requests and network bandwidth usage.

Next, we will evaluate the downsides of using SOA, and then we will end the chapter with a map of the rest of the book.

## 1.6 The Dark Side of SOA

SOA has significant advantages, but there are several problems that you should consider as well. The following is a list of SOA issues that keep me up at night.

1. **Availability.** (Note that I did not write High Availability, which is something else.) A service earns its keep by delivering good service. Good service is rated by the consumer and typically includes questions such as: Was the service available when I made a request? Did the service answer

the request with a valid response? Was the data returned from a service accurate? The right answers to these questions determine the service value to a business. Availability means being reliable and trustworthy.

2. **State**. The method to persist data behind a service interface may introduce sessions and transactions. Any time your SOA application needs to maintain the state of a service, you are guaranteed to face performance and scalability problems in the future.
3. **Versions**. Service interfaces and document definitions change over time. Each change should be controlled through a change management system. For instance, a registry, repository, or concurrent versioning system (CVS) keeps track of service versions and provides software architects and developers with programmatic interfaces for access by other applications and services.
4. **Performance Testing**. Service interfaces are a great place to incorporate performance instrumentation in an SOA application. Most SOA applications I have worked with use a stack of services that call each other in a serial fashion. This is an ideal architecture for a service to be instrumented to allow a service management tool to gather statistics on requests and responses.
5. **Graininess.** Composite applications and data services need to reach a careful balance between offering too many broad functions and being too narrow. Services need to offer functions somewhere in the middle.
6. **Localization.** Document definitions are often not precise. For instance, the order that comes into a service using U.S. dollars but thinks the order is in Australian dollars incurs a huge liability.
7. **Logging.** Debugging multithreaded, highly concurrent networks of services is made possible with logging debuggers, easily available transaction logs, and an easy method to query logged data. Without these, the software developer's life is a nightmare.
8. **Remote Management Interfaces.** These allow services to be queried remotely to determine their current operational state and controlled remotely to change their operating parameters.

## 1.7 The SOA Checklist

While the previous section may keep me up at night, the following list may help you know where things stand. Here is a checklist to understand the quality of a software architect's SOA design.

1. Is there a document that I may read (or that a program I write may find) to learn the location of a service, the types of input the service will take, the type of data the service will return, and the exceptions the service may throw in case of problems?
2. Do you know the group, or even better, an individual person who will respond to a phone call or email message when the service fails?
3. Is the data I send to the service in a format that is easy for me to write a program to manipulate?
4. Do I understand the semantic meaning of a service's function? Understanding the service interface is a good thing, and understanding the meaning of the service's function is much better.
5. Does the service use security and session data in a form that I can create and manipulate with my programming language?
6. Does the service require another service?
7. Is the service synchronous or asynchronous?

If I were ever to offer an SOA certification program, then you would need to answer the above questions to pass. So how did you do?

## 1.8 Summary

This chapter defines the viewpoint I have on SOA: While SOA is a wonderful design, SOA has issues. The wonderful part of SOA is its ability to pull together adopted and well-understood protocols, software development coding techniques, and a governance model. These lead to common use of SOA message patterns to exchange standards-based business documents in a business process. The problematic issues in SOA are driven by the gap between management's buy-in to SOA and the ability of software architects and developers to deliver production-worthy software code that achieves user satisfaction.

This book introduces SOA from a performance and scalability perspective, because that is my background. The next chapters take on the reasons why today's SOA tools fail to deliver production-worthy code and what you can do about it.

- Chapter 2 looks at the explosion of XML schemas and their impact on performance, compatibility, and flexibility.
- Chapter 3 shows the most common SOA messaging patterns.
- Chapter 4 explains the problems I encountered that drove me to need the FastSOA architecture.
- Chapter 5 explains the FastSOA architecture and the XML-centric tools needed to build it.
- Chapter 6 shows my testing methodology (with real-world examples fully implemented) to understand SOA scalability and performance.
- Chapter 7 makes the case for using XML, XML Query (XQuery,) and native XML database technology to build well-performing and flexible SOA.
- Chapter 8 shows the tools and techniques your business needs to evaluate to be ready for SOA.

Chapter

# 2

# Managing the XML Explosion

*Although* there is no SOA standard to recommend using XML, most software developers, architects, and CIOs I meet believe SOA means XML. SOA applications I see and test use XML to define service interfaces, messages, documents, and service management (often also called governance). Software architects and developers of all kinds are in love with XML. From a CIO's perspective, the world is experiencing an explosion of XML that needs to be governed. In this chapter, I show what drives the software developer community's excitement behind XML, and I make the case that XML is a good thing for SOA designs. I then demonstrate the problems XML introduces for performance, scalability, and developer productivity. This will prepare you for the SOA performance testing methodology I present in Chapters 3 and 4.

## 2.1 A Love Affair with XML

Most software developers know what it is like to write a program that reads unstructured and undocumented application data from a file, not really knowing the file format, and finding mistakes in the file contents. They also remember having to keep a bunch of relations between several database tables in their head. Wherever a name/value pair in a properties file seems too complicated and a relational database seems to be overkill, there is XML. Wherever a data description language is cumbersome to learn and use, there is XML. Whenever applications, servers, and services need to provide easy programmatic interfaces, there is XML. Ah, XML. How I love thee!

Software developers' love affair with XML is only a few years old, but it has already had a large impact on the software development community. Developers rapidly embraced XML and found exciting new applications for it, including XML file formats, XML-based message-oriented middleware (MOM) for business process integration, remote procedure calls (RPC), service asset management, Web site content syndication (RSS), and even podcasts. XML is a language for defining languages. Figure 2-1 gives a rough epidemiology of XML-related technologies.

When XML appeared on the scene in the late 1990s, software developers liked what they saw: a simple way to write self-describing structured data. They looked for a way to use it. The earliest use was to describe the contents of a file. For instance, today XML is used to store application configuration and preferences settings such as the Apache Web server configuration files. At the time, the alternative was to use a flat file key/value database, such as the Microsoft Windows Registry, to use a text-based properties file of name/value pairs, or to use a proprietary directory service technology. XML is easy, quick, and self-describing. XML is a winner.

A second early use for XML was to facilitate making remote procedure calls (RPC) between applications. Various attempts to make this happen were put into use, including Dave Winer's attempt to build a standard for XML RPC. Developers gave widespread attention to XML RPC when IBM, Microsoft, Sun, BEA, and others came together around the Simple Object Access Protocol (SOAP). Developers are still experimenting with the best way to use XML to make a remote procedure call. Current experiments include the Representational State Transfer (REST)[1] and Asynchronous Java and XML (AJAX)[2] efforts. REST is an XML-based messaging protocol for application-to-application communication that uses short stateless RPC-style messages to incrementally share knowledge between applications. AJAX is a technique to make browser-based user interfaces much more interactive without requiring the typical submit/post/

1 See http://webservices.xml.com/pub/a/ws/2002/02/06/rest.html for details.
2 See http://www.adaptivepath.com/publications/essays/archives/000385.php for details.

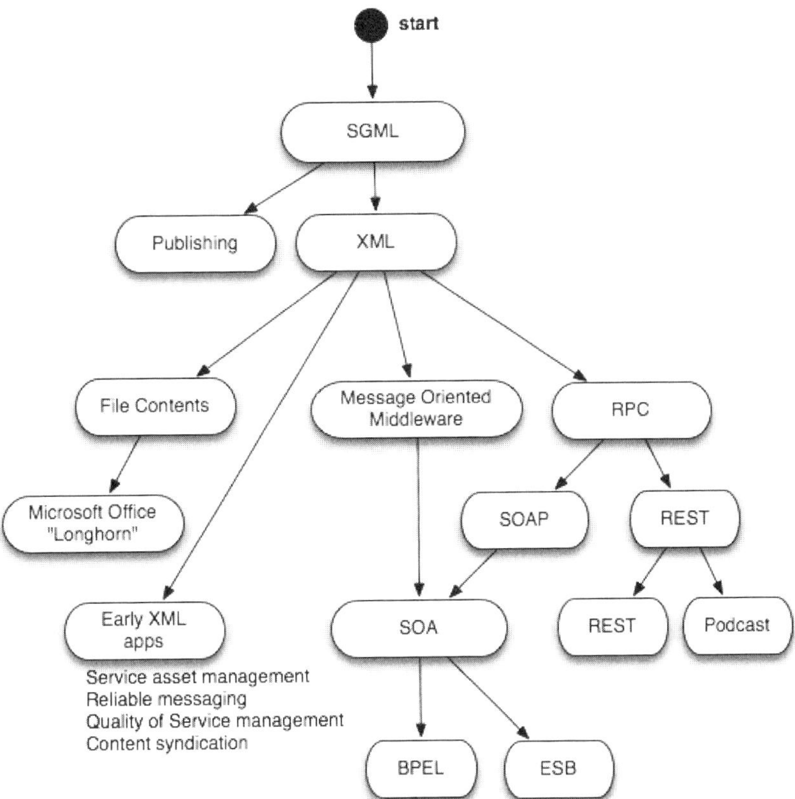


***Figure 2-1*** *In its first few years, XML excited software architects and developers and rapidly delivered several successive XML-based technologies.*

redraw round-trip of an HTML interface. AJAX uses XML messages over HTTP protocols.

Enterprise-level service interfaces require security, reliable messaging, service descriptions, and data interoperability. Developers solved these problems by delivering code implementations and written specifications through the standards bodies (OASIS, W3C, and others).

Eventually, developers began pushing back on these standards because, taken together, they appear complex, even though the individual parts, such as SOAP, are simple. Developers came to agreement on a subset of all the RPC services under the Web Services Interoperability (WS-I) standards body.[3]

3 See http://www.ws-i.org for details.

This subset consists of the WS-I profiles and the Universal Business Language (UBL) standard,[4] which allows any industry or group to define the XML schema to be used in an RPC call.

Software architects and developers began to see the advantage of taking a document-centric view of service development in the early 2000s. (I describe the scalability advantages of document-centric systems in Chapter 1.) The resulting architecture uses a set of commonly understood services to exchange and operate on documents that share a commonly agreed-to definition. Taken as a whole, these patterns and techniques are the foundations of SOA.

A critical mass of services, with each delivering data through XML-based service interfaces, enables software developers to build composite applications to deliver business processes. At the object level of a composite application an Enterprise Service Bus (ESB) facilitates orchestrations of services, communication between objects, and service deployment functions.

Composite application development methods also identify the state and transitions a document goes through as each supplementary service is called while processing an overall business process. For instance, in a bank finance company, a loan processing application requests a credit report for a loan applicant and then requests a manager's approval before approving the loan. The credit report and manager approval is received by making service calls to the credit reporting service and the manager's approval service. All of this happens in a set of XML-based messages between a set of services.

XML is even used to model business workflows. The Business Process Execution Language (BPEL)[5] and many other competing formats for gluing federated groups of Web Services together yield the possibility of new economies, new markets, and greater efficiency. Figure 2-2 illustrates the orchestration of the loan processing workflow and how BPEL notates the states of the workflow in XML form.

In this case BPEL uses XML as a procedural scripting language notation. A BPEL rules engine uses the XML to step through a workflow.

---

4 See http://www.oasis-open.org/committees/tc_home.php?wg_abbrev=ubl for details.

5 http://searchwebservices.techtarget.com/originalContent/0,289142,sid26_gci880731,00.html.

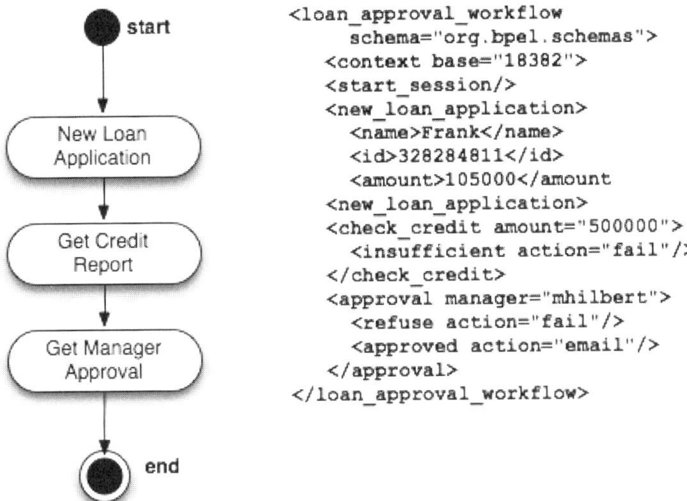


***Figure 2-2*** *A business workflow for a loan approval service and the simplified BPEL XML representation of the workflow.*

While the developer community has been energetically applying XML to a variety of problems, XML's impact on data itself is extraordinary. We will look at this in the next section.

## 2.2 XML Impact on Data

XML makes a profound impact on data, data models, and data storage. Much of the 1980s and 1990s were taken up by relational database experts convincing the world that everything should be stored in a table made up of a set number of fields and rows with the SQL language relating the data into usable knowledge. Experts such as E. F. Codd[6] and C. J. Date[7] proved to me and others that any relationship could be written in a SQL statement. I wrote a relational database back in 1988 with a SQL implementation.[8] The experience showed me SQL's richness and power. Many times I would marvel at the queries users would send me.

It did not take long to realize that while I was sufficient at implementing a SQL engine, I was pretty bad at writing SQL queries. As

6 http://www.informatik.uni-trier.de/~ley/db/about/codd.html.

7 http://portal.acm.org/citation.cfm?id=811532.

8 RegentBase was the first SQL database for 68000-based systems, including the Atari ST and Macintosh.

a software developer, I yearned for flexibility, ease of use, power, and performance.

Databases are a combination of a data model and an access language. This holds true for relational and native XML databases. Relational databases are a combination of tables composed of rows made up of fields and the SQL language. XML databases are a combination of collections of XML documents and the XML Query (XQuery) language. For instance, I model a database to describe my friends and family in a relational database using a table to hold entries for my family members and a table to hold entries for my friends. A SQL query joins the tables to show me a complete view of my family and friends. (See Figure 2.3.)

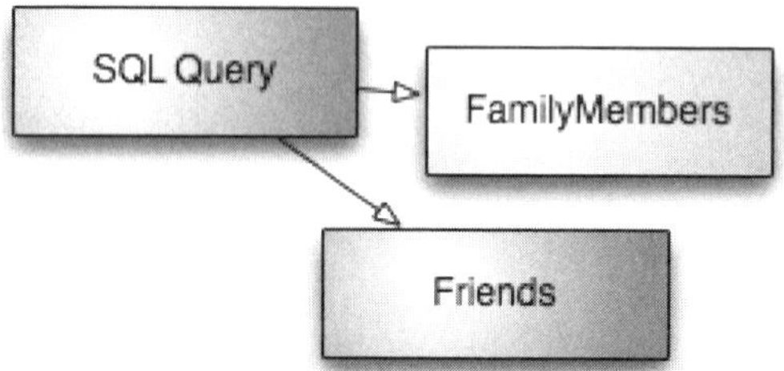


***Figure 2-3** A relational approach to the friends and family example.*

When I repeat the above example using an XML approach, I use a single XML document with two nodes. One node stores my family members and a second stores my friends. The following XML document shows the relationship between my family, my friends, and myself.

```
<father name="Frank">
  <family_members>
    <spouse>Lorette</spouse>
    <daughter>Madeline</daughter>
    <son>Jack</son>
  </family_members>
  <friends>
    <friend>Carol</friend>
    <friend>Sean</friend>
    <friend>Nichollaaa</friend>
    <friend>Sadie</friend>
  </friends>
</father>
```

I prefer the XML data model approach for two reasons:

- I understand the data in the XML document without needing to run a query. It is apparent to me from the document that I am the father and have relationships with my family members and friends.
- XML is ready for change. For instance, I hope that eventually my son will find the same joy I found by getting married. If that happens, then I can add a new category to the <family_members> element for <son> to include his <family_members> with little effort and almost no refactoring.

I also prefer the XQuery language to the SQL language. XQuery supports iterators and other modern language constructs as part of the XQuery language standard specification. These constructs are necessary for complex joins, queries that go beyond a few levels of hierarchy, and inserting records that conform to multiple schema. The same constructs are available in the SQL procedural languages delivered by the database vendors, but they are each different, not part of a standard, and offer a wide variation of performance and scalability.

To many software developers, the XML data model appears to be a more common-sense way of storing the contents of documents, forms, and data. Many new XML document-oriented architectures are about to emerge. Consider the following scenarios, where the XML data model may benefit your efforts.

- **Complex Data-Interchange Schemas**. Many industries have formed alliances and standards bodies to create and adopt XML document interchange between applications and services using complex industry-specific schema. For instance, in the automotive industry, the STAR BOD schema and in the healthcare industry the HL7 schema are examples of complex XML schema. I prefer using native XML tools to work with complex schemas because the effort, measured in lines of code, is less, and the resulting code performs faster when compared with object and relational database approaches. Chapter 4 shows the performance advantage, and Chapter 7 shows the developer productivity advantage.
- **New Kinds of Dynamic Documents.** Microsoft Office is one of the world's greatest producers of documents. Post-

2006 versions of Office will use an XML file format. Microsoft touts a glorious future in which Office documents include XML references to dynamic data. For instance, a market economics report includes a view of home interest rates for the past two years. The XML document contents tell the browsing application where to find the most recent interest rates.

- **Data Fidelity.** Several government bodies in the United States now mandate support for an ePedigree on medicines. An ePedigree benefits businesses by providing important data for customer knowledge and recall management. The pedigree of a drug shows who has held a medicine as it moves through the set of distributors from manufacturer to customer. Maintaining the XML data in its original form as the medicine moves from place to place through a variety of supplier systems is often required. Native XML storage delivers coding and flexibility advantages for storing the pedigree in its native XML form.

These scenarios show ways the XML data model benefits enterprises, organizations, and institutions. Next, I show how the XML data model benefits efforts to deliver Master Data Management.

### 2.2.1 Master Data Management and XML

From my experiences working with large enterprises and groups of developers, I find that most large enterprises have silos of data. It is pretty common to find different systems holding duplicate data with different formats, owners, uses, and values. As a result, the enterprise operates as a group of discrete businesses. In these scenarios I advocate for the customer. If an enterprise cannot view all of the data for each customer in a single view, then customers may find the business difficult to do business with. Even worse, the enterprise may miss significant opportunities, such as taking advantage of global supplier discounts, providing appropriate discounts to its largest customers, maximizing profitability within a product group, or making good management decisions with fresh and complete data. Master Data Management (MDM) resolves these issues by leaving existing applications, data stores, databases, and integration technologies (EII, EAI, and ESB) in place and superimposing an infrastructure for common enterprise data.

MDM benefits an enterprise by governing core data, which is used to update all other data stores in the enterprise. MDM may have a centralized architecture where all master data is centrally stored and all other data stores are updated from this central data store. Alternatively, MDM may have a federated architecture, where master data is stored and updated from different legacy systems but managed and coordinated by MDM. In this case, master data could reside in multiple instances of the ERP system and other master data could reside in a central CRM system.

MDM handles data in "real time" and synchronizes changes across data stores. MDM enables enterprise managers to make decisions quickly, because all key data across the enterprise is viewed as one database—either a virtual database through federation or a central database through aggregation or some combination of the two. Figure 2-4 illustrates XML data services in an MDM design.

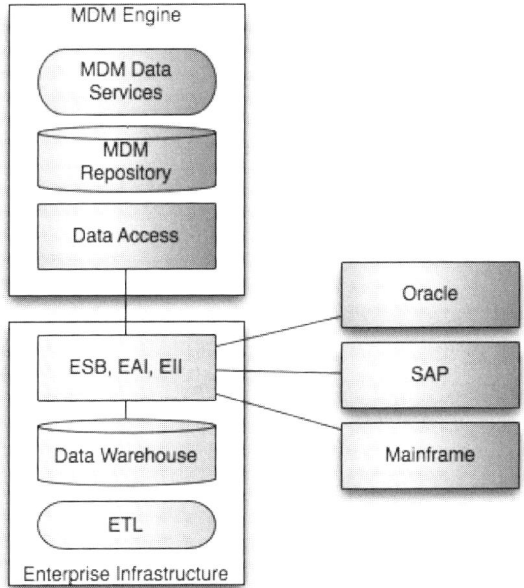


***Figure 2-4*** *Master Data Management (MDM) manages core data and updates enterprise data through ESB, EAI, and EII tools.*

MDM solutions benefit greatly from the XML data model's flexibility. For instance, many enterprise information managers and architects I meet see defining the initial data interrelationships as the most significant challenge to being successful with MDM solutions. The very nature of data models in SOA tells me that the more significant challenge to MDM success is in the effort to maintain the data inter-relationships over time as the data values and relationships change from new and changing business requirements. For example, consider what happens when an enterprise data model needs to change. Figure 2-5 illustrates changing an existing data model to add a new address field for customer vacation home addresses.

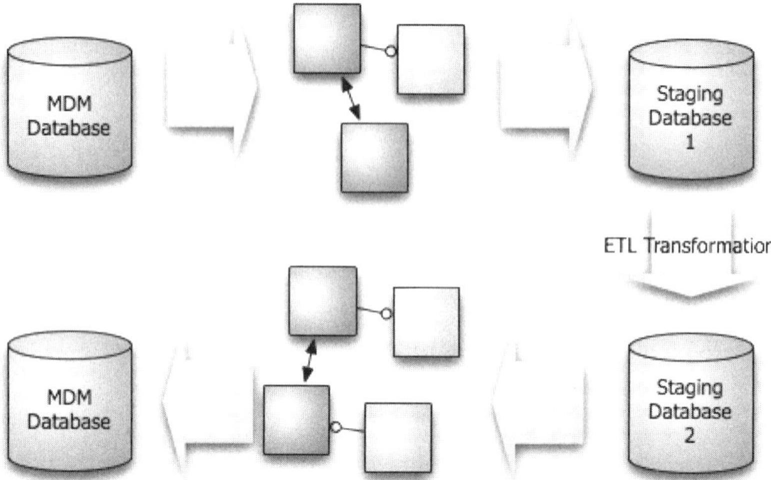


***Figure 2-5*** *A complex multistep process to add new fields to an existing relational database using ETL and MDM techniques.*

In this example, the existing database has three tables: customer, orders, and credit history. The customer table currently stores one address. The company needs to store a second address for customers and possibly more addresses: home address, ship-to address, bill-to address, and summer vacation home address. To accomplish this change the database administrator changes the schema by adding a new table to hold addresses.

The database administrator uses an ETL transformation to add the new table to an existing database. The ETL transformation moves the database contents to the second staging database, creates a new table to hold the new address fields, changes the SQL code to establish the relationship between the existing schema and the new table, and simulates and quality tests the impact to systems accessing the new schema. The final step is to move the database from the second staging database system into the master database. I have spent more than one sleepless night waiting for this ETL transformation to complete.

Compare the above example to an MDM system that uses an XML data model. Figure 2-6 illustrates the relative ease to add a new node to an existing database.

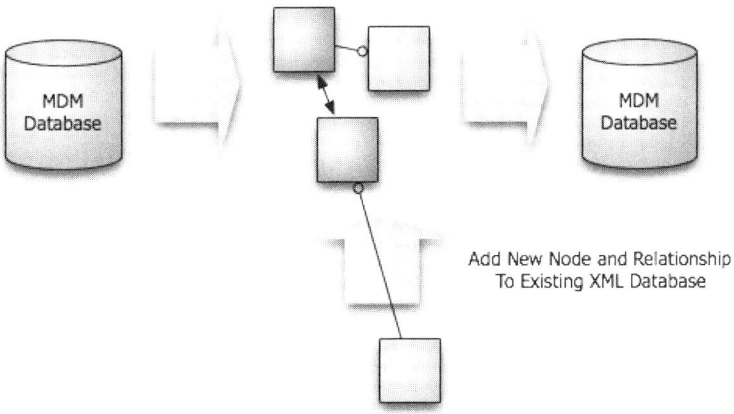


***Figure 2-6*** *XML data models are ready for change, including changing the database schema without needing the downtime and hardware.*

Using an XML data model, the database administer adds the new addresses by inserting new address nodes to the MDM database. The existing query scripts, written in XQuery, need no major changes to support storing the new addresses.

While developers love XML for its flexibility, you should be aware of the explosion in XML schemas, the driving forces behind the explosion, and what it means to your SOA efforts in terms of performance and scalability.

## 2.3 XML and the Nature of Software Developers

While it may seem like XML is leading the IT industry toward standardization, uniformity, and predictability, XML is really more subversive than that. XML encourages freedom. So while the IT industry moved toward creating standard uses of XML in Web Services, most software developers invented their own XML-based remote procedure call mechanisms because doing so was easy and simple. There is no gatekeeper to how XML may be used, only a convention on how XML describes data.

Web Services were borne from the belief that developers would use XML to build services that dynamically find other services to provide fine-grained information needed to solve a problem .[9] The Universal Description, Discovery, and Integration (UDDI) protocol from the OASIS standards body is an XML-based registry of available services categorized by taxonomies specific to an industry. UDDI is combined with the Web Service Description Language (WSDL) XML definition of how to interface with the service and the Simple Object Access Protocol (SOAP) to send requests and receive responses from dynamically bound services. Unfortunately, the Web Services vision has not yet been realized.

At the end of the day, the taxonomy experts never showed up for the party. Even a system like a public library's use of the Dewey Decimal system for categorizing books is not available through a UDDI registry. Without the taxonomy to describe the semantic knowledge available from a service, software developers need to figure out the meaning of each service for themselves.

Web Services ran aground trying to live up to its original vision of dynamic, self-discoverable, fine-grained services while still satisfying the nature of software development. Consider my theory of the nature of software development in the following axioms.

1. There is no single best practice to software architecture and development methods, tools, and techniques. Instead, there is an ever-changing set of best practices.
2. Software architects and developers constantly crave something new, even if it duplicates existing technology.
3. New inventions never die. All existing software technology will eventual ride again.
4. Simple wins over elegant.

While Web Services began as a noble use of XML, developers noticed Web Services began to get bogged down in terms of change and complexity. It was not long before enterprises and tools vendors began to work on the Web Services Interoperability (WS-I) standards to identify an agreed-to set of Web Service protocols, encoding styles, security standards, and process integration protocols. By

9 Fine-grained is a term used to describe small packets of data that answer part of an overall problem. For instance, rather than send a medical patient's entire health record, a fine-grained service sends only the date of the patient's last health check with a doctor.

the time this happened, the thought leaders had had enough. They argued for simplicity.

Tim Bray, co-inventor of XML; Adam Bosworth, architect at Google; and Jeff Barr, manager of services at Amazon, spoke at the Software Development Forum's Web Services Conference in May 2005.[10] SDForum is the Silicon Valley's largest association of software developers, entrepreneurs, and investors. Bray, Bosworth, and Barr discussed the state of affairs in the Web Services world.

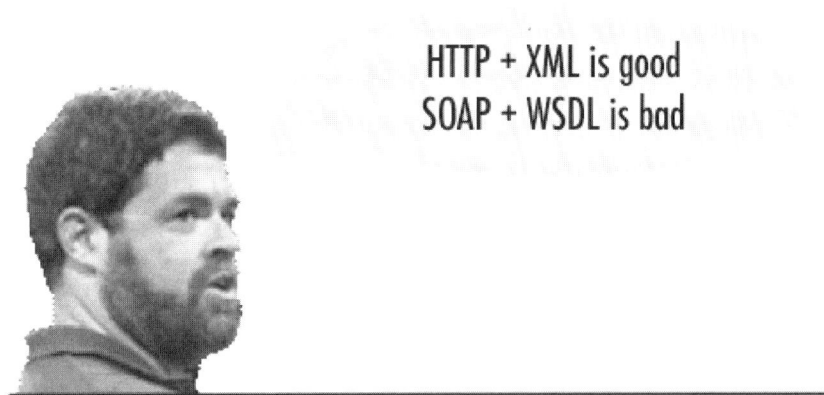


***Figure 2-7*** *Adam Bosworth urges developers and architects to use XML technology for services without the complexity of SOAP and WSDL.*

At the conference, Bosworth directed software architects and developers to look at the value of services in the knowledge they convey, not in the method it takes to convey the message. While there is a lot of activity and excitement over the work at the standards bodies (W3C, OASIS, and WS-I), these are efforts to work on how to convey the message, not how to develop knowledge. Bosworth looks at the overhead just to convey the message as a detractor from letting developers apply their effort to building knowledge. His summary observation is that HTTP and XML are good enough to convey the message and that SOAP and WSDL are impediments because they are too complex. (See Figure 2.7.)

Tim Bray began the next session by asking the audience, "Raise your hand if you understand WSDL." (See Figure 2.8.)

10 Browse http://www.sdforum.org for details.

***Figure 2-8*** *Tim Bray speaking to a room full of Web Services developers.*

This was the venerable Tim Bray asking the question, so I would bet that some people were too intimidated to raise their hands. Still, only two people in a room of hundreds raised their hand.

"Houston! I think we have a problem," Bray said. "How can you expect to do anything with the Web Services Interoperability standards when no one in the room understands one of the key underlying basic protocols?!"

Some would argue that there are plenty of tools out there to help you use WSDL. My survey of the tools available to developers using Java, Perl, .NET, Python, Visual BASIC for Applications, C, and procedural languages is that WSDL tools are not universally available. The tools to facilitate WSDL are generally for Java and .NET users. That leaves developers trying to decipher WSDL files by hand. That is not fun.

Bray was not arguing *against* WS-I, but instead, *for* simplicity. At the end of his talk, Bray said, "Simple wins." Actual Web Services deployment is a good indication that Bray is right.

Jeff Barr noted that Amazon provides service interfaces for its online store. Amazon publishes WSDL definitions of SOAP-based service interfaces. Amazon also publishes an HTML page that shows how to use REST protocols to access the same services. REST uses XML data in a simple HTTP POST protocol. REST has no description language. In the Amazon case, a developer reads a Web page to learn which values to include in the XML document sent in the payload of a simple HTTP request.

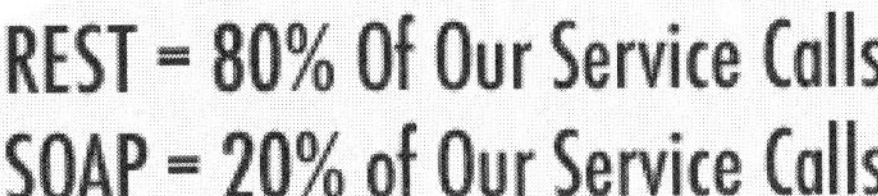

***Figure 2-9*** *Jeff Barr talks about adoption and use of the service protocols Amazon exposes for external developers to use.*

Barr notes that 80% of the service calls to Amazon come in using the REST protocol. (See Figure 2.9.) The developer community using Amazon services voted and the answer is that the simpler alternative won. This should tell all of us something about the nature of software development: Simple wins.

Many software developers, architects, and CIOs today use Web Services technologies to accomplish business process reengineering, construction of business processes in composite applications, and construction of composite data services. This can work well in environments where concurrent transactions are low, message schema are simple (not complex or very deeply nested), and message payload sizes are small. Break past any of these constraints and slow performance and big scalability problems come quickly.

## 2.4 Why XML in SOA Makes Sense

Some software architects and developers look at issues surrounding XML and reject it for SOA. The following are some of the issues I commonly hear.

1. XML is too verbose. Each element within an XML document includes a text string to tag the element. When a document contains 500 elements, then 500 fully named tags come along with the data. This is wasteful and inefficient to process.

2. XML programmatic interfaces (APIs) are difficult to use. Java developers have at least four choices in XML handling APIs to choose from, and they each have a learning curve and quirks.
3. There is no standard for XML compression to make data interchange more efficient.

I expect that these are short-term technology problems that will be solved with new approaches to XML. Here are my reasons why XML in SOA makes sense.

1. Engineering software projects that use XML take less time to build and cost less to maintain over time. This is a reflection of the software development community's love affair with XML. There is a huge pool of software engineers who understand and can skillfully work with XML data.
2. Software developer XML literacy means reduced support costs when a developer from another team (internal to your company or at a supplier or customer location) writes integration code to use your service.
3. XML facilitates self-describing data. This makes software developers more productive and reduces maintenance costs, as the service code encapsulates a function that operates with the knowledge of the semantics of the data. For instance, an agent-based service that finds a movie you are interested in that may be ordered through eBay is much easier to write and maintain when the eBay interface uses XML.
4. Document definitions and service interfaces evolve as developers maintain services. XML is well suited for versioning, support for schemas, and namespaces. Your alternative to XML in SOA needs to deliver these features.

In the following sections, we will dig into XML to explain the benefits and problems with XML's flexibility.

## 2.5 What XML Is Not: A Language for Semantics

XML is a wonderful thing. However, XML can be messy and is no panacea. XML is great at making data description easy, because it expects the data to be messy, not normalized, and sometimes adhoc.

Once you get past the schema for XML's syntax—element naming, closing element tags, attributes, and CDATA sections for binary data—there are few or no best practices for designing a good XML document. Table 2-1 shows three different techniques that are all perfectly valid XML.

***Table 2-1*** *Consider these XML techniques to express the same data.*

| One Size Fits All | Add One, Add Them All | Inclusion |
|---|---|---|
| salesorders.xml<br><orders><br><order part="173" loc="UAV"/><br><order part="221" loc="UCC"/><br></orders> | salesorders.xml<br><order><br><part>173</part><br><loc>UAV</loc><br></order><br><order><br><part>221</part><br><loc>UCC</loc><br></order> | salesorders.xml file:<br><orders><br><include file="order1.xml/><br><include file="order2.xml/><br></orders><br><br>order1.xml file:<br><order><br><part>173</part><br><loc>UAV</loc><br></order><br><br>order2.xml file:<br><order><br><part>221</part><br><loc>UCC</loc><br></order> |

In the "One Size Fits All" technique, a single XML document expands in size for the number of <order> elements to be stored. The more <order> elements the larger the document. This works fine for a while, but imagine if the same technique applied to a server log file several megabytes long! This poses a serious problem when a parser needs to validate the document by finding the closing </orders> tag.

"Add One, Add Them All" is an additive approach. As new <order> elements become known, they are appended to the salesorders.xml document. This approach eases validation and scalability, as parsing the document may be done in bite-sized chunks, each <order> being one chunk. However, imagine an XML document with millions of orders.

The "Inclusion" technique uses an XML schema include operation to reference external files that will hold the data. The salesorders.xml file references the order1.xml and order2.xml files. This approach is flexible, but it also requires an understanding of the relationships between the included files. If a developer ran across order1.xml and not salesorders.xml, it may not be obvious at first what order1.xml is all about.

Although there may never be a common and widely used pattern for structuring XML data, the XML tag notation makes data more semantically accessible than previous data notation attempts. The tag notation makes it easier to write software code to understand the semantic meaning of the data. And the XML data model makes it easy to root around in XML data to find the data we need. Sometimes our programs will need to jump right into the middle of an XML structure and then search above, below, and in parallel to the data in the document. In another instance, code may use the full-text query capability of an XML parser or query language to find an element in an XML document and understand its information by using a query to find the parent of the element.

XML was the first of a new generation of data models to make it easier to build semantically aware applications. For instance, the following XML document contains information about a friend.

```
<contact>
  <firstname>Kim</firstname>
  <lastname>Witthaus</lastname>
  <city>Campbell</city>
  <country>USA</country>
</contact>
```

Semantically aware applications know that my friend lives in a city named Campbell just by looking at the document.

XML tag notation excited many software developers and architects past what XML is able to deliver. In reality, XML does not deliver semantic information about the data it encodes. For that, we need a combination of XML; a convention on the definition and use of metadata (data about data); and a basis for encoding, exchanging, and reusing structured data and metadata. One candidate for semantically aware application development is the Resource Description Format (RDF)[11] and SPARQL[12] query language. RDF is to semantic applications what HTML is for the Web. SPARQL is a query language featuring semantic constructs to derive knowledge from RDF data sources. RDF and SPARQL are currently only experiments. For now, XML notations for <element> tags and other constructions do not deliver semantic information about the data. That leaves it up to software developers to build semantic applications with today's existing tools and XML.

In my experience, 8 out of every 10 developers I meet are procedural programmers, scripters, and macro developers. They found little excitement in the idea of discoverable, loosely coupled, finely grained Web Services. Instead, for them the semantic knowledge that links together services exists only in their head and is expressed in procedural code that makes requests to statically identified services, transforms the data in code, and exposes a result in a static interface. (Maybe that is why Amazon gets 80 percent REST requests compared with 20 percent SOAP-based Web Services requests.)

Let me give you an alternate view of the service-oriented universe. I imagine a world where services are discoverable; are document oriented; and use SOAP, JDBC, Message Queue, and other data protocols to communicate. In this world, many things are possible. If your application needs to do a 20-gigabyte file download over a SOAP call, then go for it. If you want to do it using ZIP as a file format, then go for it. I fully anticipate an explosion of document definitions where anyone who wants to publish a schema will. Services will even federate. And each service will answer a piece of a business process. Figure 2-10 illustrates a use case.

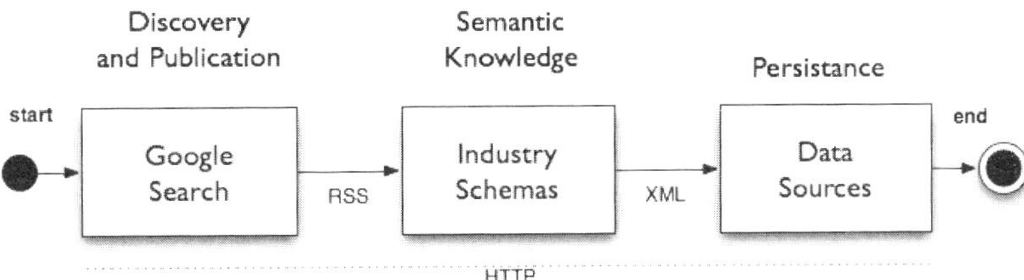


***Figure 2-10*** *An alternative to the current Service-Oriented Architecture proposals that uses RSS and document-oriented XML protocols to enable the service-based IT bus.*

11 See http://www.w3.org/RDF.

12 SPARQL is a strange acronym for *SPARQL Protocol and RDF Query Language*. Details at http://www.w3.org/TR/rdf-sparql-protocol.

In my alternative universe, services are discoverable through a search engine. For example, Google provides access through a Real Site Syndication (RSS) interface to its search functions.

The discovery and publication of services on the Web is something best left to Google, rather than trying to implement a UDDI solution. Let Google deal with the complexity of all of the services that are out there. They seem to do a good job of it today. I do not want to wait around for UDDI and for the ontologists to figure out what makes up all of the things that are categorized on the Internet.

With today's Web, tools, and techniques, I write programs that understand the schema of the domain of my interest. My program uses Google to find data sources. When it needs additional information such as data stored in a relational database or accessible from a SOAP-based Web Service, then the program uses Web protocols to retrieve the XML-formatted data. The program learns and persists data through service calls to an object—for instance, a Java or .NET object—or perhaps a message queue such as a Java Message Service (JMS) message provider. All of this interaction with my program happens over HTTP protocols.

This services vision has programs automatically finding services that are fine grained and programs that are able to search out all these services and deal with the semantic knowledge of mapping them all together. What I would put to you is that you are still going to use Java or .NET or C or any of the scripting languages to write this middle tier. This middle tier is the glue between the discoverable services and the data sources that are out there. This glue is what gives you the answer to the question, "Where may I buy the least expensive Toyota Camry within a 10-mile radius from where I live?" It is those kind of services we will build. Unfortunately, XML does not reduce the need for a live human brain to build this service. The semantics between the discovery of the service and the data source that tells you which sort of information is out there today only exists within the developer's brain. There is no part of the XML, SOA, or other stacks that tell you how you map together the discovery of services to the information that you try to find.

## 2.6 XML Benefits in a Service World

There are three reasons why XML benefits a service universe: mid-tier persistence, multiple schema support, and service federation.

### 2.6.1 Mid-Tier Persistence

After the invention and adoption of client/server technology, many software architects referred to the Web as n-Tier architecture. Figure 2-11 illustrates the differences.

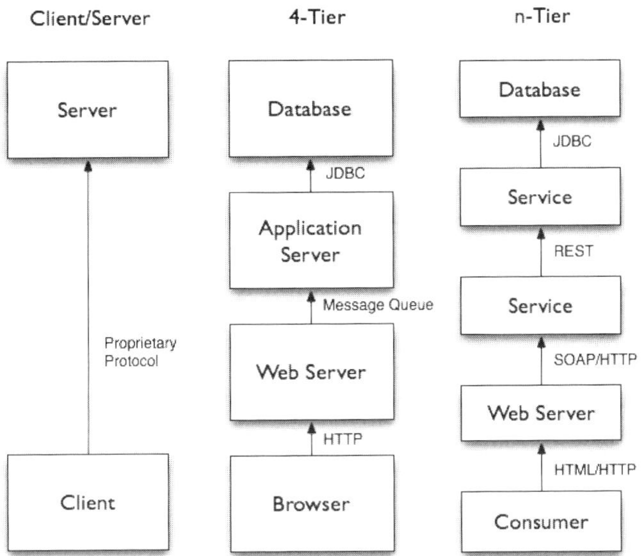


***Figure 2-11*** *Software architects and developers often talk about the Web as n-Tier architecture, when they are really only talking about a structure with fixed servers rooted in a database back end.*

While software architects and developers talk about the Web as n-Tier architecture, they usually are talking about a monolithic database that provides access to data through a strongly bound application server and Web server to a browser. In n-Tier architecture, a service consumer makes a request through several service tiers to answer a request. Many times the services called will be different for each type of request.

For instance, Figure 2-11 shows a service consumer making a request to a service over HTTP protocols. The Web Server unpackages the request and marshals a request over SOAP protocols to a service. That service uses REST protocols to request a response from another service. The REST service retrieves persisted data from a database server. This is the nature of the Web today: services making requests to a variety of services. In fact, the consumer may not be an end user but instead a data aggregation service.

In such a service environment the time it takes to perform each request is the sum of the time each subsequent service request makes up the chain of calls. Adding a mid-tier cache to the n-Tier design enables two benefits: improved performance and off-line browsing.

1. **Improved Performance**. The n-Tier architecture in Figure 2-11 requires that each request from the consumer be handled through the chain of service requests each time. The total time to process all of these requests is the sum of the time it takes each tier to respond. If any of the service tiers were intelligent enough to know that the response it recently gave is still valid, then the service could respond with a cached response. Responses from the cache are much faster than going through the chain of service requests.
2. **Off-line Browsing**. One could make the case that the weakest link in n-Tier architecture is *every* tier. If any one of the tiers loses connectivity or responds slowly, then the entire response back to the consumer suffers. With a mid-tier cache, a service accesses data from previous up-stream responses and can later query against that cache instead of going back to the original service. For instance, imagine a field repair technician for a cable television service. The farther away from his office, the worse the connectivity to the service that provides him with answers to a repair. Instead of running queries against the service in the office, the technician can query locally against the results already received from prior queries.

Improved performance and off-line browsing are benefits for considering mid-tier XML persistence in your architecture.

### 2.6.2 Multiple Schema Support

In the wild XML world, anyone can write his or here own schema that defines the format and rules for the XML data. There is no gatekeeper to the schemas for the world's XML data formats. The thought-leaders I wrote about earlier in this chapter encourage developers to write their own XML data formats. Additionally, schemas change over time as developers maintain software. We need to make an assumption for the systems we design and build that there are going to be billions of schemas out there.

There is some proof that schemas are about to get out of control. Post-2006 versions of Microsoft Office make XML the standard file format. The Microsoft file format implements a schema identifying paragraphs and other attributes of a document. However, the schema will not tell you where the word you are looking for is within the paragraph. So, literally, every time you save a file you create a new schema. It will still be up to your program to understand how to read into that XML data and extract the needed information.

### 2.6.3 Federated Service Requests

In my alternate XML world, the ability to connect to a number of different data sources—some XML and some not—is important. Most of the models proposed in the Web Services world still come down to a 3-tier architecture, where a consumer makes a request to a middle tier. And the middle tier makes a request to a single database. If that is all your architecture needs, then great. There are many object-relational frameworks to choose from. When you need to query against several data sources and present a single view of the composite data back to a service consumer—for instance, a composite application in SOA—then a federated service request approach is better. Federated service requests provide flexibility, performance, and data mitigation benefits to the enterprise. Chapters 3 and 4 show how.

## 2.7 Summary

This chapter showed the impact the software development communities' love affair with XML is having on SOA development. While there is no SOA standard to mandate using XML, most SOA applications I analyze use XML to define service interfaces, messages, and documents. XML impacts software application and service architecture and development. The Web made it fashionable to move XML messages from application to application. Today, we easily access the entire Internet in XML form using RSS, REST, and SOAP protocols, including new use cases for SOA Federation, SOA Acceleration, and Data Transformation, just to name a few.

# Chapter 3

# Understanding SOA Patterns

SOA applications typically use XML to encode data and a variety of messaging patterns to deliver it. In this chapter, I explain the building blocks of SOA in more depth by covering the SOA players, actions, message exchange patterns, intermediaries, and data and schema. This chapter prepares you for Chapter 4, where I discuss the findings from my SOA performance and scalability studies.

## 3.1 SOA Players

Components in SOA fall into one of three roles: consumer, service, or service broker. This section describes these roles and the actions associated with each.

- **The Consumer Role**. Consumers make requests to services. A consumer is a software application or another service that binds to the service using a predefined service interface and document schema.
- **The Service Role.** Services provide functions to consumers. Services accept consumer requests through their service interface using a document schema and execute an opera-

tion on the document. Services are available at known endpoints defined with a Universal Resource Locator (URL.)

- **The Service Broker Role**. Brokers bring consumers and services together by providing a registry of known services. The registry provides a search function for consumers to discover services. The registry provides the consumer with the URL to the service endpoint, the service interface definition, and document schema.

Consumers, services, and service brokers form the basic three roles in SOA. Next, we will see how these roles interact with each other.

### 3.1.1 Actions: Publish, Discover, Bind, and Execute

Each role uses actions to interact with the other roles. For instance, a consumer may use a broker directory service to discover a service that offers a specific type of interface. Figure 3-1 shows consumers, services, and service brokers interacting.

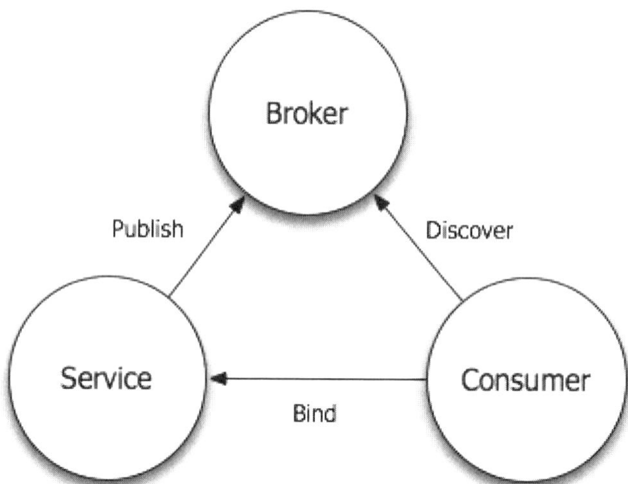


***Figure 3-1*** *Consumers, services, and brokers use actions to interoperate.*

The software development community continually improves its skills at designing and building SOA-based applications. When SOA was young, most consumers bound to a service using hard-coded endpoint URLs. This kind of static-to-static service design is appropriate when the consumer and service are well known, offer high quality-of-service availability, and rarely change.

As developers mature in their understanding of SOA, they usually adopt service broker technology to dynamically learn the endpoint URL at run time. In this case, a consumer initiates a service request by contacting a service broker. The consumer passes parameters of the service being sought, including the service name, method name, and document schema type. In this environment, services make themselves known to consumers by registering their supported interfaces with the broker. The consumer binds to the interface returned by the broker and a makes a service request using a proxy pattern.

Next, I will present several patterns for exchanging messages between consumer and service.

## 3.1.2 Messaging and Message Exchange Patterns

The SOA roles show consumers making requests to services and receiving responses using messages. There is no SOA standard to define a message pattern. Instead, several messaging patterns have emerged.

### *Synchronous Pattern*

The synchronous pattern is the most widely know mechanism for a consumer to use a service. A consumer makes a synchronous request and waits until it receives a response from the service. Figure 3-2 shows the sequence diagram of a synchronous message pattern.

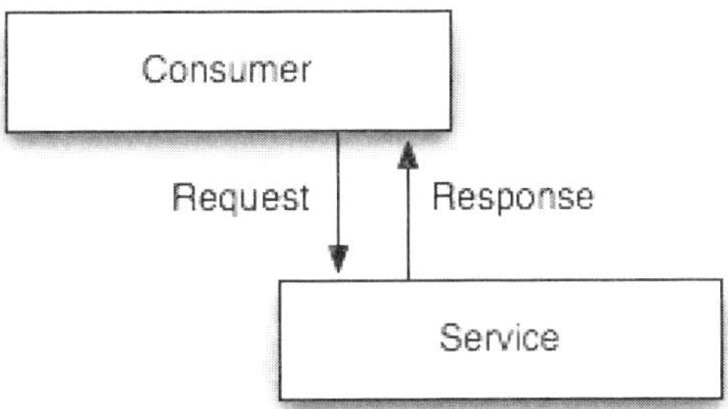


***Figure 3-2*** *A consumer making a synchronous request waits until it receives a response from the service.*

Synchronous message exchange is easier to develop and debug than the other message exchange patterns. Transaction processing and rollbacks are easier to build with synchronous message exchange.

Synchronous message exchange is the most stateful pattern and that presents a scalability and performance problem. Usually, consumer requests are executed using a thread pattern. Since the consumer blocks the thread until the service responds, the overall system risks running out of threads and other resources (memory, network sockets) if connectivity to the service runs slow or the service goes down.

### *Asynchronous Pattern*

The asynchronous pattern is popular with high-volume applications, because systems that use the asynchronous pattern do not require state; therefore, load-balancing patterns and message queues provide good scalability. In an asynchronous message exchange a consumer makes a request to a service. The request contains the message. The service receives the request and ends the connection. Asynchronous messages do not need to receive a response from the service. Figure 3-3 illustrates the asynchronous pattern.

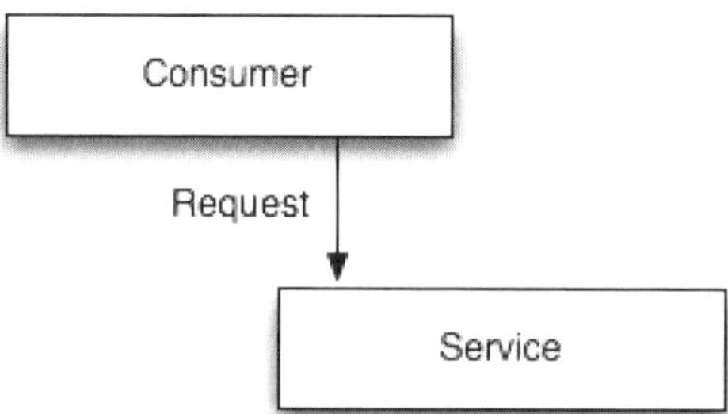


***Figure 3-3*** *Asynchronous message exchange is a one-way operation.*

Asynchronous message exchanges are popular because the consumer can continue to work on other tasks once it sends the request to the service. Also, the pattern reduces the need to keep network sockets open as in the synchronous pattern.

If the consumer needs confirmation that the service received the request, then the consumer must use a polling or callback pattern. In these situations the synchronous request-acknowledge message exchange pattern is a popular alternative pattern to asynchronous messages. Figure 3-4 shows the synchronous nonblocking pattern.

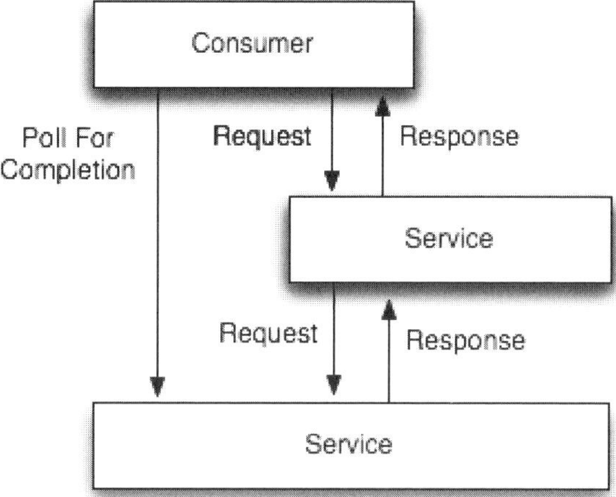


***Figure 3-4*** *The synchronous request-acknowledge pattern is often confused for asynchronous message exchange.*

In the synchronous request-acknowledge pattern the consumer sends a request to the service and receives an immediate response. The response is a simple acknowledgment message that the service received the request. With this pattern the consumer blocks for the short time it takes to receive the acknowledgment message. The consumer then quickly gets back to work on other tasks.

An optional variation on this pattern implements a polling mechanism at the consumer. The consumer makes the request to the service and receives the acknowledgment, which includes a session-tracking number. The consumer uses the tracking number to poll the service for completion of the requested function.

### *Reliable Message Patterns*

A lot can and does happen when moving messages across networks using Hypertext Transfer Protocol (HTTP) and synchronous message patterns. For instance, it is possible that a consumer makes a request to a service and receives a response to the previous request to the service. HTTP does not guarantee the order of delivery, the path for the message to take depending on the quality of service of the connection, or a guaranteed reply. HTTP does not guarantee reliability.

Reliable messaging patterns are important for many SOA applications, because they provide guaranteed delivery, only-once delivery, delivery in correct order, and guaranteed replies.

While there are many types of reliable message protocols available, I favor the OASIS Group specification for Web Services Reliable Messaging (WS-RM).[1] You will find open-source and commercial off-the-shelf technology (COTS) implementations. The specification defines patterns for reliable message exchanges and reliable reply message exchanges. In the OASIS Reliable Messaging Model, the service consumer (the sender) sends a message to the service (the receiver node). Upon receipt of the message and at the appropriate time, the receiver node sends back an acknowledgment message or fault message to the sender node. WS-RM uses a proxy pattern to layer the reliability protocols on the normal messaging patterns so the consumer and service concentrate on their tasks and leave the reliability to the Reliable Message Provider (RMP) proxy.[2]

The following describes the ways for the receiver to send back an acknowledgment message or a fault message to the sender.

### Response RM-Reply Pattern

In the Response RM-Reply pattern, the consumer sends a message and expects a response that includes an Acknowledgment message or a Fault message. The service responds with a service reply and the Acknowledgment. Figure 3-5 shows the Response RM-Reply pattern.

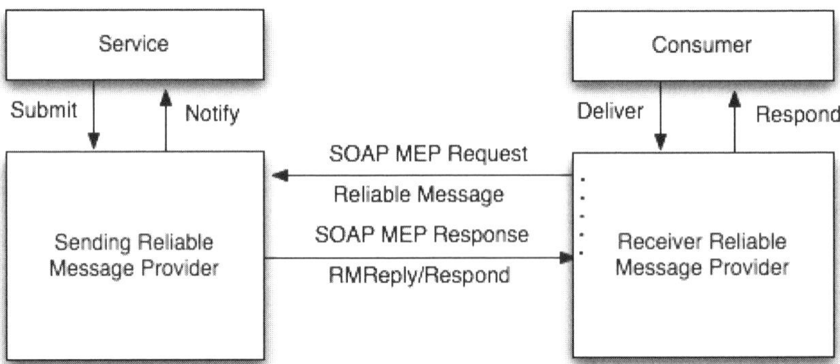


***Figure 3-5*** *The Response RM-Reply pattern uses a Reliable Message Provider proxy to guarantee a reply to the message. This is a synchronous pattern, which blocks until the reply is received.*

1 See http://www.oasis-open.org/committees/tc_home.php?wg_abbrev=ws-rx.

2 By proxy I mean a piece of software that acts as an intermediary between the message transport layer and the application, as opposed to a proxy server, which acts as a firewall on a corporate network.

The consumer's Reliable Message Provider (RPM) sends a Request to the service's RPM. In the event of an error, the consumer RPM tries to send the message again until it gets a response from the service's RPM. Of course, how many times and which action the RPM takes is configurable by the Reliable Messaging implementation.

### Callback RM-Reply Pattern

In the Callback RM-Reply pattern the consumer sends a message and expects a response that includes an Acknowledgment message or a Fault message. The service later contacts the Reliable Message Provider (RMP) proxy when the service has a response to the request. Figure 3-6 shows the Callback RM-Reply pattern.

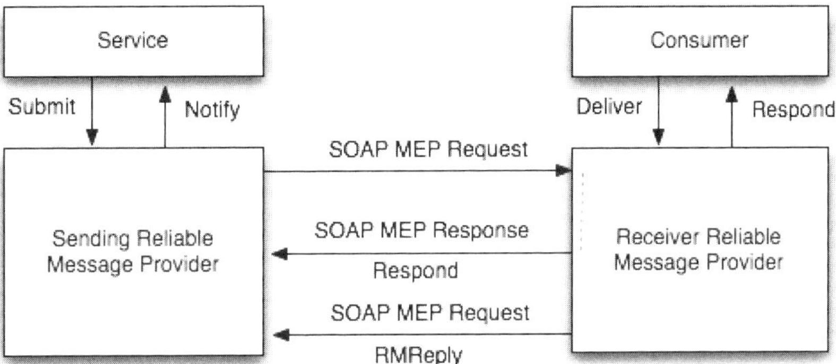


***Figure 3-6*** *The Callback RM-Reply pattern makes the request to the service and then waits for the service to call back to the consumer with a response.*

The consumer Reliable Message Provider (RPM) sends a Request to the service's RPM. In the event of an error, the consumer RPM tries to send the message again until it gets an acknowledgment response from the service's RPM. The service RPM makes a callback to the consumer RPM when a response is ready. This pattern is very useful to reduce network connection usage, since the consumer RPM does not hold open a socket connection to the service while the service works on a response. I have also seen the callback pattern used for one-way request message patterns and for batching Acknowledgment and Fault messages.

### Polling RM-Reply Pattern

While the Callback RM-Reply pattern may be attractive, there are conditions where it may not be used. For instance, when the consumer runs behind a firewall that restricts callbacks from the service, another approach needs to be taken. In the Polling RM-Reply pattern, the consumer sends a message and expects a response that includes an Acknowledgment message or a Fault message. The consumer RMP polls the service Reliable Message Provider (RMP) proxy until the service has a response to the request. Figure 3-7 shows the Polling RM-Reply pattern.

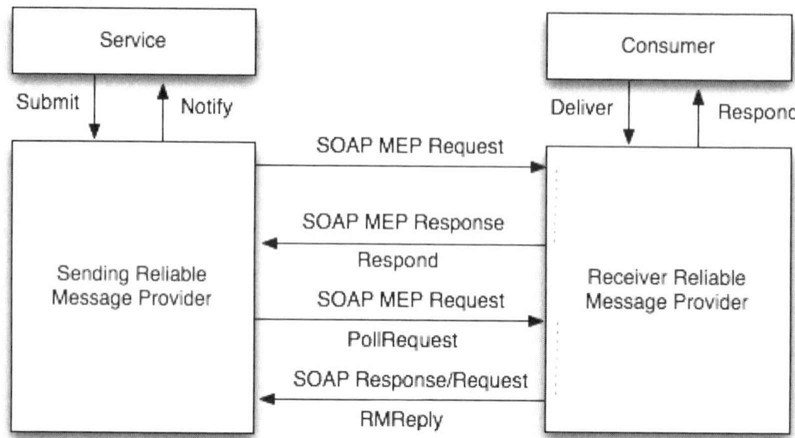


***Figure 3-7*** *The Polling RM-Reply pattern is useful when the consumer and service are separated by a firewall.*

The OASIS standard for Reliable Messaging also includes patterns for polling that use synchronous and asynchronous messaging, which you may find useful. See the specification for details.

The Reliable Messaging patterns give your SOA applications the flexibility to send reliable request/response or one-way messages using standard open protocols (SOAP and HTTP). Similar standards exist for non-SOAP protocols.

### 3.1.3 Three Popular Message Exchange Patterns

Among messaging and message exchange patterns section, I will cover three message exchange patterns that are popular in SOA designs: request/response, publish and subscribe, and broadcast or multicast.

### Request/Response Pattern

The Request/Response pattern is the simplest and most widely used messaging pattern, because it most resembles the way software developers make method calls to an object. In this pattern, the consumer and the service talk to each other directly as peers. Figure 3-8 illustrates the Request/Response pattern.

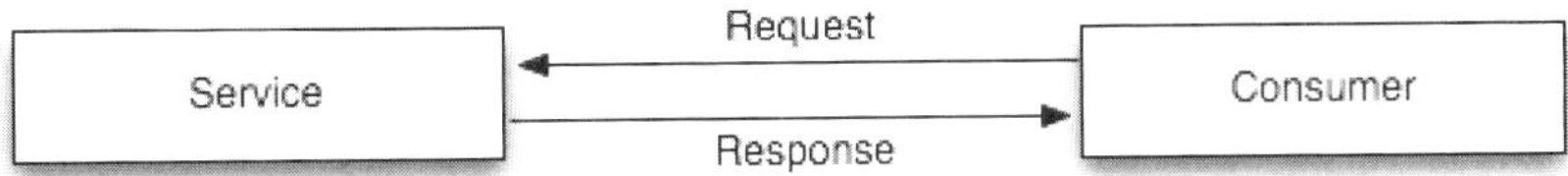


***Figure 3-8*** *The Request/Response pattern.*

The Request/Response pattern has a downside too. Software architects and developers often miss performance and scalability advantages of using the next patterns because the Request/Response pattern is so easy. The next two patterns usually require a little more effort to implement and provide their own unique advantages.

### Publish and Subscribe Pattern

In a Publish and Subscribe pattern, the service offers a set of functions to which the consumer may register. When a function has data to deliver, the service delivers the data to the consumer. Figure 3-9 illustrates the Publish and Subscribe pattern.

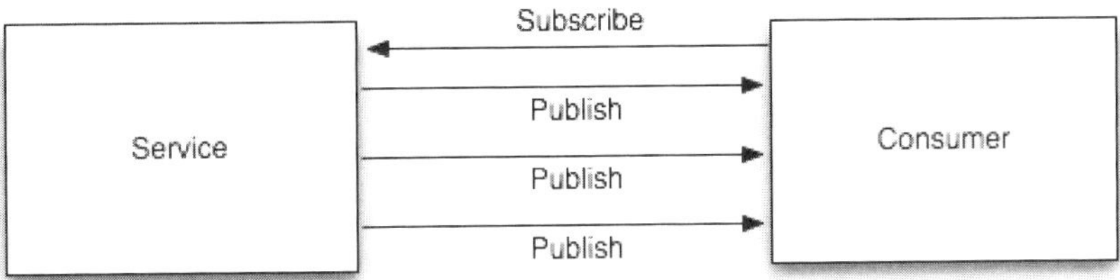


***Figure 3-9*** *The Publish and Subscribe pattern.*

Publish and Subscribe may also be implemented using a polling, where the consumer polls the service for changes. This is different from the Request/Reply pattern in that the service prevalidates the consumer and readies data specific to the consumer without requiring a connection to be open between the consumer and service.

### Broadcast or Multicast Pattern

The Broadcast pattern, sometimes called the Multicast pattern, sends the same message to a group of consumers. The message is identical to all of the consumers and no response is expected. Figure 3-10 illustrates the Broadcast pattern.

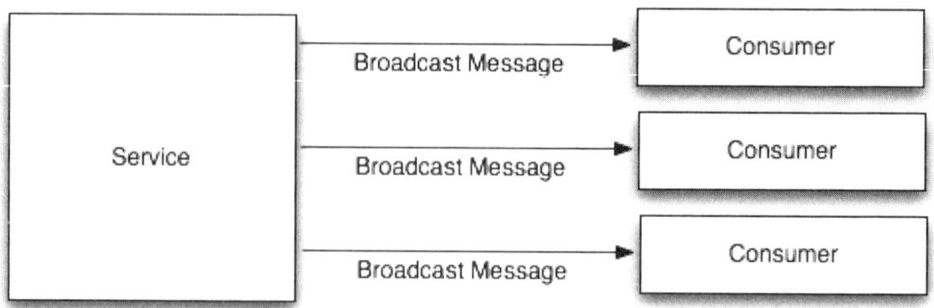


***Figure 3-10*** *The Broadcast pattern.*

The Broadcast pattern has the largest possibility of improving scalability and performance of an information system. However, it also has the most challenges. For instance, broadcast and multicast pattern implementations often relies on the underlying network technology to enable delivery of a single message to all the listening consumers. Additionally, corporate firewalls often block true multicast service as part of a commonly adopted security policy.

I often see a combination of the Publish and Subscribe pattern with the Broadcast pattern in an information system that needs to efficiently and rapidly deliver the same content to a group of consumers. Consumers subscribe to a broadcast channel and poll the service for new data.

## 3.2 Summary

This chapter showed the building blocks of SOA in more depth by covering the SOA players, actions, message exchange patterns, intermediaries, and data and schema. In the next chapter, we will discuss the findings from my SOA performance and scalability studies.

# Chapter 4

# Identifying And Avoiding SOA Performance Problems

The previous chapters showed the key drivers for SOA and XML. Business and information managers love SOA design patterns for their promise of agility and speed to build composite applications and integrate systems, and software developers love XML's simplicity and subversive nature. Unfortunately, the choice of both SOA and XML often leads to scalability and performance problems.

This chapter presents the findings from my SOA performance and scalability studies and introduces a new architecture—FastSOA—to solve the problems. I discuss the experiences that led me to develop FastSOA and the common traps that you can avoid by following a set of software development patterns when building SOA application. This chapter prepares you for Chapter 5, where I discuss the FastSOA architecture and patterns.

## 4.1 Patterns and Experiences That Led to FastSOA

Many times the software development tools we use to build software introduce scalability and performance problems of their own. It's easy! The lazy software developer in me finds it pretty easy to accept an Integrated Development Environment (IDE) default setting to write an object for me. My first reaction to SOAP and WSDL was elation. In a Web Services world I imagined letting my development tools generate code from WSDL interface definitions to build distributed applications. Looking at the results of my scalability studies showed me that relying on development tools alone was a good way to innocently introduce scalability and performance problems. I sat in my cubicle satisfied in the knowledge that I delivered functional code, while at the datacenter a truckload of servers arrives to run my application. Sound familiar?

If so, let me introduce you to patterns that require little or no additional work and accelerate XML and SOA performance.

### 4.1.1 Use SOAP Document-literal Encoding—Avoid SOAP RPC Encoding

In 2002, Darin MacBeath of Elsevier commissioned my company, PushToTest, to run a study of SOAP scalability and performance.[1] Darin is Elsevier's Chief Architect. To my knowledge, Elsevier operates the largest deployment of XML and Web Services technology in the commercial sector. Darin found me by reading my early articles on Web Services interoperability and scalability problems. He steered Elsevier to adopt SOAP as a standard service interface years before Web Services and SOA emerged as a popular architecture. Darin's thesis was that SOAP encoding styles greatly impact the scalability and performance of Web Services. He was right.

SOAP uses XML encoding to marshal data that is transported to a software application. The XML Protocol Working Group at the World Wide Consortium (W3C) standards body split between two architectural patterns when it developed the SOAP specification. One group viewed SOAP as document-oriented architecture enabling technology. Chapter 1 introduced the topic of document-oriented Web Services, where services pass a document from service to service and each service operates on its part of the document. I call this the document model. The second group viewed SOAP as a mechanism to make remote procedure calls (RPC) between objects running on a distributed group of server applications. The W3C codified the split between these two groups in the SOAP standard by defining two encoding styles:[2] SOAP Document-literal and SOAP RPC encoding.[3]

---

1 Full disclosure: Darin worked for a division of Elsevier that later acquired Morgan Kaufmann, the publishers of this book.

2 The standard actually defines variations of document and RPC encoding styles. I limit the discussion to these two in reflection of the real-world's adoption of these two encoding styles.

3 The SOAP standard defines RPC encoding in Section 5 of the standard document.

The encoding styles tell a SOAP stack how to transform from XML data into a serialized stream of characters that is sent over a network transport protocol—for instance, HTTP—to a remote service and application. The encoding style tells the receiving application how to transform the stream of characters back into XML data.

Shortly after I concluded the SOAP study, IBM developerWorks published my article describing the SOAP encoding scalability problem.[4] Figure 4-1 shows the results and an indication of the size of the problem.

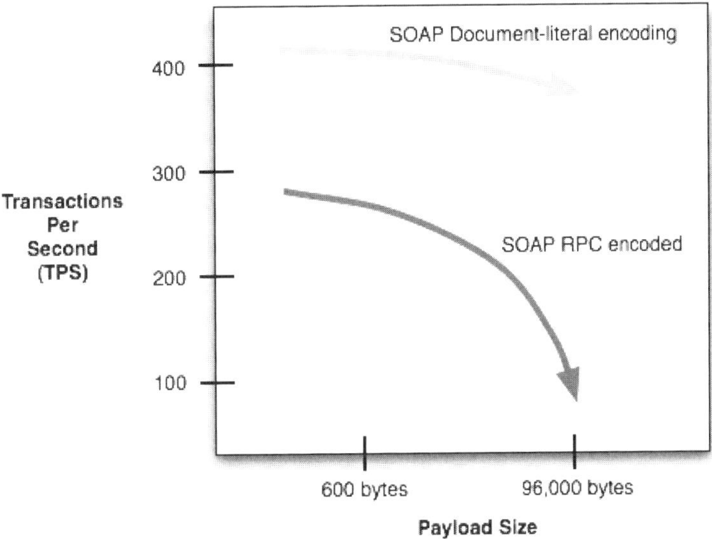


***Figure 4-1*** *SOAP encoding styles profoundly impact the scalability and performance of Web Services.*

The SOAP encoding study found that a developer's choice of encoding style determines to a large extent the scalability and performance a Web Services. The problems are most pronounced when using SOAP RPC encoding as payload size increases.

As Figure 4-1 shows, the test recorded 294 transactions per second when making requests where the response SOAP envelope measured 600 bytes of SOAP RPC–encoded data. As the test increased the response size, the transactions per second (TPS) ratio plummeted. When making requests of 96,000 bytes of SOAP RPC–encoded data, the test measured only 9.5 TPS.

4 See http://www-128.ibm.com/developerworks/webservices/library/ws-soapenc

When the test used SOAP Document-literal encoding, the performance fared much better. With 600 bytes of SOAP Document-literal–encoded data, the test measured 446 TPS. Additionally, SOAP Document-literal encoding did not show the plummeting TPS function of SOAP RPC–encoding performance. At 96,000 bytes of SOAP Document-literal encoded data, the test measured 387 TPS.

To see the test run in your own environment, you can download the test from the PushToTest Web site. Almost all of the scalability and performance studies commissioned by Elsevier, BEA, Sun, IBM, and others are available for download there. For instance, I built the Elsevier test environment by customizing my free open-source TestMaker tool to support SOAP RPC encoding and SOAP Document-literal style requests, as well as by implementing a Test Web Service (TWS) to respond to requests in these encoding styles.

Why would any software developer or architect purposely use SOAP RPC Encoding if they know that doing so adds a huge scalability and performance problem to the resulting service?

One reason is that SOAP RPC encoding is the style that offers the most simplicity for developers. The developer makes a call to a remote object, passing along any necessary parameters. The SOAP stack serializes the parameters into XML, moves the data to the destination using transports such as HTTP and SMTP, receives the response, deserializes the response back into objects, and returns the results to the calling method. Whew! SOAP RPC encoding handles all the encoding and decoding, even for very complex datatypes, and binds to the remote object automatically.

Building a Web Service using SOAP RPC encoding is easier for the developer too. For instance, Apache Axis, an open-source SOAP library, introspects Java code in files ending with .jws and creates a SOAP RPC–encoded service. When a consumer calls the service, the SOAP stack unmarshals the request parameters into objects and passes them to the method call of your object. The same service built with Document-literal encoding requires the developer to write code to parse through the XML tree to find the data elements needed, instantiate input objects, find the target object, and call one of its methods.

In the above example, the Apache Axis library is being *helpful* in publishing a service by introspecting a .jws source code file. The problem here is that the Axis tool chooses to use SOAP RPC encoding without explicitly telling the software developer. If the developer knows enough to look at the Axis-generated WSDL document for the new service, the developer will see the encoding style. But, I refer you back to Tim Bray's ironic question from Chapter 2: "Who knows WSDL?"

Another reason you may not want the tool to choose the encoding style regards the interoperability of the finished service. Services built with tools that default to SOAP RPC encoding are incompatible with tools that only marshal a Document-literal–encoded request. Many of the SOAP tools on the Java platform default to SOAP RPC encoding styles. For example, when using IBM WebSphere Application Developer, the default encoding style to publish a Java object as a Web Service is set to SOAP RPC. On the other side of the divide, Microsoft .NET development tools implement Document-literal style SOAP calls by default. This makes the consumer's encoding incompatible with the service. Both can be made to interoperate, but developers need to be wise to the different encoding styles to avoid problems.

At work in the above example is a fundamental difference in approaches from the software development tools vendors. In their attempt to make software developers' lives easier, the tools may be making decisions for you that affect scalability and performance of the finished service. This was highlighted when Microsoft and Sun debated the relative virtues of JEE and .NET at an event hosted in Silicon Valley by the Software Development Forum.[5] Microsoft made the argument that it serves developers best by being the sole supplier of a complete solution. At the other end of the spectrum, Sun posited that developers should have a choice of tools that they can assemble into a solution. This top-down versus bottom-up argument permeates into both companies' development tools. For example, representatives from Sun and Microsoft were asked to explain why developers would choose SOAP RPC encoding over SOAP Document-literal–style encoding. Microsoft's reps gave a somewhat technical answer, but conceded that they thought the issue was moot, since developers should rely on their development tools to make decisions about encoding styles.

Software developers serve themselves best by making informed decisions about how helpful their development tools and environments should be. Understanding each tool's handling of SOAP encoding styles is an important factor in delivering well-performing and reliable software projects.

---

5 See http://www.sdforum.org.

The test results from Figure 4-1 show the throughput when a SOAP stack uses RPC encoding and Document-literal encoding on the same data. The service composes a response by encoding all of the elements in the response. The better pattern is to parse the XML data yourself. Since you know the data in the XML tree best, your code will parse that data more efficiently than a generalized SOAP stack code using RPC encoding. Document-literal encoding with custom parsing logic yields even faster and more scalable results.

Next, I will describe a common problem when using HTML/HTTP tools in an XML environment.

### 4.1.2 Use XML Tools to Build XML Services—Java App Server Tools Handle XML Data Poorly[6]

Many information systems strategies (including the U.S. Department of Defense Net-Centric Data Strategy, known as NCES[7]) aim for rapid integration, flexible data management, systems interoperability, and lower total cost of ownership (TCO) through the use of SOA practices. Unfortunately, existing commercial off-the-shelf (COTS) and open-source Java solutions do not perform well enough to become viable platforms for SOA development.

For instance, General Motors is a proponent of ebXML in SOA, and its early designs—using the Universal Business Language (UBL)—created XML messages that are 150 kilobytes to 10 megabytes or larger. In 2004, I determined that the Java application server technology of the day did not deliver sufficient throughput and exhibited scalability and performance problems in the GM Web Services Performance Benchmark that I authored.

At the time, XML-based Web Services technology was still fairly new and I expected the performance problems to be resolved with new generations of the application server technology. Most of these problems still exist.

In 2005, BEA commissioned a new SOA performance study that shows how applications built with current Java application servers deliver performance that is not production worthy when dealing

6 This may be better explained as "Object-Oriented Application Servers Handle XML Data Poorly," as all indicators point to the same scalability and performance problems in .NET.

7 Details found http://www.disa.mil/nces/ne4.html.

with complex XML messages.[8] The problems are the same as those in earlier studies:

1. Simple Object Access Protocol (SOAP) bindings are inefficient and slow.
2. Every request requires an entirely new set of resources (objects, CPU, and network bandwidth) to process a response. There is no caching pattern.

To understand these problems, consider how software developers build and deploy an XML service using Java Enterprise Edition (JEE) application server tools.[9] These tools introduce a significant scalability problem in the SOAP service interface bindings (essentially a proxy) generated by tools found in Java application servers.

Since its introduction 10 years ago, Java has become the predominant server-side programming language to enable the Web. Most organizations today deploy JEE architectures for Web browser-based applications, including technology components of a relational database management system (RDBMS) in combination with an application server. Figure 4-2 illustrates the standard Web browser-based 3-tier architecture. These are reliable and scalable systems that deliver performance of 60 transactions per second (TPS) on an entry-level server.

As organizations move to SOA, they want to extend existing technology investments. Most application server publishers promote the use of JEE development tools to build SOA.

While there are a variety of techniques for building an XML-based Web Service, many of the tools state a preference to begin from a Web Services Description Language (WSDL) definition of the service. Java application servers provide a utility that inputs a WSDL definition and generates a binding class. The binding receives a SOAP request and routes the request to a Java object or Enterprise Java Bean (EJB) for processing. The SOAP binding is a Java class that is called through a servlet interface. Figure 4-3 shows the process to create a SOAP binding using one of these tools.

Figure 4-4 shows a JEE environment extended to support SOA development with an auto-generated SOAP binding in place.

---

8 Details found at http://www.pushtotest.com.

9 In 2005 Sun renamed Java 2 Enterprise Edition (J2EE) to Java Enterprise Edition (JEE) by dropping the version number from the title.

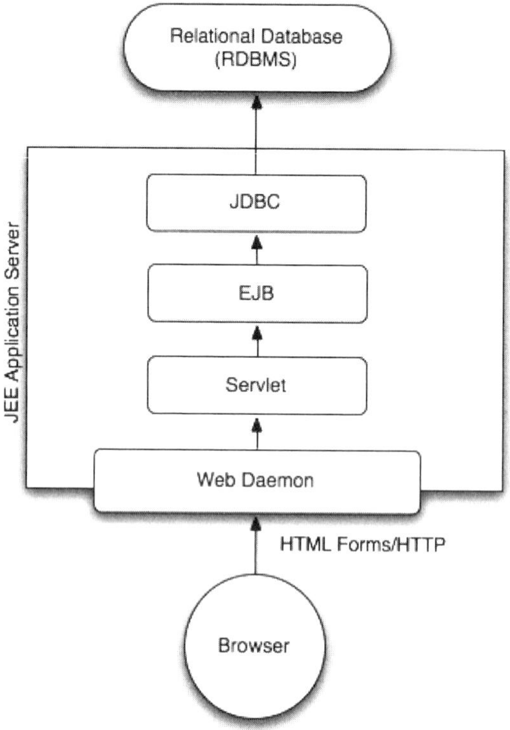


***Figure 4-2*** *Traditional JEE application server technology responds to Web browser requests across open protocols in a well-understood architecture.*

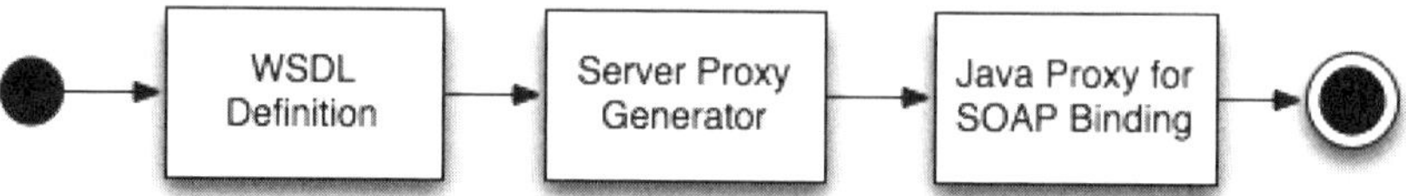


***Figure 4-3*** *Software developers take advantage of easy tools in JEE application servers to build SOAP bindings.*

The SOAP binding deserializes the XML content from the SOAP message body. This is processor-intensive and complicated because the message body often includes complex datatypes. For instance, the consumer may send a hash map containing multiple values to the service. The SOAP binding needs to decode the hash collection and instantiate Java objects for each value contained. A collection may contain other collections, so the process of decoding SOAP mes-

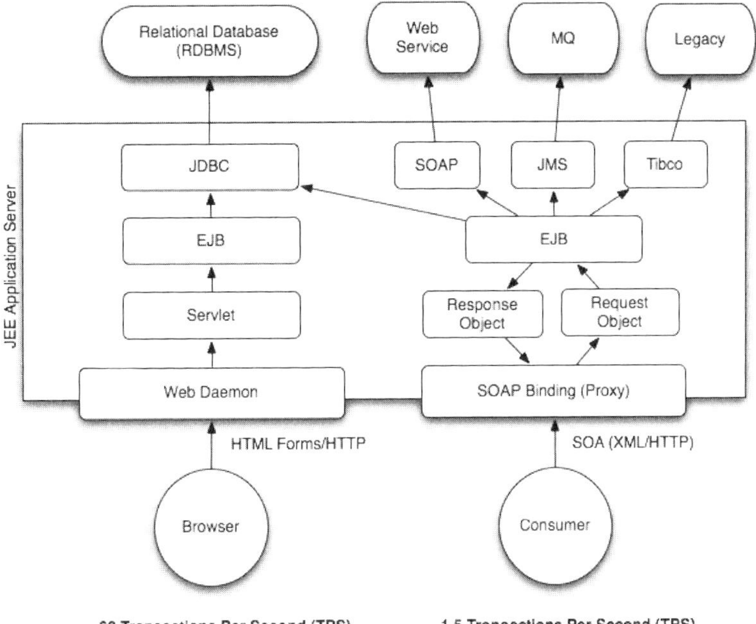


***Figure 4-4*** *Performance decreases dramatically when using a Java Web application server to handle XML and Web Services data.*

sage contents is not easy. Don't believe me? Take a look at the source code to the Apache Axis deserializer. It is huge!

The SOAP binding instantiates a Java Request object that contains the SOAP message body contents. The SOAP binding calls the target method in the target class and passes the Request object as a parameter. The target EJB or Java object provides all of the processing necessary to create a response to the request. The SOAP binding serializes the return value from the EJB or Java object into a SOAP response message. The SOAP binding goes through the same complexity to decode the values in the response object into values it can serialize into a SOAP response message.

In a 2005 study of SOAP bindings created with utilities from the popular Java application servers, I found these problems:

1. The SOAP bindings generated by the application server utilities are inefficient. For instance, certain SOAP bindings create multiple copies of the SOAP request, with each request instantiated as a String object, for no apparent rea-

son. Some of the SOAP bindings instantiate up to 15,000 Java objects to deserialize the SOAP request that contain 500 elements in the SOAP message body.

2. A server equipped with dual CPU 3.0-GHz Intel Xeon processors delivered throughput of 15 to 20 transactions per second (TPS) when processing simple SOAP messages, where the 10-kilobyte payload contained 50 elements. As the complexity and size of the SOAP messages grew, I observed significant scalability and performance problems. Throughput fell to 1.5 TPS for SOAP messages with a 100-kilobyte payload containing 750 elements. The larger the number of elements and the depth of each element in the SOAP message body, the worse is the problem.

The performance problem multiplies in SOA designs. SOA is a technique for component software reuse. Often one service calls another service in a chain to determine the response to a request from a consumer, as shown in Figure 4-5. Not only will the performance problem appear in a single service, but each service adds the same overhead as it serializes and deserializes requests and responses. The performance problem multiplies with the number of layers of services called.

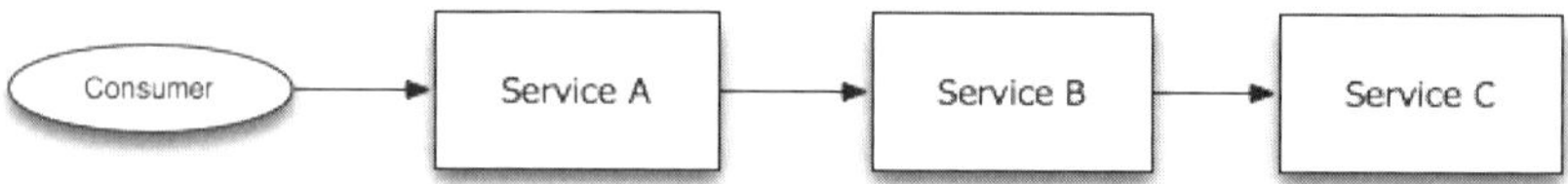


***Figure 4-5*** *SOA design patterns emphasis service reuse, which in-turn amplifies scalability and performance problems.*

You may think I am headed toward a conclusion that includes throwing out your JEE application server to handle XML data. Rest assured I am not advocating the end of JEE application servers.

## 4.2 Mitigate Performance Problems with the FastSOA Architecture

I am advocating an XML data mitigation strategy, which adds an XML-specific mid-tier to your SOA designs to deliver needed scalability and performance. Figure 4-6 illustrates the FastSOA architecture running alongside—not replacing—the JEE application server.

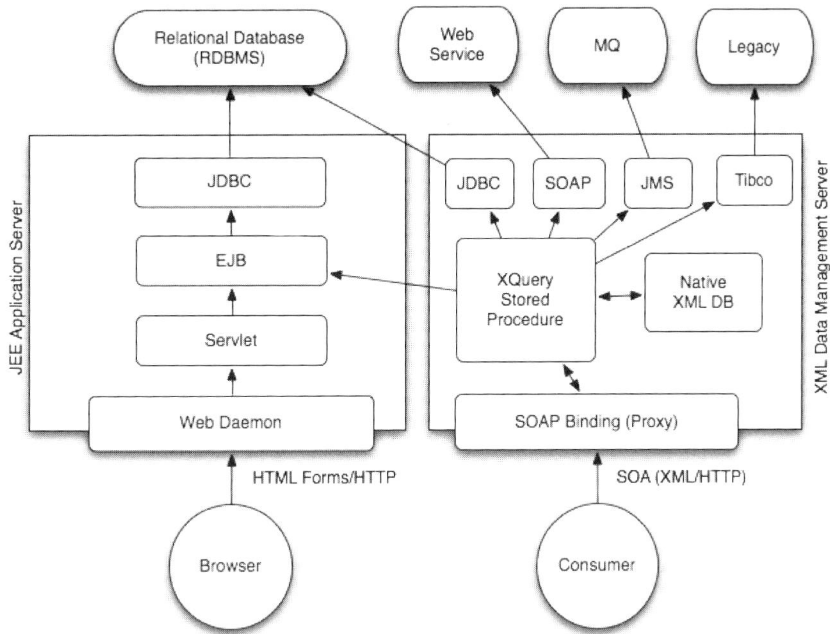


***Figure 4-6*** *The FastSOA pattern uses XQuery and native XML database technology to deliver acceptable scalability and performance.*

The FastSOA architecture runs in tandem with existing Web-based infrastructure. Chapter 5 explains the FastSOA architecture in great detail. For the moment I will illustrate one advantage of using the FastSOA architecture in your SOA designs.

The FastSOA architecture built with native XML tools is an ideal way to expose SOAP service interfaces. In such a design, the consumer makes a SOAP over HTTP request to a SOAP binding. The SOAP binding calls an XQuery stored procedure to directly handle the XML request document in the XQuery engine. The XQuery processes the native XML request, including possibly making queries to other services, to JEE objects, and data sources via JDBC, SOAP, and JMS protocols. The XQuery generates an XML response document and returns it to the SOAP binding as the response to the consumer.

I tested this design and found the FastSOA implementation delivered a minimum of four times the performance of the same service built on JEE servers. Table 4-1 compares performance.

The FastSOA approach uses native XML technology. Avoiding a transformation from XML-based SOAP messages into Java objects

***Table 4-1*** *Comparing Java to FastSOA Performance*

| FastSOA Performance | JEE Application Server Performance | Analysis |
|---|---|---|
| 6–9 TPS | 1.5 - 2 TPS | 4 to 4.5 times faster |

for the request, and the opposite for the response, solves a major bottleneck to good performance. Additionally, the SOAP bindings provided by the JEE application server were highly inefficient and introduced their own performance problems.

Later in this chapter, I show how even greater performance increases are possible using the FastSOA pattern when you consider the impact of mid-tier data caching. The FastSOA pattern includes a native XML database to store requests for commonly requested data. Most SOA and XML data include a time-to-live (TTL) element. This determines the time when the data within a service expires.

When the service receives requests for the same document multiple times, the FastSOA service returns a response that is cached in the mid-tier native XML database. This delivers SOA acceleration through caching for quick SOA performance.

### 4.2.1 Use Unencoded XML Elements with Strings—Avoid JAX-RPC SOAPElement

Building SOA with Java technologies has three problems:

1. The Domain Model pattern and other patterns that use object-oriented code to bind, parse, and build XML data deliver poor performance and scalability.[10]
2. There are many competing technology choices for the software developer to make, and each choice impacts scalability and performance in different ways.
3. All the existing approaches may crumble when Sun Microsystems (Java's benevolent dictator) finally picks an XML approach that everyone will fall inline with.

None of these problems is insurmountable. Let me explain these problems in detail and offer my approach to solve them.

10 Chris Richardson explains the Domain Model pattern in his book *POJOs in Action.*

You may be wondering why I chose XQuery as part of the FastSOA pattern. Many developers have asked me if they could implement FastSOA using Java. My original approach to solve SOA scalability and performance problems used Java to implement a fast and efficient SOAP binding and XML data handler. With each attempt I bumped up against two problems: XML is not a native type in Java, so each request uses additional resources and time transforming the message into objects, and that reduces performance. Second, every year the Java thought-leaders would get behind a new technology for building XML-based applications and services. Each technology was viable, had its own product road map, release schedule, and scalability and performance profile. Keeping track with the current XML handling flavor of the year was very difficult and time consuming.

If you are a .NET developer and shaking your head at the folly of so many XML handling approaches in Java, don't be so smug. Microsoft is approaching XML from many different directions too. For instance, Erik Meijer[11] is leading the XLinq[12] project to deliver an XML programming interface for .NET developers. From my view, Microsoft's efforts to deliver XLinq as a standard way to work with XML data using SQL-like operators looks analogous to the JDOM project in the Java world.[13] XLinq does not replace the existing methods to work with XML data in .NET. With both Java and .NET, it seems likely to me that developers will have to choose an XML technology strategy and work to integrate the various offerings. For instance, even though JDOM is part of the official Java Community Process mechanism to become part of Java, developers still need to write code to use JDOM when building service interfaces with JAX-RPC and SAAJ (the service interface building components in the Java Web Services Developer Pack – JWSDP).[14] The JAX-RPC APIs do not directly use JDOM object types to represent XML data.

For Java developers today, the JAX-RPC API has Sun's official seal of approval to build SOAP-based service interfaces. Sun is not isolated from the reality that the development community cleaves into two around the Remote Procedure Call (RPC) versus document-oriented service interfaces (issues described in Chapter 1 and earlier in

---

11 See http://research.microsoft.com/%7Eemeijer.

12 See http://research.microsoft.com/~emeijer/Papers/XLinq%20XML%20Programming%20Refactored%20%28The%20Return%20Of%20The%20Monoids%29.htm.

13 See http://www.jdom.org and JSR 108 at http://www.jcp.org.

14 See http://java.sun.com/webservices/jwsdp/index.jsp.

this chapter). Sun will rename JAX-RPC to JAX-WS in the next release to reflect the merged support for both RPC and document-oriented service architectures.

Some of the confusion over SOAP encoding styles goes back to the days when the W3C standards body argued over the SOAP design. SOAP was intended to be an RPC protocol and never had in mind using SOAP with large documents. Instead, SOAP was supposed to be used for simple method calls with a few parameters. Document-style encoding made it into the SOAP specification as an alternative to RPC. Consequently, many tools for building SOAP-based services offer tricks to enable software developers to use document-style encoding. Consider the following three tricks when using JAX-RPC to send an XML document (parameters) to the service.

1. **Using SOAPElement.** The developer writes a WSDL definition of the service using xsd:anyType and JAX-RPC creates a SOAPElement object representing the XML document.
2. **Using String.** The developer writes a WSDL definition of the service using xsd:string and JAX-RPC creates a String object representing the XML document.
3. **Encoded Array of Bytes.** Using the JAX-RPC Source type delivers an interface that uses SOAP with Attachments (SwA). SwA is a nonstarter in most cases, because few non-Java SOAP stacks implement SwA encoders directly.

The above approaches deliver acceptable performance and scalability when the XML data is cute and cuddly.[15] For instance, an XML document with 50 elements and less than 5 kilobytes of data will deliver the same performance regardless of encoding style or WSDL type definition. The problems surface when using JAX-RPC to handle 100 kilobytes or more and complex multiple orders of hierarchy in an XML document.

When working with moderate and huge XML documents, as described in Figure 4-7, most software developers I work with wonder how it could be that JAX-RPC does not offer something better than String, DOM, or SOAPElement to handle these large payloads. Who in their right mind would be sending 10-megabyte Strings through Java code and expect it to perform?

15 Inspired by the film *Madagascar,* "cute and cuddly" is part of my lexicon to describe simple and small XML data.

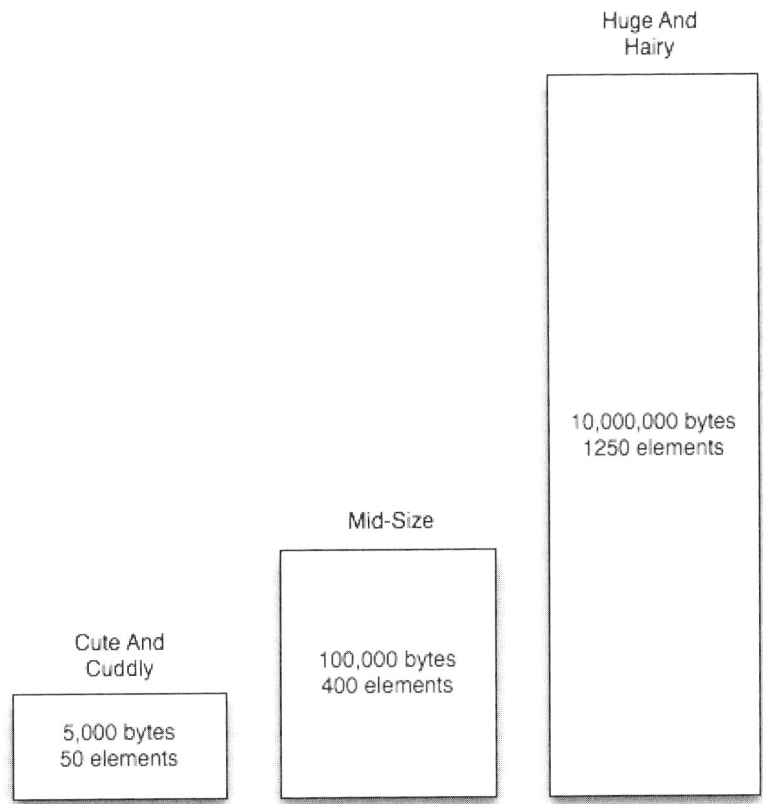


***Figure 4-7*** *JAX-RPC APIs work acceptably for the cute-and-cuddly level of XML documents but run into significant problems dealing with huge-and-hairy documents.*

This is exactly where the rubber meets the road. I have found no way to generate a SOAPElement (xsd:anyType) element efficiently from the JAX-RPC specifications. When Simon Tuffs,[16] a colleague, compared the performance of SOAPElement, String, and SWA using the JAX-RPC reference implementation in the JWSDP 1.5, he found that SOAPElement performance was a nonstarter.

The results shown in Table 4-2 and Figure 4-8 are astonishing. SOAPElement avoids XML entity encoding (all those < and > signs transformed to < and >) but more than makes up for it with the massive load of building a DOM document as part of its strategy to transform XML data between the consumer and service.

16 See http://www.simontuffs.com

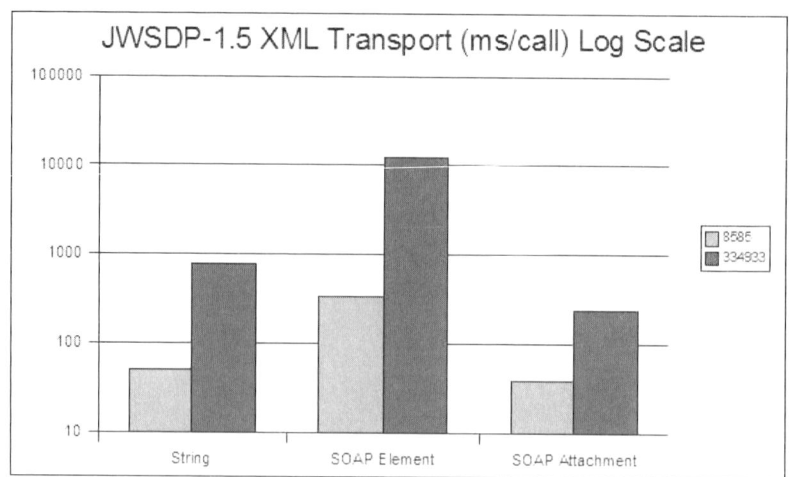


***Figure 4-8*** *SOAPElement is a poor choice for performance.*

***Table 4-2*** *Contrasting JAX-RPC Performance Using Various XML Datatypes*

| | **8,585 bytes** | **334,933 bytes** |
|---|---|---|
| String | 50 milliseconds | 773 milliseconds |
| SOAP Element | 331 milliseconds | 12,284 milliseconds |
| SOAP Attachment | 39 milliseconds | 243 milliseconds |

That leaves software developers who choose JAX-RPC to build service interfaces with few choices to efficiently handle moderate to huge payloads. Even if SOAPElement performance were good in the JWSDP reference implementation, I still would not recommend its DOM approach, which requires the entire document to be in memory before the service starts transmitting it across the wire. For these moderate to huge XML messages, a streaming solution appears the most likely candidate for FastSOA.

A far superior choice in Java would be to stream an XML document into a SOAPElement (xsd:anyType) element; however, that could lead to badly formed SOAP documents and potential security holes. For moderate and huge XML messages, String appears to be the safe choice for security, interoperability, and performance.

Unfortunately, this means that all of the SOAP stacks that adopted the JAX-RPC specification have the same problems handling moderate to huge XML messages. The JAX-RPC specification is widely implemented, both by open source projects—for example, Apache Axis—and by commercial vendors such as Sun, IBM, and BEA.

Finally, if the above discussion makes you think about writing your own SOAP binding, then please stop. Consider these issues before choosing to write your own SOAP binding.

1. It will be up to you to maintain your SOAP binding code when the SOAP specification changes and/or software developers begin to widely use different and incompatible implementation styles.
2. You will need to publish and maintain a service interface development kit (akin to a Software Development Kit—SDK) for your service. Many software developers need example code they have previous experience using to really understand an SDK.
3. When tools emerge to rapidly build service interfaces, you will missout on their advantages while you maintain your custom code.

While this section discussed the JAX-RPC APIs and datatypes, the next shows how choosing the best parser that is appropriate to your data impacts performance and scalability.

### 4.2.2 Use the XML Parser That Is Appropriate to Your Data

Often SOA designs overlook the impact an XML parser has on the performance and scalability of the finished system. Chapter 1 urged, among other things, a document-centric approach to building SOA-based information systems. Earlier in this chapter I showed the scalability and performance problems of using remote procedure call (RPC) patterns in SOA. Adopting these patterns does not automatically deliver good performance and scalability.

Software developers have a variety of approaches to XML message parsing, including the Streaming API for XML (StAX), XML binding compiler, Java Architecture for XML Binding (JAXB and JIBX), and Document Object Model (DOM) techniques. Some provided better performance than others. For instance, many StAX parsers deliver 2 to 10 times faster performance than DOM parsers. Much of the performance difference came from matching the right XML parser to the type of data being parsed. For instance, parsing a complex document that uses the automotive industry Business Object Document (BOD) schema[17] will highlight performance of some XML parser implementations, while working with simple RSS feeds will show other parsers in a favorable light.

Testing XML parser implementations against three use cases delivers useful performance and scalability knowledge:

- Parsing moderate to huge XML documents. The documents are typically 10 kilobytes to 5 megabytes—for instance, an HL7 document or BOD. In this case, I recommend using an XML binding compiler such as JAXB, which addresses elements directly.
- Parsing XML documents that contain many elements that are not nested deeper than two or three elements deep. Think of a stream of data where skipping unwanted elements yields a performance advantage. In this case, a Streaming XML (StAX) approach works best.
- Parsing medium-sized documents with a little bit of complexity—for example, a purchase order from a manufacturer where you need to evaluate every element in the order. In this case, an XML parser using DOM may be best.

### 4.2.3 Use a Database That Is Tuned to Your Data Definition—Native XML Databases Help Relational Databases

While there is no SOA standards body to recommend XML, most of the SOA applications I work with use XML to exchange messages and provide service interfaces. The strong focus on XML in SOA makes relational database technology look like a square peg in a field of round holes.

Consider how foreign XML datatypes and operators look to a relational database. For instance, writing SQL commands to insert and query XML data require specialized nonstandard SQL commands. Additionally, relational databases have a rich history of tools to provide adhoc queries and complex joins. Unfortunately, these tools typically do not allow the same rich features when querying

17 The Standards for Technology in Automotive Retail (STAR) organization, comprised of companies supporting retail automotive operations, contracted to the Open Application Group (OAGi) to build an XML schema that describes the operations between auto retailers and supplier.
Details are at http://www.starstandards.org.

XML data stored in a relational database, because the XML data model is too different for them.

While none of these issues is overly difficult to understand and overcome for the average software developer native XML technology offers better developer productivity and operating scalability and performance to the software developer, architect, or CIO who chooses SOA, even if his or her organization is standardized around a relational database. Native XML technology mitigates and aggregates data in a way that accelerates relational database performance, scalability, and developer productivity.

For example, consider a mid-tier data service built with native XML technology as an alternative to using relational XML datatypes. In the mid-tier, a service receives the XML data, breaks it down into relational datatypes, and stores the data in relational tables. The XQuery needed to do this may then optimize the storage techniques, index techniques, and data loading techniques specifically for your data and database. This technique also takes into account differences in XML support that vary by relational database vendor and version of the database.

Native XML technology is a viable strategy to supplement relational database storage. For instance, the relational database holds the metadata for queries and the native XML database holds the original XML data for retrieval.

There is no reason to think of native XML technology as an either or proposition. For instance, some relational databases provide XQuery as an alternative to SQL. Many times the results of combining native XML technology with relational technology leads to better developer productivity, scalability, and performance.

Mid-tier active SOA approaches to SOA may even be the way to solve the supposed impedance mismatch between XML, object, and relational data models. Thought-leaders such as Steve Loughran[18] and Edmund Smith do not believe that Object/XML mapping is possible with Java and .NET. Loughran and Edmund describe many incompatibilities that are native in the object world that are incompatible with XML, including the following: sometimes it is just impossible to map XML constructs to Java objects, XML Schema namespaces are incompatible with Java object names, performance problems prevent deployment of services that use larger payloads

18 See http://www.hpl.hp.com/techreports/2005/HPL-2005-83.pdf.

and when network latency increases, and WSDL descriptions of these services are too complex for the average software developer.

The above issues led me to identify the need for FastSOA. Next, I describe the FastSOA pattern itself.

### 4.2.4 Understanding the FastSOA Pattern

FastSOA is an architecture and software coding practice (pattern) that addresses these problems:

1. FastSOA solves SOAP binding performance problems by reducing the need for Java objects and increasing the use of native XML environments to provide SOAP bindings.
2. FastSOA introduces a mid-tier service cache to provide SOA service acceleration.
3. FastSOA uses native XML persistence to solve XML, object, and relational incompatibility.

Figure 4-9 illustrates the FastSOA architecture.

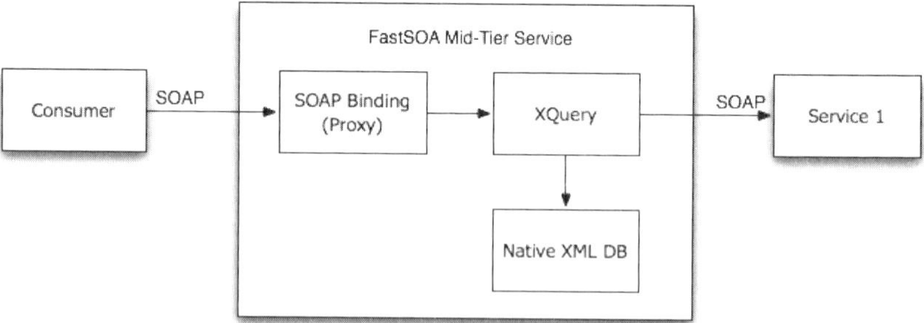


***Figure 4-9*** *The FastSOA architecture.*

FastSOA is an architecture that provides a mid-tier service binding, XQuery processor, and native XML database. The binding is a native and streams-based XML data processor. The XQuery processor is the actual mid-tier that parses incoming documents, determines the transaction, communicates with the "local" service to obtain the stored data, serializes the data to XML, and stores the data into a cache while recording a time-to-live duration. While this is an XML-oriented design, XQuery and native XML databases handle non-XML data, including images, binary files, and attachments. An equally important benefit to the XQuery processor is the ability to define policies that operate on the data at run time in the mid-tier.

The FastSOA architecture runs in tandem with existing Web-based infrastructure and deploys in the mid-tier of a set of services to quickly handle service consumer requests. For instance, a consumer makes a SOAP request to a service. The mid-tier FastSOA service provides a SOAP binding. The binding calls an XQuery to handle the XML request document in the XQuery engine. FastSOA enables you to write business processing logic in the XQuery to form a response to the request. Additionally, FastSOA enables the XQuery to check the cache to see if the request was previously received; in this case, the FastSOA service is able to return the response from the cache without having to go upstream to make the request to the service. This process delivers SOA acceleration through native XML SOAP bindings and caching for quick SOA performance.

The advantages of the FastSOA approach are:

1. Your SOA environment runs faster and requires less CPUs and network bandwidth. FastSOA is a native XML environment.
2. Service end points are standards based. To the rest of your applications, the FastSOA mid-tier system looks like a SOAP service.
3. No need to replace your existing systems or code. The FastSOA mid-tier cache fits into your existing datacenter as a data aggregation and mitigation service.
4. In the event that the upstream service is temporarily unavailable, the FastSOA approach provides an easy mechanism for browsing cached data while the service is off-line.
5. Requests that are served from the cache lower the amount of bandwidth normally needed to support communication between consumer and service.

To understand FastSOA from a practical standpoint consider the following example application.

### 4.2.5 Mid-Tier Cache Pattern and Example

Earlier in this chapter, I described the performance advantage in using native XML to provide SOAP bindings. The resulting service enjoyed four times better performance. In the following example, I show how to provide even better service acceleration through mid-tier caching.

General Motors (GM) created a service using SOA patterns to enable automotive dealerships to order parts from a manufacturing facility using ebXML-based patterns and protocols. The service understands an XML schema from the Software Technology in Automotive Retailing (STAR) organization.[19] STAR is a combined effort of the big automotive manufacturers, including GM. STAR created and maintains the Business Object Document (BOD) schema and defines, among many other things, a request for an inventory check.

The CheckInventory request validates the requester and checks inventory levels and status. The service consumer creates an inventory request document according to the BOD schema. The consumer marshals the document in a request and sends it over a network to the service. The service sends an inventory status response that shows the parts that are in stock.

The parts ordering service benefits from the FastSOA patterns by reducing network bandwidth needs and mitigating the service bandwidth needed to respond to redundant requests.

For instance, the inventory response for the parts from an automotive dealership includes a time-to-live (TTL) element. The TTL element defines the number of seconds that the response is valid. For example, GM may have set this value to 60 seconds. During those 60 seconds the mid-tier server responds to inventory requests from the stored cache of inventory responses from the mid-tier. The service avoids unnecessary bandwidth use and improves the time to respond to requests.

Table 4-3 shows how to calculate service acceleration metrics in a network where the service resides on a server external to the local network and a FastSOA data mitigation aggregation service resides on the local network.

***Table 4-3*** *Metrics to Calculate Service Acceleration*

| Action | No Caching | Caching Enabled |
|---|---|---|
| Time to Process First Request | 1,765 | 2,218 |
| Time to Store the Request in Cache | n/a | 453 |

19 See http://www.starstandard.org.

*Table 4-3 Metrics to Calculate Service Acceleration (continued)*

| Action | No Caching | Caching Enabled |
|---|---|---|
| Subsequent Identical or Redundant Requests | 1,765 | 320 |
| Internet Bandwidth Used | 30,400 Kbits | 304 Kbits |
| Total Time Used | 2,941 minutes | 533 minutes |
| All times are in milliseconds unless noted.<br>Assumptions:<br>100-Mbit Ethernet connection from consumer to Cache Service and DSL connection at 1.5 Mbits/second up and down.<br>Time to Live (TTL) of 60 seconds.<br>Request/Response is 38,000 bytes combined.<br>100,000 requests during the TTL period. | | |

In a FastSOA implementation, an XQuery implements the parts ordering service by making a request to an inventory service, reading the content of the response, and determining at run time if a previously stored response may be played back instead of going to the inventory service again.

As with all other software architecture and patterns, you should determine if FastSOA will benefit your business or organization over other approaches. For instance, the FastSOA pattern in the CheckInventory example requires additional policy code to be written and maintained over time as the service and service interface schema change. Implementing the CheckInventory logic in the mid-tier may even duplicate code that exists elsewhere in your architecture.

The above example implements a FastSOA data mitigation aggregation architecture in a service environment. The combination of XQuery and a native XML database delivers a service that plays back the previously cached response data provided the request matches the previous request and the data is still fresh. The result is service acceleration.

### 4.2.6 Patterns That Accelerate SOA Performance

In the GM example above, FastSOA delivered service acceleration through mid-tier caching. Once you adopt a mid-tier service acceleration and well-performing SOAP binding strategy, additional performance acceleration and flexibility become possible.

Figure 4-10 shows the SOA design that I typically encounter.

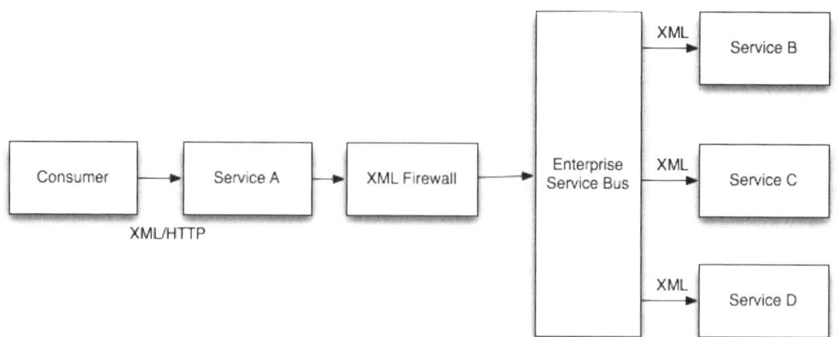


***Figure 4-10*** *Example of a typical SOA design using several tiers of services, an XML firewall, and an Enterprise Service Bus (ESB) for connectivity to multiple services.*

The design shown in Figure 4-10 works well for simple SOA services where connectivity is plentiful, you have what seems like an unlimited number of CPUs to run the application, the XML messages use simple schemas and have small message sizes (less than 5 kilobytes), and the consumers and services support common message data schemas. In general, this design works well when service performance, management, and compatibility issues are under control.

Figure 4-11 introduces the FastSOA pattern by including a mid-tier service for data acceleration, transformation, and mitigation.

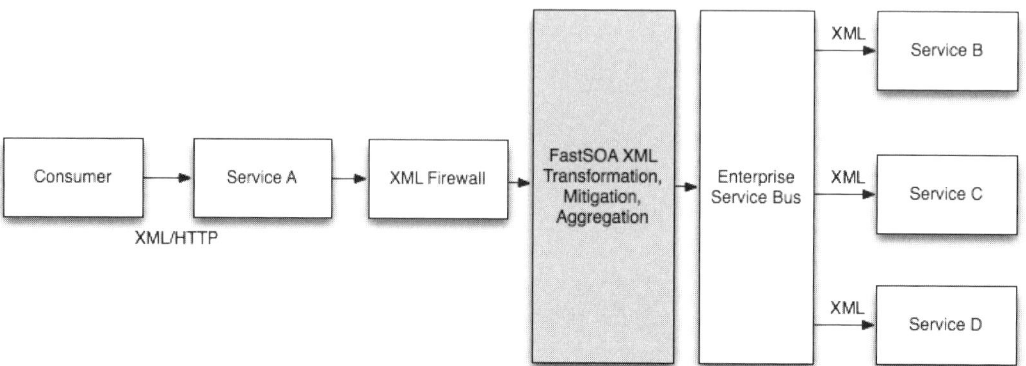


***Figure 4-11*** *FastSOA adds a mid-tier service for data and metadata aggregation, transformation, and service acceleration.*

The design in Figure 4-11 adds a mid-tier service. The advantages to this design are that FastSOA works with existing application servers and enterprise service bus technologies. To these the Fast-SOA tier looks like a service providing value-added functions. To management services, which control the operation of a network and group of service, the FastSOA tier looks like a service management and security policy mechanism. Chapter 5 shows how to implement this mid-tier service in detail using XQuery and native XML data-base technology.

Your decision to incorporate a FastSOA mid-tier service enables possibilities to solve service incompatibility, service federation, and service discovery issues too. For instance, Figure 4-12 shows Fast-SOA providing mid-tier transformation between a consumer that requires one schema and a service that only provides responses using a different and incompatible schema. The XQuery in the Fast-SOA tier transforms the requests and responses between incompatible schema types.

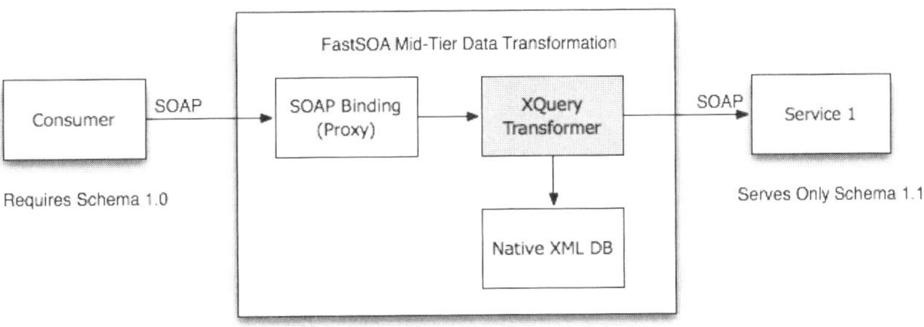


***Figure 4-12*** *An example where FastSOA solves a data schema incompatibility between a consumer and service.*

I have run into the example shown in Figure 4-12 many times. For instance, a directory service used by two organizations within the same company relies on a human resources service to provide updates that appear in the directory. When the human resources group updates its system to use a new schema—and does not provide backward compatibility to the original schema—it requires the directory service group to update its code. FastSOA mitigates the need to work on the code by doing schema transformation in the mid-tier.

Another advantage to implementing FastSOA in the mid-tier is flexibility and efficiency, as shown in Figure 4-13.

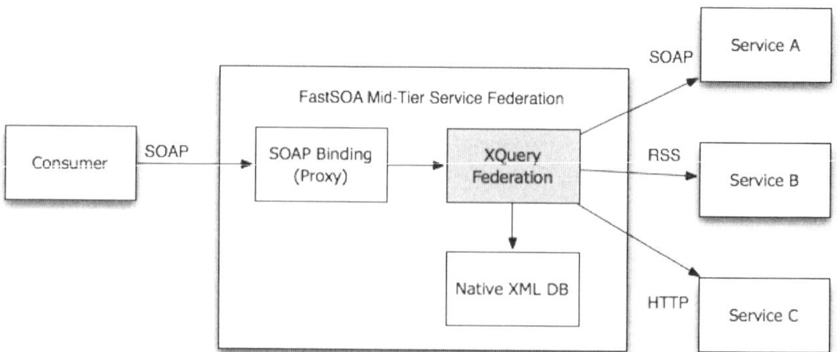


***Figure 4-13*** *FastSOA federates data from multiple sources over multiple protocols into one service.*

When a service commonly needs to aggregate the responses from multiple services into one response, FastSOA provides service federation. For instance, many content publishers such as the New York Times provide new articles using the Rich Site Syndication (RSS) protocol. FastSOA may federate news analysis articles published on a Web site with late-breaking news stories from several RSS feeds. This can be done in your application, but is better done in FastSOA because the content (news stories and RSS feeds) usually include time-to-live values that are ideal for FastSOA's mid-tier caching. Chapter 6 describes data aggregation and federation in detail.

SOA environments that use XML data the metadata for the messages exchanged between consumer and services can become a laborious and error-prone effort. Figure 4-14 shows FastSOA applied to solve storage and querying of metadata.

FastSOA is an appropriate pattern for service discovery, interrelationships, and policies. Intelligent policies written in XQuery enable services for devices requiring incompatible XML schema types. Chapters 7 and 8 describe metadata transformation, querying, and aggregation in detail.

## 4.3 Summary

This chapter showed software architects and developers patterns to accelerate XML performance and reduce service maintenance, including patterns that work at the SOAP binding layer, patterns that deliver performance with complex XML schemas, and XML parsing patterns. It also covered patterns to accelerate SOA performance and mitigate SOA performance problems, mid-tier service caching, native

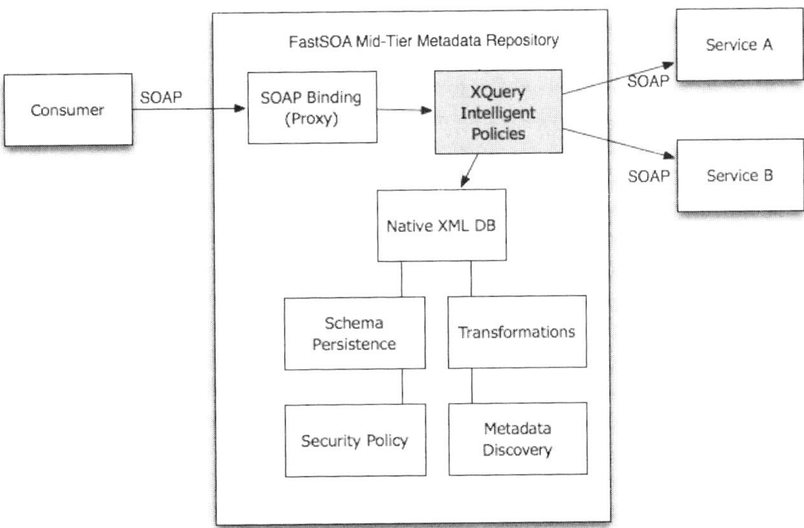


***Figure 4-14*** *Using FastSOA for storing metadata to provide fast performance in discovering services, transforming schemas, and implementing security policy.*

XML persistence, and mid-tier data transformation, aggregation, and federation. In the next chapter, we will compare performance of SOA built with Java application servers against FastSOA built with native XML technology.

# Chapter 5

# Solve Performance Problems with FastSOA Patterns

The previous chapters described the FastSOA patterns at an architectural level. This chapter shows FastSOA mid-tier service and data caching architecture applied in three real-world scenarios. The scenarios show how to accelerate SOA performance and mitigate performance problems through mid-tier service caching, native XML persistence, and mid-tier data transformation, aggregation, and federation.

## 5.1 Three Use Cases and the FastSOA Pattern

In this chapter, I describe three use cases where FastSOA is an appropriate solution for SOA performance and scalability challenges. Each use case shows how pure XML technology used in the mid-tier mitigates and solves performance and scalability problems and delivers flexibility unavailable with object and relational technology.

While there are many (sometimes contradictory) definitions for SOA, the majority of software developers and architects I have gotten to know over the years recognize and support SOA as a pattern built around consumers, services, and brokers. Figure 5-1 shows this relationship.

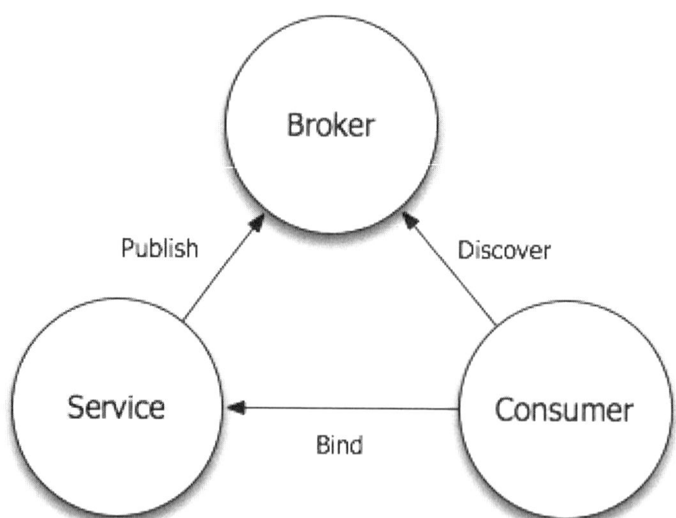


***Figure 5-1*** *The basic SOA pattern.*

The basic SOA patterns make sense for developers building services, Web services, and composite applications and data services. The pattern allows a consumer that makes a request to learn the location and interface message schema of a service. The consumer binds to the service by sending a request message. The service returns a response message to the consumer's request. The service makes its location known by publishing ontology of its functions and interface message schema to the broker. SOA is an abstract architecture—for instance, SOA does not define a specific protocol such as SOAP in the Web Services standard—but most SOA designs I have seen use XML as the message format between consumer, broker, and service.

To understand the SOA pattern in practice, we will look at three scenarios and show how FastSOA solves scalability, performance, and flexibility challenges in each.

- Accelerating service interface performance and scalability
- Improving SOA performance to access services
- Flexibility needed for semantic web, service orchestration, and services dynamically calling other services

## 5.2 Scenario 1: Accelerating Service Interface Performance and Scalability

In this scenario, a business operates a parts ordering service for customers. The service provides a Web browser user interface to enter a new order and learn the status of an existing order. Behind the user interface is a SOAP-based Web Service using ebXML message schemas to track order status from a vendor's legacy inventory system. The service stores orders and customer information in a relational database. Figure 5-2 illustrates a typical use case.

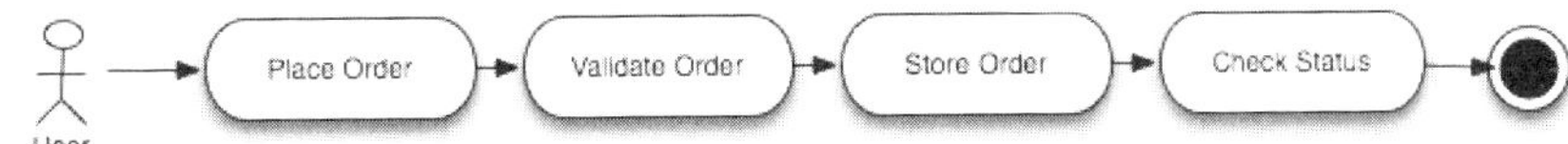


***Figure 5-2*** *A typical use case for a parts ordering service.*

The use case begins with a customer placing an order. The service validates the order against the current inventory to make sure the part being ordered is in the parts catalog. The service stores the order until the company places a consolidation of all the orders in a nightly batch process with the parts vendor. The service ends the use case by checking the status of the order.

Figure 5-3 illustrates an n-Tier architecture often recommended in the Java development community to implement the parts ordering service.

The architecture divides into three portions: A presentation tier, an application tier, and a data tier. The presentation tier uses a Web browser with AJAX and RSS capabilities to create a rich user interface. The browser makes a combination of HTML and XML requests to the application tier. Also at the presentation tier is a SOAP-based Web Services interface to allow a customer system to access the parts ordering functions. At the application tier, an Enterprise Java Bean (EJB) or plain old Java object (pojo) implements the business logic to respond to the request. The EJB uses a model, view, and controller (MVC) framework—for instance, Struts or Tapestry—to respond to the request by generating a response Web page. The MVC framework uses an object/relational (O/R) mapping framework—for instance, Hibernate or Spring—to store and retrieve data in a relational database.

There are three problem areas that cause scalability and performance problems when using Java objects and relational databases in XML environments. Figure 5-4 illustrates these problems.

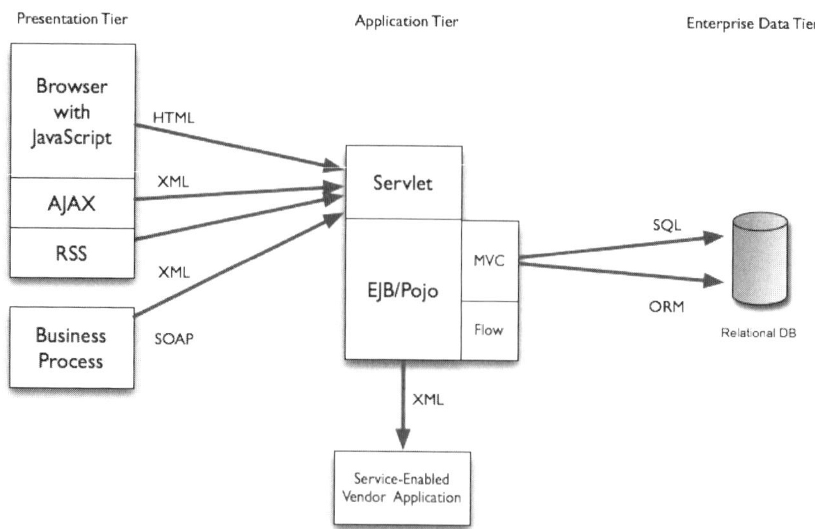


***Figure 5-3*** *Building the parts ordering service using the Domain pattern.*

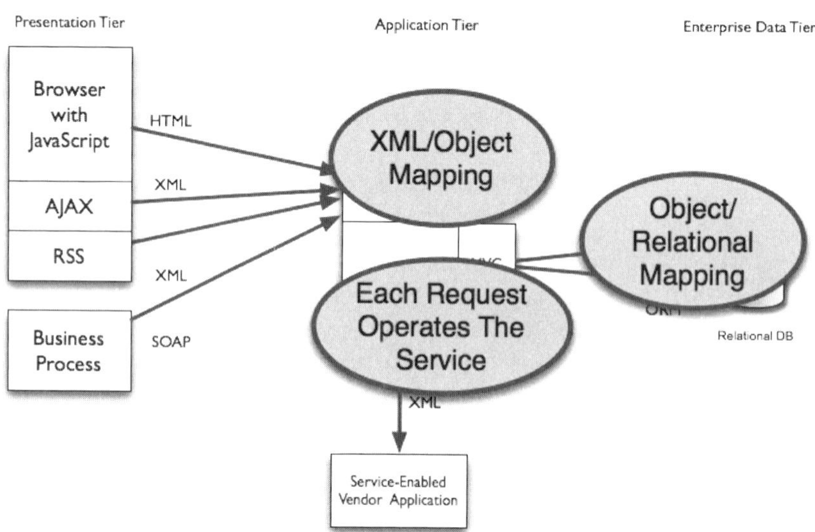


***Figure 5-4*** *The source of scalability and performance problems… all that mapping and transformation.*

Using the Java/relational architecture leads to performance and scalability problems as the XML messages grow in complexity and size.

- XML/Java mapping requires increasingly more processor time as XML message size and complexity grow.
- Each request operates the entire service. Many times the user will check order status sooner than any status change is realistic. If the system kept track of the most recent response's time-to-live duration, then it would not have to operate all of the service to determine the most previously cached response.
- The vendor application requires the request message to be in XML form. The data the EJB previously processed from XML into Java objects now needs to be transformed back into XML elements as part of the request message. Many Java to XML frameworks—for instance, JAXB, XMLBeans, and Xerces—require processor-intensive transformations. These frameworks challenge developers to write difficult and complex code to perform the transformation.
- The service persists order information in a relational database using an object/relational mapping framework. The framework transforms Java objects into relational rowsets and performs joins among multiple tables. As object complexity and size grow, many developers need to debug the O/R mapping to improve speed and performance.

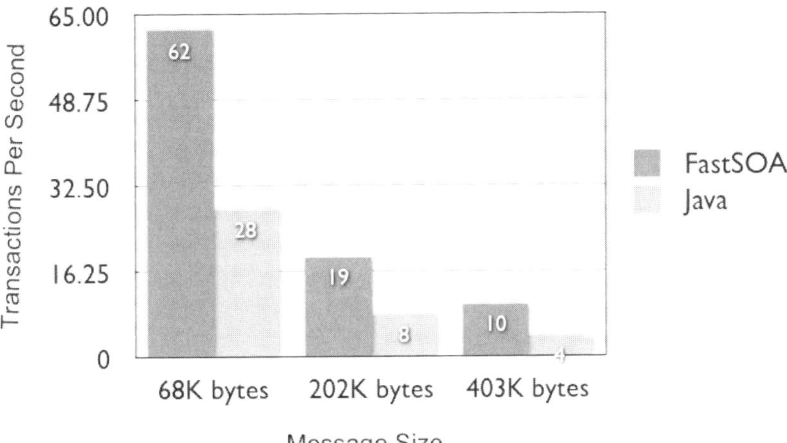


*Figure 5-5* Contrasting service interface performance between techniques.

To give you an idea of the extent of the problem, consider the performance advantage of using native XML technology to respond to service requests. Figure 5-5 contrasts the performance difference.

The results in Figure 5-5 contrast native XML technology and Java technology to implement a service that receives SOAP requests. The test varies the size of the request message among three levels: 68 kilobytes, 202 kilobytes, and 403 kilobytes. The test measures the round-trip time to respond to the request at the consumer. The test results are from a server with dual CPU Intel Xeon 3.0-Ghz processors running on a gigabit-switched Ethernet network. I implemented the code in two ways:

1. **FastSOA technique**. Uses native XML technology to provide a SOAP service interface. I used Raining Data TigerLogic's XML query (XQuery) engine to expose a socket interface that receives the SOAP message, parses its content, and assembles a response SOAP message.
2. **Java technique**. Uses the SOAP binding proxy interface generator from a popular commercial Java application server. A simple Java object receives the SOAP request from the binding, parses its content using JAXB-created bindings, and assembles a response SOAP message using the binding.

The results show a 2 to 2.5 times performance improvement when using the FastSOA technique to expose service interfaces. The FastSOA method is faster because it avoids many of the mappings and transformations that are performed in the Java binding approach to work with XML data. The greater the complexity and size of the XML data, the greater the performance improvement.

FastSOA is equally applicable to improve the performance of SOA application requests that require access to data. FastSOA implements a mid-tier cache to commonly accessed data.

Caching is a powerful and proven technique for database systems. For instance, RDBMS tools vendors perform caching strategies at three points in an SOA environment, as illustrated in Figure 5-6.

RDBMS vendors recommend caching at three places. In the presentation tier, a Web cache provides cached data to Java Server Faces (JSF) dynamic pages. At the application tier, it recommends caching at the object/relational mapping (ORM) and in the connection layer to the relational database (RDBMS) using an in-memory

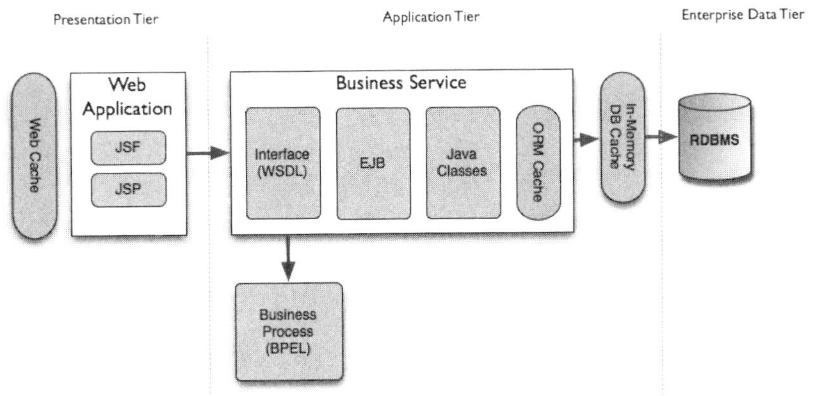


***Figure 5-6*** *Mitigating relational performance through caching.*

cache. Caching in this environment works well to mitigate relational performance problems.

These caching techniques should, but don't, take advantage of the unique features of XML data. Many SOA XML messages include a time-to-live value in the message itself. This gives the cache intelligence about the lifetime of data that is usually unavailable in generic data caching approaches. To achieve this cache intelligence requires a programming language and persistence engine of its own.

Figure 5-7 shows the FastSOA architecture that uses native XML technology to provide a service interface, to accelerate service performance by caching response data, and implements flexible and rapidly changed policies to operate the cache engine.

The advantage to using the FastSOA architecture as a mid-tier service cache is in its ability to store any general type of data, as well as its strength in quickly matching services with sets of complex parameters to efficiently determine when a service request can be serviced from the cache. The FastSOA mid-tier service cache architecture accomplish this by maintaining two databases.

- **The service database.** Holds the cached message payloads. For instance, the service database holds a SOAP message in XML form, an HTML Web page, text from a short message, and binary from a JPEG or GIF image.
- **The policy database.** Holds units of business logic that look into the service database contents and make decisions on servicing requests with data from the service database or passing through the request to the application tier. For

instance, a policy that receives a SOAP request validates security information in the SOAP header to validate that a user may receive previously cached response data. In another instance, a policy checks the time-to-live value from a stock market price quote to see if it can respond to a request from the stock value stored in the service database.

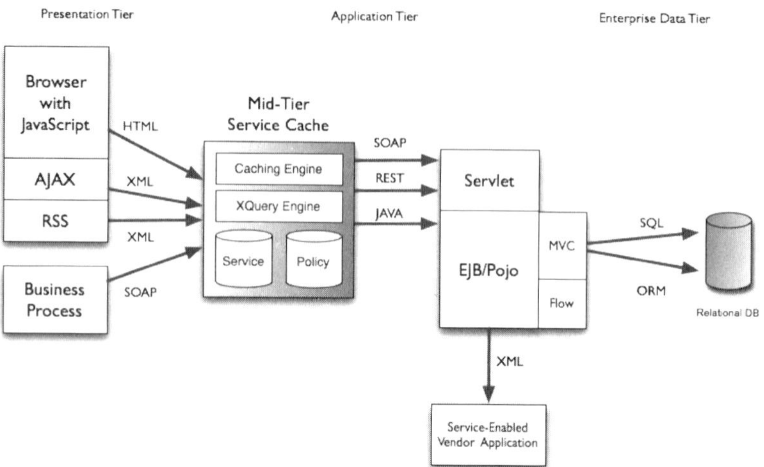


*Figure 5-7 Using XML technology to provide service acceleration through caching.*

FastSOA uses the XQuery data model to implement policies. The XQuery data model supports any general type of document and any general dynamic parameter used to fetch and construct the document. Used to implement policies, the XQuery engine allows FastSOA to efficiently assess common criteria of the data in the service cache, and the flexibility of XQuery allows for user-driven fuzzy pattern matches to efficiently represent the cache.

FastSOA uses native XML database technology for the service and policy databases for performance and scalability reasons. Relational database technology delivers satisfactory performance to persist policy and service data in a mid-tier cache provided the XML message schemas being stored are consistent and the message sizes are small. To understand this in more depth, consider the following results from a comparison of native XML database technology to relational databases.

The test runs multiple test cases where each test case varies the number of concurrent requests made to the database host and varies the size of the XML message. The test environment makes requests to a relational database and a native XML database. For the relational database the test used an XML CLOB field type. The use case is modeled around a mid-tier cache's need to rapidly persist and query an unknown quantity of data with multiple and unknown schemas.

The test environment monitors the time it takes to receive a response at the consumer. The test produces a report showing transactions per second (TPS) at each level of concurrent requests and message payload sizes. Figure 5-8 shows a scalability index report for querying a database of stored XML documents.

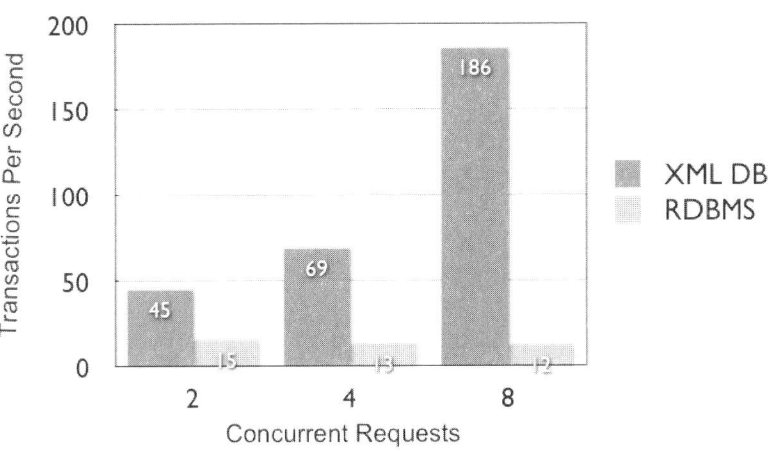


***Figure 5-8*** *Comparing query performance between a native XML database and a relational database management system.*

In the query performance test, the native XML database starts at 45 TPS and goes up to 186 TPS while the relational database stays at 15 TPS or less. Figure 5-9 compares performance characteristics while inserting XML documents into the database.

The insert document performance test shows that native XML database and relational database performances are evenly matched at 20 and 17 TPS at the lowest number of concurrent requests. At 32 concurrent requests, the native XML database performs 3.4 times (48 TPS/14 TPS) as many inserts than the relational database performs.

These results are not meant to knock relational database technology out of the running for XML persistence, because there are

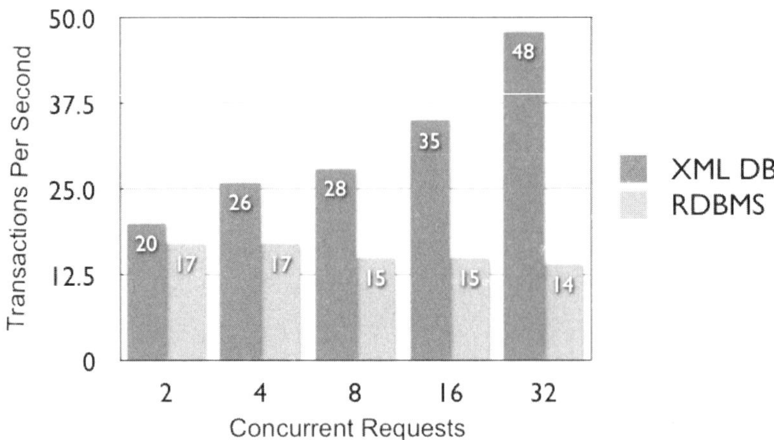


***Figure 5-9*** *Comparing insert performance.*

undoubtedly a large number of optimizations that could be employed to improve performance. Instead, I show these numbers to prepare you for the performance and scalability challenges in SOA environments that use an unknown variety of XML message sizes and schemas. There is no gatekeeper to the number and form of XML message schemas in an SOA environment. Mid-tier caching strategies need the best performing and most flexible database available that can handle multiple and unknown message schemas and data formats.

The benefits to a business running a FastSOA mid-tier service cache include:

- Less CPU licenses for commercial application servers
- Less network overhead
- Improved performance as compared with other mid-tier cache architectures
- Advanced SOAP in-line processing for a 2–3 times performance improvement over binding proxies created with Java application server utilities
- More efficient relational to XML transformation processing

The next scenario shows how FastSOA is used as a service data cache to improve data retrieval performance.

## 5.3 Scenario 2: Improving SOA Performance to Access Services

In this scenario, a business operates a portal for employees to sign up for a retirement plan, medical insurance plan, and other programs. The portal application interfaces to an external database using a JDBC driver to retrieve company news. It also interfaces using REST protocols (XML over HTTP) for employee benefits data from the human resources service. The portal allows single sign-in to these services by interoperating with the corporate directory using LDAP protocols. Figure 5-10 illustrates a typical use case.

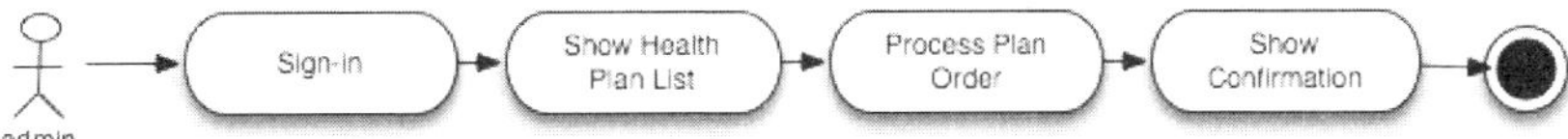


***Figure 5-10*** *The employee portal use case.*

The use case begins with an employee signing in. The portal application validates the user credentials. Validated users sign up for alerts to enable the system to send an email notification when new healthcare plans become available. The employee uses the portal to browse healthcare plans and choose a plan. The service ends the use case by confirming the plan choice.

Figure 5-11 illustrates an architecture often recommended in the Java development community to implement the employee portal.

The architecture divides into three portions: a presentation tier, an application tier, and a data tier. The presentation tier uses a Web browser with AJAX and RSS capabilities to create a rich user interface. The portal application also presents data to systems in other departments using SOAP and Java interfaces. At the application tier, an Enterprise Java Bean (EJB) implements the business logic to respond to the request. The EJB interoperates with a relational database, security manager, and human resources service. Corporate mandates require the system to store the plans offered to the employees in its original XML form.

This architecture puts a lot of emphasis on the EJB. The EJB must produce aggregated views of the healthcare plans according to the user's position in the company. The views are assembled from XML data sources (the human resources system) and LDAP security provider. There are three problem areas that cause scalability, performance, and developer productivity problems when using Java objects and relational databases in what is otherwise an XML environment in this scenario:

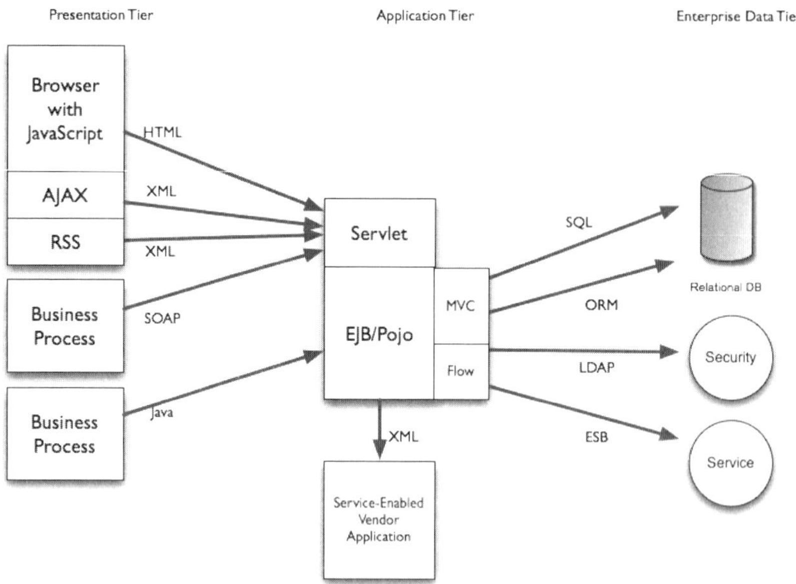


*Figure 5-11* *The employee portal built with Java and relational technologies*

- **Slow object/relational mapping.** The views from the aggregated XML services need to be mapped into objects and then mapped into relational rowsets. This requires much coding and processing.
- **Every request accesses the services and database slowly.** There are only so many types of employees. Yet, the EJB assembles the views into the plan data each time a user requests a page.
- **Schema changes cause coding changes.** Every change to the human resources system message schema requires you to be right back in the code for the EJB.

Figure 5-12 shows an architecture that uses XML-centric technology to efficiently and rapidly create aggregate views of data from multiple data sources, accelerate data source performance by caching commonly used view data in the mid-tier, and implement flexible and rapidly changed policies to operate the data cache.

The mid-tier data cache stores XML, non-XML (such as binary), and other general types of data in two databases:

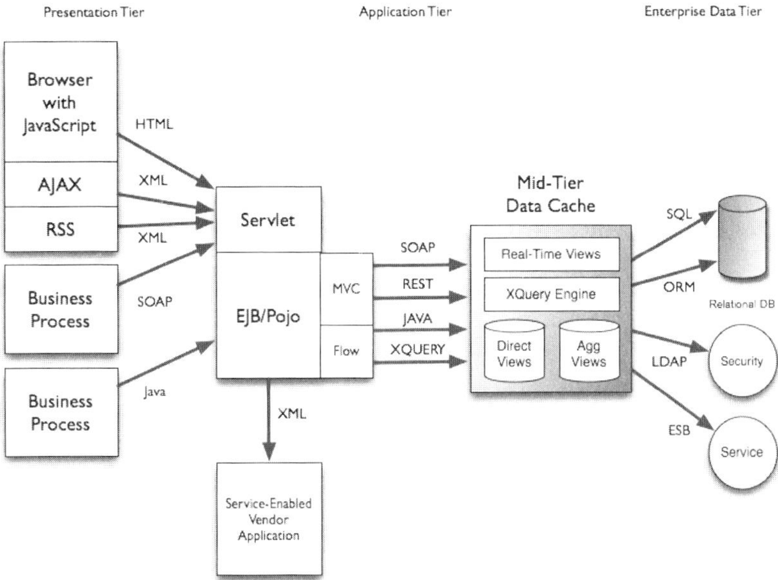


***Figure 5-12*** *Implementing a data cache for aggregate views*

1. **Direct views database.** Holds views of the data from the upstream data source providers. For instance, when the human resources health care plan services go off-line, the mid-tier data cache still services the last available view of the data. In another instance, the EJB may need a healthcare plan using a more modern schema and the direct views database holds a transformed healthcare plan from the human resources service emitting plans in an older schema. The direct views database may also hold an aggregated view of two plans and an archive of how the plans have changed over recent time.
2. **Aggregate views database.** Holds data views that are intelligently composed as data is served to the EJB. For instance, in the employee portal scenario the aggregate views database stores the most recent plans viewed, keeps a list of popular plans, and keeps a list of high-quality plans as ranked by employee feedback.

The mid-tier data cache uses a set of policies to determine the contents of the direct and aggregate views databases. Each policy holds the business logic to look into upstream data sources and make decisions on which data to update and how frequently. The policy system is efficient at processing the business logic and storing the resulting XML views of the data from its use of native XML technology.

Choosing the FastSOA architecture for a mid-tier data cache in this scenario delivers a way to mitigate XML schema migration problems, reduce the amount of object-to-relational-to-XML mapping and transformation, and provides off-line data browsing capability. All of this comes without requiring you to be back in the EJB writing code.

The benefits to a business running a FastSOA mid-tier data cache include:

- Direct and aggregated views of the data model
- Real-time and near-time access between data and application tiers
- Two to 20 times performance advantage

In the next scenario, I will show how FastSOA is used as a platform for building high-performance and scalable dynamic services.

## 5.4 Scenario 3: Flexibility Needed for Semantic Web, Service Orchestration, and Services Dynamically Calling Other Services

Over the past two years, the software development community has enjoyed a renaissance of creativity from new XML-based technology, including mashups (for instance, combining Google maps with photos from Flikr), AJAX for better user interfaces, and REST for easy application-to-application interoperability. Much of this creativity pushes software development in the direction Tim Berners Lee espoused in the semantic Web.

When services communicate with other services, XML is the interoperability standard. FastSOA has much to offer a software developer working in an XML environment. Figure 5-13 illustrates an architecture that adds fast, efficient, and flexible XML capabilities to an otherwise Java and relational database architecture.

The FastSOA architecture enables developers to write business logic using pure XML technology. The FastSOA architecture provides the XML interface to the existing Java and relational database systems. For instance, when a browser makes an XML request from an

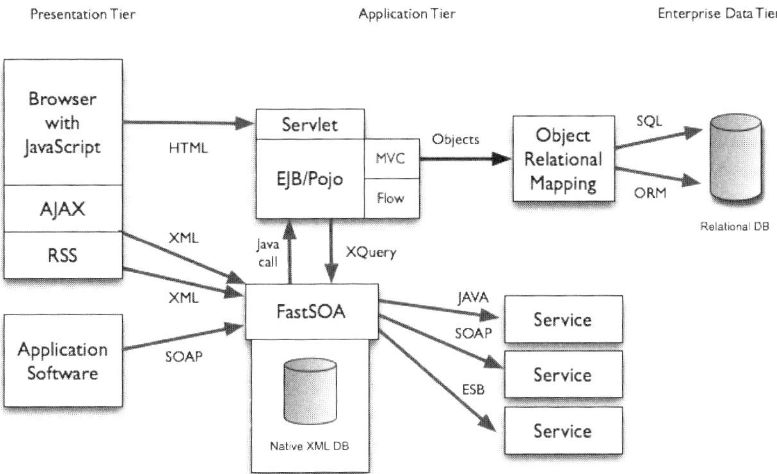


***Figure 5-13*** *FastSOA in a semantic Web environment.*

AJAX component, FastSOA receives the request, sees if the response is cached and still valid, and responds with the cached response. If the request requires data provided by a Java object (in the EJB), then FastSOA makes a direct Java call to the object and method.

FastSOA as a service interface and component development environment for semantic Web applications brings the following business benefits.

- One hundred percent native XML environment
- Avoiding object/relational/XML mapping reduces need for expensive application servers and network bandwidth
- Reduced software maintenance over time as message schemas change

The above three use cases show where FastSOA is an appropriate solution for XML performance and scalability challenges. We saw how native XML technology used at the mid-tier mitigates and solves performance and scalability problems and delivers flexibility unavailable with object and relational technology. The following are the business benefits for FastSOA.

- Solves SOA scalability problems for fast throughput and good scalability

- Works within existing infrastructure to avoid replacement costs
- Easy to customize with enterprise business processes using XQuery-based components
- Improves business agility and flexibility by maintaining interoperability and accelerating performance

## 5.5 Summary

This chapter showed three real-world scenarios where FastSOA improves performance, mitigates service bottlenecks, and improves developer productivity. In the next chapter, I show my PushToTest methodology to test and quantify performance in an SOA environment.

# Chapter 6

# The PushToTest Method to Identify SOA Scalability and Performance Metrics

The previous chapter showed the FastSOA patterns for accelerating SOA performance and mitigating performance problems in three use cases. Each pattern has a performance, scalability, developer productivity, and flexibility benefit. This chapter shows the scalability and performance test methodology I developed at PushToTest to identify and quantify the FastSOA benefits.[1] This is the same test method used at General Motors, BEA, Lockheed Martin, Sun Microsystems, and the European Union. The methodology makes apparent the tradeoffs a software developer makes when choosing SOA coding techniques, code libraries, and APIs.

## 6.1 The Method to Identify SOA Performance Metrics

It frequently surprises me how few enterprises, institutions, and organizations have a method to test services for scalability and performance. One Fortune 50 company asked a summer intern it wound up hiring to run a few performance tests when he had time between other assignments to check and identify scalability problems in its SOA application. That was their entire approach to scalability and performance testing.

1 See http://www.pushtotest.com.

The business value of running scalability and performance tests comes once a business formalizes a test method that includes the following steps:

1. Choose the right set of test cases. For instance, the test of a multiple-interface and high-volume service will be different from a service that handles periodic requests with huge message sizes. The test needs to be oriented to address the end-user goals in using the service and deliver actionable knowledge.
2. Accurate test runs. Understanding the scalability and performance of a service requires dozens to hundreds of test case runs. Adhoc recording of test results is unsatisfactory. Test automation tools are plentiful and often free.
3. Make the right conclusions when analyzing the results. Understanding the scalability and performance of a service requires understanding how the throughput, measured as transactions per second (TPS) at the service consumer, changes with increased message size and complexity and increased concurrent requests.

All of this requires much more than an adhoc approach to reach useful and actionable knowledge.

This section teaches the PushToTest methodology for understanding the scalability and performance of SOA in multiple environments and configurations. You will learn how to identify the use cases, test cases, and test scenarios to understand the scalability and performance of your SOA. And you will learn how to analyze the results.

The PushToTest methodology is available to you in a set of developer scalability and performance kits. These kits are either available for free download under an open-source license or available as a commercially licensed product. Details on the available kits can be found later in this chapter.

### 6.1.1 An SOA Industry Supporting the PushToTest Methodology

PushToTest is a software publishing and services company I founded in 2001. Enterprise information technology managers were in a bind. They already used up their capital budgets through the 1990s buying huge volumes of equipment and building huge datacenter capacity. Now they needed to increase productivity of their existing information systems without engaging huge integration projects such as those of the past. Against this backdrop I founded PushToTest as a test automation solutions and enterprise services business with three goals.

1. Use open-source distribution and development techniques to build a test tool. I used on-line community development techniques to build an audience to sell services and product license up-sells.
2. Conduct scalability and performance studies of information systems and development tools and libraries for software tools vendors and enterprises that use the tools.
3. Convince the software development tools vendors and enterprise users that it is in their best interest to release performance and scalability testing results and the software developed of the studies they commissioned to the software development community as a "kit."

PushToTest developed a community of approximately 110,000 software developers, quality assurance technicians, and IT managers who use the open-source TestMaker framework and utility to build automated Web Service, and SOA tests. The scalability and performance kits use TestMaker and garnered interest from the software development community and CIOs. The kits deliver immediately usable reference software code to developers and best practices and a total cost of ownership (TCO) analysis to business managers. PushToTest became the company that tools vendors such as BEA, Sun, and IBM turned to for independent validation of their competitive standing, and enterprises turn to PushToTest for independent validation of the tools vendors claims.

Many of the tools vendors released the resulting software to the software developer community. Use Google to search for "scalability and performance kit" to find these. Here are URLs to the publicly available kits:

- BEA SOA Performance and Developer Productivity Kit:

  `http://dev2dev.bea.com/soa/toolkit.html`

- The SOAP Encoding Performance Kit featuring IBM WebSphere:

  http://www.pushtotest.com/Downloads/kits/websspherekit.html

- Web Service Performance and Developer Knowledge Kit:

  http://www.pushtotest.com/Downloads/kits/origperfkit.html

- Additional kits are available at:

  http://www.pushtotest.com/Downloads/kits

The most recent kit implements the FastSOA pattern using a variety of native XML and relational tools. This kit is available under a commercial license from Raining Data.

- Raining Data FastSOA Performance Kit:

  http://www.rainingdata.com/products/soa/soatestkit

The PushToTest methodology implemented in these kits follows a user goal-oriented testing (UGOT) philosophy to determine the scalability, performance, and reliability of a service and application software. The following sections describe this in detail.

### 6.1.2 User Goal Oriented Testing (UGOT)

In my previous book, *Java Testing and Design,* I introduced the user goal-oriented testing (UGOT) method.[2] UGOT contrasts user goals with what a service (or application) actually delivers. I developed the idea for UGOT testing after hearing Alan Cooper describe his techniques for user goal-oriented software interface design.[3] Alan argues that software developers should design user interfaces against the needs of a single archetypal user. I enjoy watching Alan spar with developers on this issue. Most developers argue with Alan that they should be designing their interfaces for all possible users. Alan counters by saying, "If you design for every possible

2 Prentice Hall Publishers, ISBN 0131421891, published in 2004.
3 See http://www.cooper.com.

user, no individual user will have his or her goals met when using your software application!"

The same controversy exists when applying Alan's techniques to testing. Most software developers I have met are predisposed to want maximum coverage of all features when testing new software. When this happens, I point out that coverage tests are usually pointless. Users always take a path through the functions in a service. They never use every feature. They use a chain of features, one after another.

The agile development community approaches this problem by recommending a "test first" strategy. Test first urges developers to write a unit test of a class before writing the class itself. At build time, the compiler environment compiles the object code for the class and then runs the unit test against the compiled code. The unit test completes successfully by receiving example data and validates the response. When the class returns an invalid response, the unit test throws an exception that the build and deploy environment handles.

Unit testing and agile development methods help but are not a complete solution to UGOT techniques. For instance, test first is usually only carried out at a unit level. SOA deploys applications as a collection of services, so testing individual units misses most of the big problems that occur during SOA integration and deployment. UGOT-modeled tests check a service as an individual user would—by picking one feature after the next in a chain of service requests.

UGOT is ideal to understand SOA performance and scalability testing. UGOT treats ad-hoc testing of software as the slippery slope to madness. In all that we do to understand performance and scalability in SOA, every step must deliver real value to the decision makers who build and operate services.

Convincing your organization to use UGOT requires a little persistence and then a whole lot of explanation. Which software architect, developer, and IT executive will refuse the results of a test that would immediately benefit the business or institution? First ask the question, "What do I need to learn from a performance test and how will it benefit my company, business, or institution?"

This question gets directly to the heart of the reason why we test SOA at all. It may be more difficult to answer than it first appears. In the test projects I have run, sometimes the answer took longer to find than the time it took to run the actual test and understand the results.

The question challenges us to understand what we are actually testing. For instance, Figure 6-1 shows many of the building blocks found in Java development tool set for building SOA.

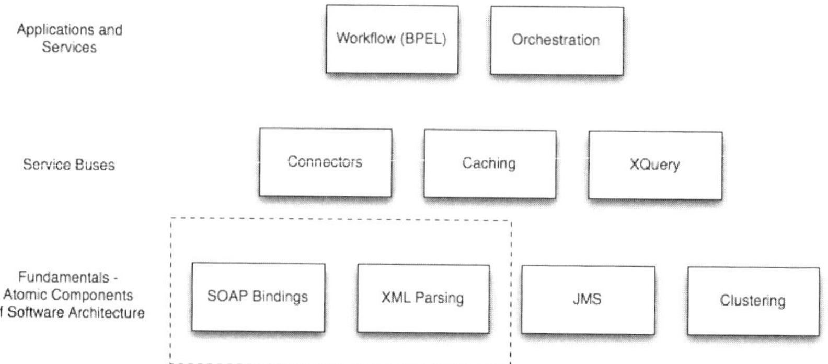


***Figure 6-1*** *The possible architectural components of SOA designs that could be tested for performance and scalability.*

The components build on each other in three tiers: At the bottom are the fundamental components for SOAP bindings, XML parsing, Java inter-application messaging services (JMS), and clustering. Building on these are service bus components for services to interoperate at a message level. The top tier provides interoperability at an application level. Given these building blocks and tiers, where would you start testing to understand the scalability and performance of an SOA implementation?

For instance, would it make sense to test only the connectors and caching objects at the service bus level exclusively? If you did so, you may miss key performance bottlenecks in the SOAP Bindings and JMS service. Each of the components in Figure 6-1 impacts the scalability and performance of the resulting SOA implementation.

Another way to understand the goal of your test is to review the definition of SOA I first presented in Chapter 1, now shown here in Figure 6-2.

Figure 6-2 shows that SOA is a consumer, service, and broker architecture. Performance tests normally check at least two. For instance, one performance test may check a consumer and service, and, in another example, you may test a consumer and a broker. Table 6-1 lists options to understand which part of your system would benefit most from a scalability and performance analysis.

Table 6-1 covers the SOA test goals I most often encounter. However, there are many more possibilities, and the pace of innovation within SOA building tools is fast.

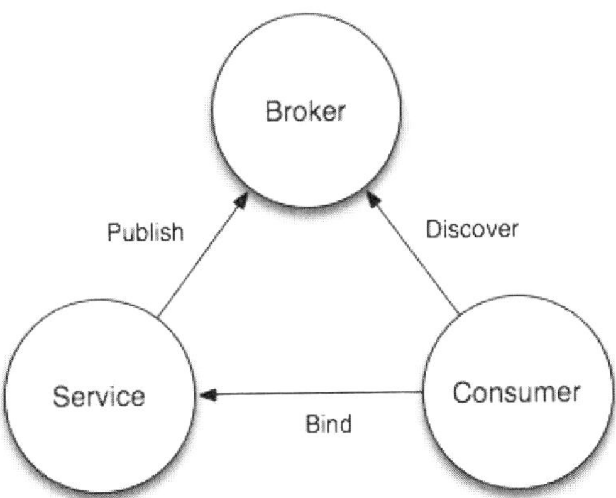


*Figure 6-2* SOA is a consumer, service, and broker architecture. So what do you test first? And when?

*Table 6-1* Understanding Your Test

| What you want to test | Benefit of this kind of test | Type of test | Parameters to understand the scalability index |
|---|---|---|---|
| Service Interface | Decrease response times for each request to a service to lower network bandwidth and server hardware costs. | Stateless | Message size and concurrent request levels |
| XML Parsing | Decrease the time it takes to route a message to a service handling object to lower network bandwidth and server hardware costs. | Stateless | Schema complexity (depth and element count), document size, concurrent request level |
| Data Persistence | Decrease the time it takes to store and retrieve messages to lower network bandwidth, server hardware, and disk costs. | Stateful | Schema complexity (depth and element count), document size, concurrent request level |
| Data Transformation | Decrease the time it takes to transform a message into a given XML schema to lower network bandwidth and server hardware costs. | Stateless | Source and destination schema complexity (depth and element count), request and output document size, concurrent request level |

***Table 6-1** Understanding Your Test (continued)*

| What you want to test | Benefit of this kind of test | Type of test | Parameters to understand the scalability index |
|---|---|---|---|
| Data Aggregation and Federation | Decrease the time it takes to respond to service requests that require inputs from several upstream data sources. Reduces network bandwidth and server hardware costs. | Stateful | Schema complexity (depth and element count), for each upstream service, data persistence quantities, time-to-live (TTL) values for each message |
| Data Mitigation | Improve service availability and user satisfaction by reducing the times when a service is unavailable at times of peak usage. | Stateful | Schema complexity (depth and element count), for each request, document size, concurrent request levels |

The name of the test and its benefit shown in Table 6-1 should be self-explanatory. The type of test and parameters to understand the test merit some explanation.

- The type of test is either stateful or stateless. Each requires a different testing strategy and has different test goals.
    - **Stateless** testing checks the impact of concurrent requests and message payload size on a service. The service responds to each request independently from all the other requests. It is therefore stateless.
    - **Stateful** testing is similar to stateless testing; however, the service provides data persistence, workflow transaction processing, message queuing, sessions, or data indexing.
- The parameters to understand the scalability index define the inputs to a test that will show us the scalability index—the usage pattern that shows us what we can expect of our service's performance in production.

I show the scalability index, stateful and stateless testing, and the impact of changes in the test parameters in more depth later in this chapter. First, let me explain the steps to implement the PushToTest method.

### 6.1.3 The Method

The PushToTest method implements five sequential steps, each with a checkpoint milestone. Table 6-2 describes the test phases and checkpoints.

***Table 6-2*** *The PushToTest Method*

| Phase | Goal | Checkpoint |
|---|---|---|
| Planning | Answer the question, How will this test benefit my organization? | Write test plan document. |
| Definition | Identify the use cases, test cases and scenario and test environment (hardware, software, network). | Add the use cases, test cases, and test scenario to the test plan. Achieve management sign-off. |
| Calibration Test | Calibrate the test cases to the test environment. | Identify the use cases that drive the test environment to its maximum throughput (as measured in TPS from the client). |
| Optimize | Modify the service and/or test environment to optimize for best performance based on what you learned in the calibration test. | Amend the test plan to add the optimizations made. |
| Full Test | Run the test scenario. | Successful run of test scenario. |
| Results Analysis | Identify test result metrics and trends against test scenario goals. | Present results and achieve adoption by management. |

New terminology may have appeared to you in Table 6-2. Here is a brief explanation of the terminology I use:

- **Use case**—describes the functionality of a test. For instance, a test compares XML parsing techniques by including two use cases: the first using the Xerxes DOM parser and the second using the JAXB XML binding compiler.

- **Test case**—describes the inputs to an individual test. For instance, a test compares service throughput at low and high levels for message payloads by defining two test cases: the first making requests to the service using XML documents of 500 bytes and the second test using documents of 10 kilobytes.
- **Test scenario**—the aggregate of all the test cases and use cases run to complete the test.

With any test methodology, the devil is in the details. That is why the next section provides a detailed look at the method in practice. But before we dig into that, we will cover an important distinction between this SOA test method and everyday software testing.

### 6.1.4 Method for Black Box and White Box (Profiling) Tests

Testing SOA for scalability and performance is different from testing software applications and code. SOA testing is focused on understanding how a service responds to increasing levels of concurrent requests, message sizes, and response handling techniques. The nature of SOA testing is black box testing. It really does not matter what happens inside of the box.

Too often, software developers are ready to break out a code profiler to learn the location of a performance problem. Profilers have their place in testing software. However, in my experience, black box testing more often yields actionable knowledge. Here is what I recommend:

1. Create a baseline performance metric. I call this a Scalability Index, using black box performance tests that show TPS results as measured at the service consumer in a variety of message sizes, message schema complexities, and levels of concurrent requests.
2. When comparing performance and scalability between multiple servers, consumers, or brokers, it is important to identify the scalability index of each server and then to normalize the test parameters to avoid wrongly reporting slow

performance results. I call this step a calibration test, as you are calibrating the test lab to properly run the tests.

3. Once you determine the scalability index of the service, then use white box techniques to profile the largest time expensive object operations to handle requests. Optimize the software based on the profile.
4. Continue to optimize the service by repeating steps 2 and 3.
5. Run the Performance Index and analyze the results.

Profilers have a place in testing SOA. However, in my experience, developers are usually better off conducting black box tests to understand the Scalability Index of a service first and then use profilers to solve the underlying problems.

The above sections lay the groundwork for understanding the method I use to test services for scalability and performance. Next, we will see the test method applied to a real-world SOA scenario.

## 6.2 Applying the Method to SOA and Web Services

While the previous sections cover the goals and means to test services, there is nothing quite like a good example. This section shows what went into the Raining Data FastSOA Performance Kit.[4]

The Raining Data FastSOA Performance Kit—for the remainder of this chapter I will referred to as "the kit"—highlights the scalability, performance, and developer productivity differences between SOA services built with Java application servers and database tools and the same services built with native XML technology. The kit looks at SOA from two perspectives:

1. **SOAP binding acceleration**. Implements the FastSOA architecture using Java objects and XQuery technology. The use cases contrast performance and developer productivity based on the typical developer choices of XML parsing techniques (XML binding compiler, streaming XML parser, and DOM approaches for Java and XQuery parsing).
2. **Mid-tier caching for service acceleration**. Implements a use case with native XML databases (XML DB) and relational

4 http://www.rainingdata.com/products/soa/soatestkit.

databases (RDBMS) to contrast database performance across a variety of XML message sizes and database operations (insert, update, delete, and query).

The following sections explain the background and goals of the test to illustrate applying the PushToTest method in the kit.

### 6.2.1 Planning: Background and Goals

Software architects and developers make choices of XML parsing techniques, service libraries, encoding techniques, and protocols when building services using SOA techniques. Each choice has an impact on the scalability and performance of the finished service. The kit has the following three goals.

1. Explain the changing landscape of APIs, libraries, encoding techniques, and protocols to software architects and developers. The current generation of technology choices changes approximately every six to nine months. For instance, JAXB 1.0 is replaced by JAXB 2.0 and WebLogic Server 8.1 is replaced by WebLogic Server 9.
2. Identify and use real-world use case scenarios that inform software architects and developers of the most appropriate technology choices based on the goals of the intended service. The scenarios come from practical experience testing Web Services for General Motors and seeing how developers at the Silicon Valley–based Software Development Forum apply XML parsers and service interface toolkits.[5]
3. Deliver code that is compatible with software developers' existing knowledge of building functional and scalability tests, including black box, unit testing, and agile test-first (unit) testing methods. I have seen many tutorials from vendors that did not match what I used to build my own software. They were useful but always seemed to require adoption of some proprietary tool that I did not have or made use of some secret magic that only the vendor had access to internally. I resolved to use the same techniques to build the kit that I used on my open-source project and only follow the publicly available information as published on the Web.

5 See http://www.sdforum.org.

The kit delivers a reusable method for evaluating SOA performance and system scalability. And the results findings feed basic business needs for cost/benefit and feature/function analysis, including the following benefits:

- Reduce the extra cost of hardware and per-CPU licensed software to run less efficient services built with less efficient tools.
- Increase savings in efficiency from lowered network and processor bandwidth.

Save the additional time needed to solve interoperability problems caused by less effective tools.

***Table 6-3*** *Contents of the SOA Scalability and Performance Kit*

| Content | Description |
|---|---|
| Source code | Complete source code for each use case and test scenario; including Ant build scripts for you to build the kit in your own environment. |
| Developer's Journal | A Developer's Journal describing in detail:<br>▪ Detailed use cases and test scenarios<br>▪ Design decisions and tradeoffs<br>▪ XML and Java binding implementation stories<br>▪ Client-side software to call the implemented services<br>▪ Server-side software that implements the services<br>▪ Use case scenario specific findings<br>▪ Installation and performance tuning |
| Prebuilt JARs—Ready for you to press a start button and watch the results. | Prebuilt JAR and WAR files to run immediately in your own environment. |
| TestMaker and XS test scripts | Scripts to stage a scalability and performance test of each use case and the test scenario. |

The kit arms business managers and software developers with the evidence they need to recommend and adopt FastSOA solutions internally and get their projects funded. Table 6-3 summarizes the contents of the published kit.

Next, I show the kit's use cases and test scenario.

### 6.2.2 Definitions: Use Cases and Test Scenario

The kit measures SOAP binding performance and scalability of bindings created and deployed using J2EE-based tools and XQuery and native XML database. Performance testing compares several methods to receive a SOAP-based Web Service request and respond to it. Scalability testing looks at the operation of a service as the number of concurrent requests increases. Performance and scalability tests measure throughput as TPS at the service consumer.

The use cases and test scenarios contrast the TPS differences between the most popular approaches to parse the XML in a request. I chose these in recognition of the following personal experiences:

1. While Web Services standards are now more than five years old, a standard way to test services has not yet emerged. For instance, the SPECjAppServer test implements a 4-tier Web browser-based application, where a browser connects to a Web server, application server, and database server in series. SOA, on the other hand, is truly a multitier architecture, where each tier may be making multiple SOAP requests to multiple services and data sources. SPECjAppServer and similar 4-tier tests do not provide reliable information for capacity planners and software architects in SOA applications.
2. Software architects and developers are specializing their talents by service type. For instance, one type of developer works with complicated XML schemas in order processing services, while another group concentrates on building content management and publication services in portals.
3. The tools, technologies, and libraries available for a software architect are changing rapidly. For instance, a survey I conducted in 2005 shows that all Java-based XML parsing libraries will change significantly within the next year.

Responding to the above issues, the kit has use cases common to many SOA environments. These use cases highlight different aspects of SOA creation and present different challenges to the software development tools examined.

1. **Compiled XML binding using BOD schemas.** (Codenamed the TV Dinner.) In the TV Dinner scenario, a developer needs to code a parts ordering service. The service uses Software Technology in Automotive Retailing (STAR) Business Object Document (BOD) schemas.

   On the consumer side, the test code instantiates a previously serialized Get Purchase Order (GPO) request document. The test code then adds a predetermined number of part elements to the part to be ordered. On the service side, the service examines only specific elements within the GPO, instead of looking through the entire document.

   The TV Dinner scenario is so-called because the entire dinner comes all at once but the food is in compartments. The developers are writing code that addresses elements by their namespace, so they add/put only the parts of the purchase order that need to change. The other compartments—for instance, company name and shipping information—don't change from one GPO request to another. The code for the TV Dinner uses JAXB-created bindings. JAXB accesses the compartments individually. This kind of XML to object binding framework is used only to instantiate the required objects.

2. **Streaming XML (StAX) parser.** (Codenamed the Sushi Boats.) In the Sushi Boats scenario, a developer builds a portal that receives a "blog"-style news stream. Within each received request is a set of elements containing blog entries. The test code scenario parameters determine the number of blog entries inserted into the request. The developer needs to skip the entries that the portal is not interested in and take action on the entries of interest. The test code for the Sushi Boats will feature the JSR 173 Streaming XML (StAX) parser.

   The Sushi Boats scenario is so-called from our observations when one is at a Japanese Sushi Bar. The food comes in a stream past the diner, and it is up to him or her to select which boat to take food from.

3. **DOM approach.** (Codenamed the Buffet.) In the Buffet scenario, a developer writes an order validation service that

receives an order request and needs to read every element of the document to determine the response. The test code scenario parameters determine how many elements it inserts into the request. The test code for The Buffet scenario uses Xerces DOM APIs.

The Buffet scenario is so-called from our experience eating at a buffet restaurant and feeling compelled to visit all stations in the restaurant.

The kit implements the above use cases using both Java and XQuery tools.

In addition to the use cases just mentioned, the kit contrasts database performance differences between use of native XML databases and relational databases when persisting XML data with complex schemas and multiple message sizes in the mid-tier.

### 6.2.3 Additional Use Cases Considered but Not Implemented

During the planning phase of the test case, it is very easy to add use cases and wind up with a test that takes months to run! Sizing the number of use cases meant putting off some test cases until a future date. The following use cases will appear in a future edition of the kit but were temporarily put aside for the sake of time.

1. Creating XML structures from relational data. This is a very common scenario because relational databases are so widely deployed. Also, recombining data to create different structures is often very important.
2. Additional ways to return XML data. For instance, returning entire XML documents and extracting portions of a very large XML document.
3. Joins between nodes of large XML documents.
4. Returning large or complex XML structures, either by direct extraction or as the result of more complex operations.
5. Full-text queries for portions of XML structures.

The above tests will likely make it into the next performance test.

### 6.2.4 Defining the Test Scenario

The *test scenario* is the aggregate of all the use cases and test cases. For instance, the kit implements several use cases that show different approaches to XML parsing (DOM, XQuery, StAX, and Binding Compiler). So if I wanted to run the four use cases with two message sizes I would have eight test cases in my test scenario.

Figure 6-3 lists the four use cases, two technology choices, three message payload sizes, and four concurrent request levels.

| Use Case | | Technology Choice | | Request Payload Size | | Concurrent Requests |
|---|---|---|---|---|---|---|
| Java XML Binding Compiler | | Raining Data TigerLogic* | | 5 kilobytes | | 5 |
| Java Streaming XML Parser | X | Java Application Server | X | 100 kilobytes | X | 50 |
| Java DOM | | | | 500 kilobytes | | 100 |
| XQuery Streaming XML Parser | | | | | | 200 |

*See http://www.rainingdata.com/products/tl.

***Figure 6-3*** *The test scenario is the aggregate of all the use cases, technology choices, request payload size, and concurrent requests.*

The test scenario is the aggregate of all the test cases. For instance, in one test case the test uses the XML Binding Compiler running on TigerLogic at 100 kilobytes and 100 concurrent requests is a single test case. With so many parameters it is easy to see that this test scenario requires 96 test cases to be run.

If each test case takes 5 minutes to run with a 5-minute warm-up and 5-minute cool-down period, then the entire test scenario will take 1,440 minutes (24 hours) to run. I advise caution when adding use cases to a test scenario unless you are confident that the extra time will deliver actionable knowledge.

### 6.2.5 Identify the Test Environment (Hardware and Software)

The last part of defining the test concerns the test environment itself. One of the goals of the test is to follow commonly used best practices that are well known and published. I chose the following for the test environment specification:

- For service hardware, the fastest, least expensive server hardware with the best performance. At the time, this was a rack-mounted IBM 4-CPU Intel Xeon 2.8-GHz model 873 server with 4 gigabytes of memory, dual gigabit Ethernet adapters, running Windows 2003 Server, Service Pack 2.
- For load-generating consumers of the service, a white-box no-name rack-mounted 2-CPU Intel Xeon 2.1-GHz with 2 gigabytes of memory, dual gigabit Ethernet adapters, also running Windows 2003 Server, Service Pack 2. I refer to these as TestNodes.
- The choice for client-side load generating test automation framework was simple. TestMaker—my baby—is free, open-source, and supported by a large user community. The kit code comes with a set of TestMaker files, but it should be possible to implement the test scenario using any commercial or open-source performance tools.
- I chose BEA JRockit JVM 1.5 as a Java Virtual Machine to operate the server-side test software. Past performance testing on JRockit makes me impressed with its speed and stability. Additionally, an informal poll of datacenters shows many Java application servers being run on JRockit.
- For Java-specific optimizations I bumped the consumer and server memory up to 4 gigabytes, the capacity of the underlying PC, using the -Xms and -Xmx memory settings. I set these values to the same large number.
- Logging, debugging, and monitor components were disabled to reduce overhead. All servers were restarted after each scenario, to clean up resource allocations.

At this point, the test is defined to a point where coding of the use cases should begin. This is a good point to end the definition phase, build the test environment, install the test, and learn the actual levels where the server has topped out.

### 6.2.6 Using the XSTest Pattern for Performance Tests

When testing SOA for scalability and performance, the sheer number of test cases in the test scenario makes test automation a necessity. One approach to test automation is a pattern I call XSTest and is implemented as a feature in TestMaker. XSTest takes a test sequence—such as the scenario in Figure 6-3—as input, stages each test case in sequence, and records the transaction results to an XML-based log file. The XSTest implementation in TestMaker then tallies the results from the log file into a TPS report. Figure 6-4 illustrates the XSTest pattern in a UML sequence diagram.

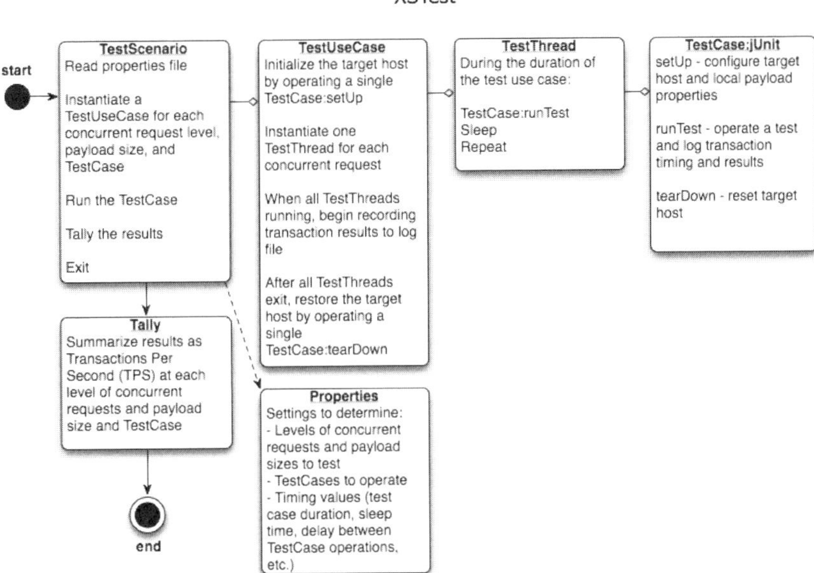


***Figure 6-4*** *XSTest sequence diagram showing how it runs a test scenario.*

A key advantage to the XSTest pattern is its use of jUnit TestCase objects. These are familiar to most developers and also easily learned. The kit implements the tests into TestCase objects for use in the load test and reuse as functional tests.

### 6.2.7 Calibration Testing

When defining the test scenario, a certain amount of speculation gets baked into the test plan. For instance, Figure 6-3 speculates that a test case can achieve satisfactory throughput (TPS) with a message payload request size of 500 kilobytes and 200 concurrent requests.

A calibration test identifies the optimum throughput—measured in TPS at the consumer—for a service against the test given test hardware and software. For instance, consider the results presented in Table 6-4.

***Table 6-4*** *Calibration Results Analysis for a Stateless Service*

| Payload Size (Bytes) | Concurrent Agents | Transactions Per Second (TPS) |
|---|---|---|
| 1,000 | 10 | 10.376 |
| 2,000 | 10 | 8.667 |
| 3,000 | 10 | 6.174 |
| 4,000 | 10 | 1.383 |
| 5,000 | 10 | 0.731 |

Table 6-4 shows the two input values for the test: the size of each message sent to the service and the number of concurrent test agents. XSTest in TestMaker uses these values to operate a test case. XSTest instantiates one thread for each concurrent request. Each thread dynamically generates data of the defined payload size and sends the data as a request to the service. The thread receives a response

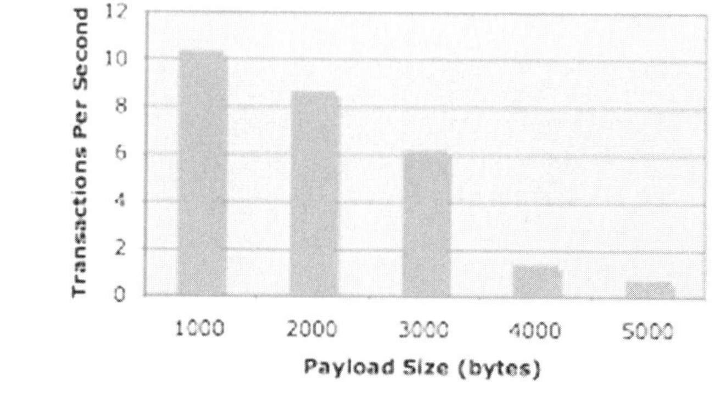


***Figure 6-5*** *A bar chart view of the results data from Table 6-4 shows the maximum throughput value more clearly.*

from the server, validates the response, handles any exceptions, and logs the response as a completed transaction. The thread repeats these steps until the test case period is finished.

Looking at Table 6-4 and Figure 6-5 tells a few things about the service under test, including the following.

1. As the payload increases, the TPS reduces proportionately. The test is not saturating or underutilizing the server, network, or consumer. If TPS were increasing, then we were testing at too low of a level; if it were flat or dropping sharply, then we were testing at too high of a level. (I explain this in detail later in this section.)
2. The reduction in TPS is not proportional to the increase in request size. If the network and consumer are not highly active, then this is an indication of a poorly performing request processor at the service. It could be that the message parsing system is not allocating resources (such as memory, network socket connections, and message queues) correctly sized to the demands of the test.
3. TPS takes a significantly larger reduction for the test cases above 3,000 bytes of payload. This is a case where I normally break out a code profiler and see which buffer has overflowed or which object list was not created to be large enough for the test.

While Figure 6-5 tells me a few things about the service, there is not enough information here to make a conclusion. I have more questions than conclusions! The test needs to provide the values listed in Table 6-5 to help determine what is going wrong.

***Table 6-5*** *Observed Parameters Required to Calibrate the Test*

| Observation | Description |
|---|---|
| Request Payload Size | Size in bytes of the message body sent in the request to the service |
| Response Payload Size | Size in bytes of the response message body sent from the service |
| Concurrent Requests | Total number of concurrent requests in this test case |

***Table 6-5*** *Observed Parameters Required to Calibrate the Test*

| Observation | Description |
|---|---|
| Transactions per Second (TPS) | Total number of completed responses divided by the number of seconds for the test case |
| Network Utilization | % network bandwidth utilized as measured from the server |
| Server CPU Utilization | % server processor bandwidth utilized |
| Consumer CPU Utilization | % consumer (client) processor bandwidth utilized |
| Average Transaction Time | Average time each response took from the service as measured by the consumer/client |
| Minimum Transaction Time | Minimum time each response took from the service as measured by the consumer/client |
| Maximum Transaction Time | Maximum time each response took from the service as measured by the consumer/client |

In a stateless system, each request to the service allocates its own memory, CPU bandwidth, network bandwidth, and other resources necessary to make a response. In a stateless calibration test, I am looking for resource bottlenecks. Table 6-6 shows the results of the test scenario with the network utilization and server and consumer CPU utilization.

***Table 6-6*** *Running the Test While Logging Network and CPU Utilization.*

| Payload Size (Bytes) | Concurrent Requests | Transactions per Second (TPS) | Network Utilization | Server CPU Utilization | Consumer CPU Utilization |
|---|---|---|---|---|---|
| 1,000 | 10 | 10.376 | 1.24% | 55% | 34% |
| 2,000 | 10 | 8.667 | 1.14% | 78% | 37% |
| 3,000 | 10 | 6.174 | 1.32% | 89% | 31% |
| 4,000 | 10 | 1.383 | 0.45% | 95% | 21% |
| 5,000 | 10 | 0.731 | 0.28% | 96% | 18% |

Aha! Looking at the results in Table 6-6 gives some idea of what is going on during the test scenario.

1. The test is *server bound* from achieving greater throughput (TPS). When payload sizes are less than 4,000 bytes, the server CPU utilization is high but not saturated. At 4,000 bytes and over, the CPU is pegged.

   Stateless tests require resources to handle the load of concurrent requests. Take away one of those resources—CPU bandwidth or possibly free memory to operate on the larger payloads—and each response takes longer and lowers overall TPS.
2. The scale of the problem tells me that there is a significant problem in the server. The payload size between 1,000 and 5,000 increases 5 times but the TPS value decreases from 10.376 to 0.731, or 14 times. In a stateless test, the TPS value should be relative to the inputs.

By the way, this is a stateless test, so each request should be served from an independent group of resources (threads, memory, etc.) Watching CPU and memory utilization levels is an appropriate way to identify scalability and performance thresholds. This is not the case for stateful services, including databases and workflow applications. Stateful services use data caches, server queues, and typically have the overhead of a session manager. Each of these impacts CPU and memory utilization levels in the service independently of the current request load from consumers.

The calibration test illustrated above helps us to determine which levels of concurrent requests and message payload sizes are appropriate for a scalability and performance test of a given service running on a defined software and hardware environment. The results we are looking for show a Scalability Index for the service.

### 6.2.8 Scalability Index

Calibration testing matches the number of concurrent requests and payload sizes in a test scenario to the underlying service software and hardware. A Scalability Index is a function of the TPS a service delivers as the concurrent requests and payload sizes change in a test scenario. Figure 6-6 illustrates a Scalability Index for a service.

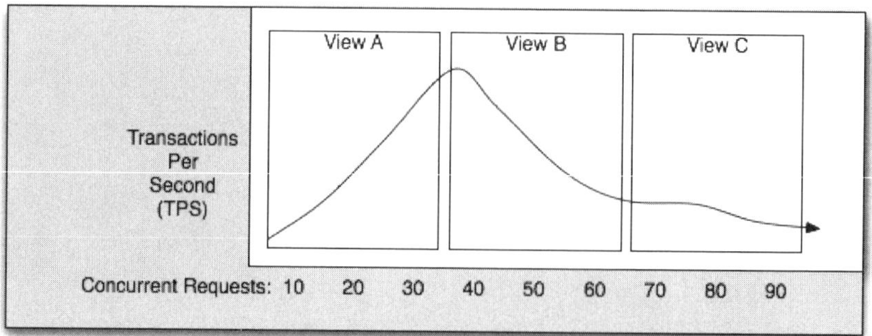


***Figure 6-6*** *The Scalability Index shows the TPS at a set of given concurrent request sizes. Calibration testing shows us the most value range of payload sizes to test the service.*

The Scalability Index in Figure 6-6 shows how the service responds to increasing levels of concurrent requests. There are three distinct parts to this Scalability Index, as follows:

- When testing the service at 10, 20, and 30 concurrent request (CR) levels, we see that TPS rises for each CR level. Figure 6-6 identifies this as View A. Imagine your conclusion if all you tested were the CR levels in View A. The TPS results would mislead you to believe that the service would scale up to handle additional CRs. In fact, when you get to 40 CRs, the TPS values begin to decrease.
- When testing the service at the other end of the spectrum—70, 80, and 90 CR levels—the TPS values do not change noticeably as the CR levels increase. Imagine your conclusion if all you tested were the CR levels in View C. I have seen information systems managers buy overly equipped server hardware to contend with situations where the server received too many responses to efficiently handle them all. The manager could save a lot of money if he or she bought many smaller machines to load balance the total CR levels into smaller CR levels sent to multiple servers.
- Calibration tests seek the TPS values in the 40, 50, and 60 CR levels shown in View B. In this range, the service responds to a moderate number of CRs at a TPS rate that is acceptable to the organization hosting the service.

The calibration test of the service illustrated in Figure 6-6 shows us that we should compare the TPS levels from View B to the other scenarios, including alternative APIs and products. The View B CR levels of 40, 50, and 60 do not underdrive the service with too few requests and do not swamp the service with too many requests. We can now take the View B CR levels as the results of the calibration tests into the full test of the test scenario.

In the above example, we found the CPU, network, and memory utilization values during the test to be helpful in determining the location of a performance and scalability bottleneck. CPU and memory bandwidth are helpful in stateless tests. In the next section, I will show that CPU and memory bandwidth are usually meaningless for stateful tests.

## 6.3 Understanding TPS

Before we move on to running the full test and doing the results analysis, I want to make sure you have a thorough understanding of transactions per second (TPS) measurement. I have seen TPS results confuse and mislead software architects, developers, and CEOs. Sometimes the results can be counterintuitive.

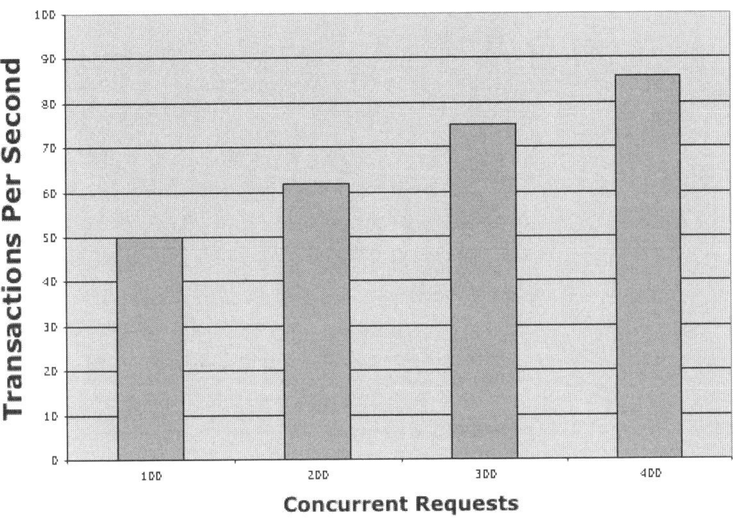


*Figure 6-7 The Scalability Index shows the function of a service's ability to respond to increasing levels of concurrent requests.*

Figure 6-7 shows the system's scalability as measured by throughput. In other words, how many transactions can the system handle as it receives more and more requests. The test measured how many TPS are being handled at four levels of concurrent requests.

A perfect information system is able to keep handling requests at the same speed regardless of how many requests come in at the same time. Charting a perfect system's scalability shows TPS rates increasing in equal proportion to the number of requests sent its way. For example, in the perfect system if you made 100 concurrent requests in a 10-second interval and the system responded to each of the requests in 2 seconds, then the perfect system should let you make 200 concurrent requests in a 10-second interval with each request still taking 2 seconds. The resulting chart of the perfect system would look like Figure 6-8.

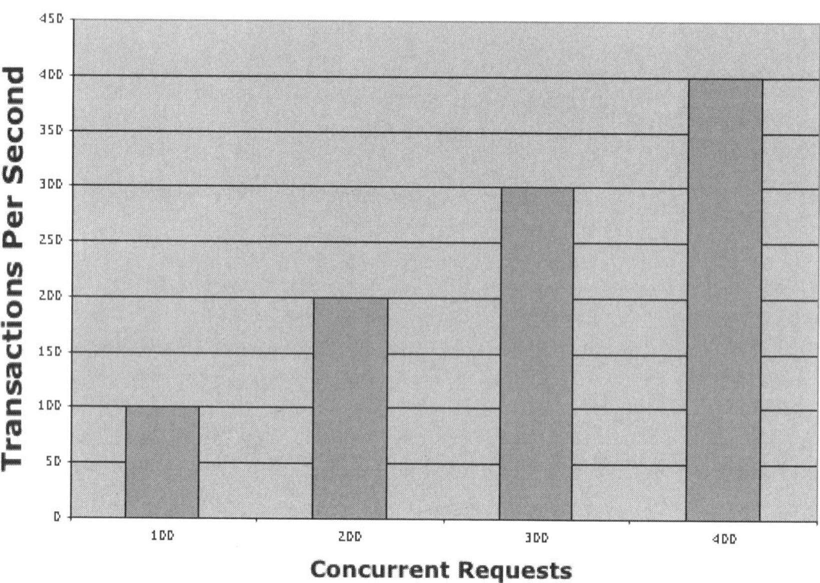


*Figure 6-8 The Scalability Index for a service exhibiting linear scalability.*

TPS keeps going up and to the right in equal proportion to the number of requests made. At each measured level of concurrent requests, the system is handling requests at a measured number of transactions per second. When you increase the number of concurrent requests, the system handles more requests and so the overall average number of transactions completed increases in equal proportion. For example, at 100 concurrent requests the system handles 1,000 requests in a 10 second period (100 TPS), and at 200 concurrent requests the system handles 2,000 requests in the same 10 second period (200 TPS). That is perfect scalability—the Holy Grail of performance testing. The additional requests you throw at the system do not slow down the proportional speed at which the system responds to the requests.

A typical system that hits a bottleneck would look like Figure 6-9.

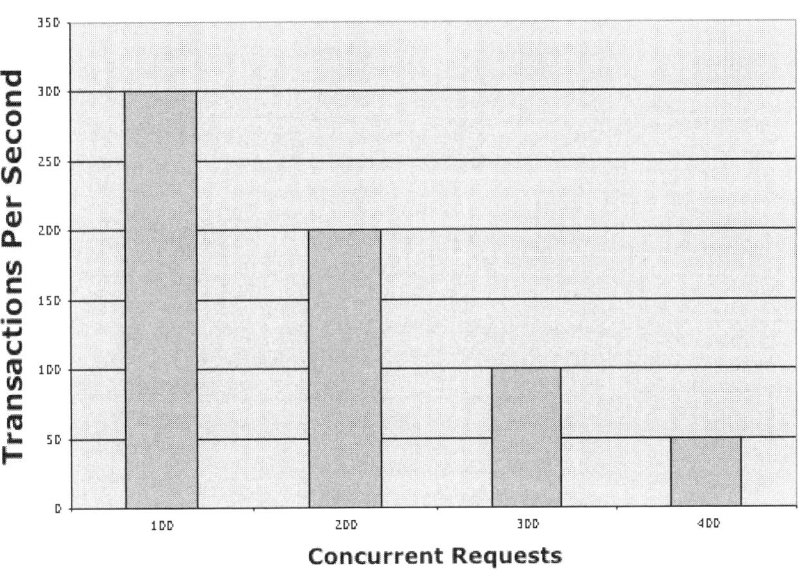


*Figure 6-9* *A service exhibiting a bottleneck in performance.*

As the system receives larger numbers of concurrent requests, it slows down on responding to all requests. If you kept going past 400 concurrent requests in this system, eventually the system would reach 0 transactions per second. Many systems I have checked for scalability have this problem. The Scalability Index shows systems managers how to plan the capacity of their systems against the desired throughput to make users happy. The Scalability Index also helps developers to understand the impact their design and coding decisions have on performance.

In my experience, the more common situation is shown in Figure 6-10. In the first three columns of Figure 6-10, the system is able to

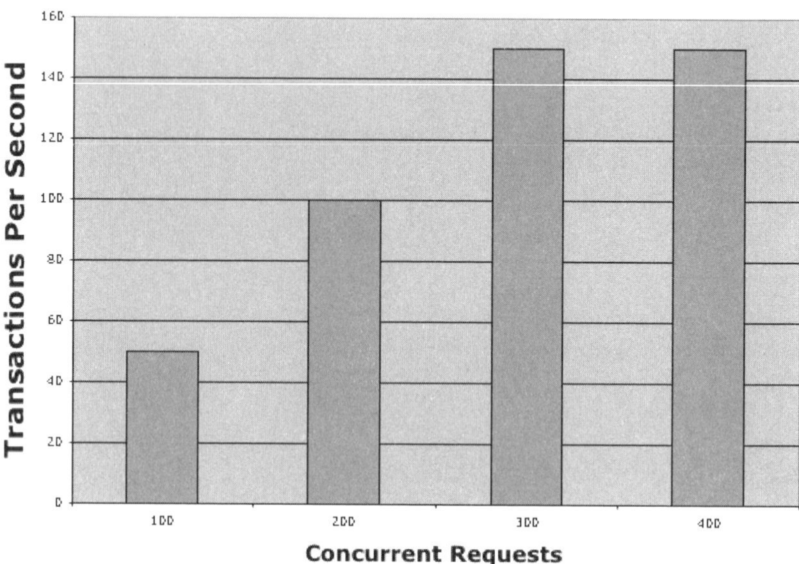


*Figure 6-10* *A service exhibiting a scalability problem.*

handle increasing levels of concurrent requests. In the fourth column, the system hits an upper limit to handle transactions. Many times this is caused by a database indexing problem, a data cache that is now full, or a network connection that is saturated.

This TPS method may seem straightforward enough to you. I will cover an example of the questions I received during a scalability and performance study from an engineer, an engineering manager, and an executive. I conducted a scalability test and determined the results presented in Table 6-7.

*Table 6-7* *The Scalability Index for a Given Service*

| Concurrent Requests | Transactions per Second (TPS) | Count of Completed Transactions | Average Response Time (Milliseconds) |
|---|---|---|---|
| 25 | .38 | 68 | 65,344 |
| 15 | .33 | 61 | 33,828 |
| 10 | .31 | 59 | 12,234 |

From the results in Table 6-7 you may wonder why the TPS increases only slightly with more concurrent requests considering the test is making 2.5 times (25/10) more concurrent requests? Why would the test not increase the TPS value by 2.5 times to 0.775 (0.31 TPS at 10 concurrent requests, times 2.5)?

Free-running threads generate the concurrent requests with no sleep time between requests, as illustrated in Figure 6-11. Their job is to keep making requests to the server during the test period. Yet, the average response time at 25 users is 5.34 times longer (65,344 milliseconds at 25 users divided by 12,234 milliseconds at 10 users). Consequently, there are fewer opportunities to log results and increase the TPS value.

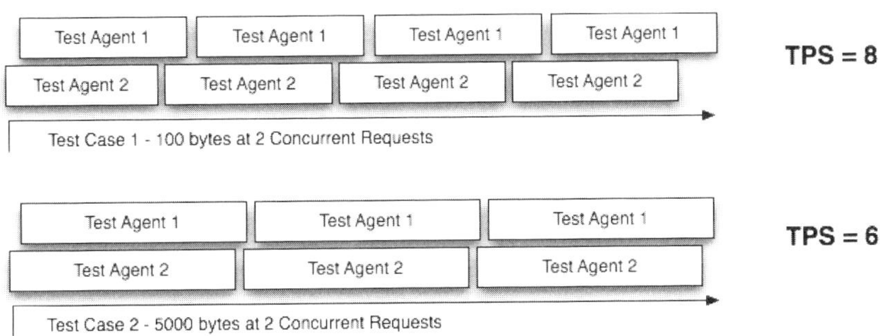


***Figure 6-11*** *Throughput as measured in transactions per second (TPS) from the consumer reduces as the service takes longer to respond to each request.*

When the test has increased concurrent users, running one of two things can happen:

1. The server responds to each request on average in a smaller amount of time than it took at the lower level of CUs. In this condition each CU finishes sooner, logs a response (a transaction), and can make its next request that much sooner. TPS goes up from the lower level of CUs.
2. The server responds to each request on average in the same time it took at the lower level of CUs. In this condition each CU takes the same amount of time but there are more CUs running concurrently. TPS goes up from the lower level of CUs proportionately to the increase of CUs.

The server responds to each request with a longer response time than it took at the lower level of CUs. In this condition each CU finishes later. There are fewer opportunities for the server to respond, because the CUs are waiting for the server to respond. TPS drops proportionately to the increase in each response time.

In the next section, I present a list of test issues and solutions from which you may take action based on the Scalability Index to your service.

### 6.3.1 Calibration What-If Chart

***Table 6-8*** *Calibration What-If Chart*

| Test Experience | Likely Problem | What to Do Next |
|---|---|---|
| Increase CRs and see a decrease in TPS | Check the average response time. | Run a test case that compares response times as CRs increase. Identify the least acceptable response time and work backward from there. |
| Increase CRs and see an increase in TPS | Your test is not calibrated to use high enough CR and payload sizes. | Run a calibration test to determine the optimal Scalability Index and correctly set the CR and payload size levels. |
| Increase CRs but see little change in TPS | CRs are set too high already. Check CPU if doing stateless test. | Run another test with half the CRs. |
| Server CPU at 95% and increase in CRs gives me increase in TPS | Likely that you are testing a stateful system. | Run a test case to determine the Scalability Index of the service under test. |
| Consumer CPU at 95% and increase in CRs gives me a decrease in TPS | CRs are set too high already for the number of load-generating consumers. | Add more load-generating consumer machines to the list. |
| Consumer CPU at 15% and server CPU at 30% and increase CRs gives me little change in TPS | Likely that your network is saturated. | Check the network bandwidth utilization. Add network adapters to server or consider a faster network. |

It is beyond the scope of this book for me to teach you everything that might happen during a calibration test. However, Table 6-8 lists a few good ones to know.

## 6.4 Summary

This chapter presented the PushToTest testing method to identify and quantify the scalability, performance, and developer productivity benefits available behind choices of technology to implement SOA applications. The methodology helps to make apparent the tradeoffs a software developer makes when choosing SOA coding techniques, code libraries, and APIs.

By now my hope is that you are so excited about the performance findings from this chapter that you want to learn all you can about XML, XML Query (XQuery), and native XML database technology. The next two chapters show you these technologies and how to use them in your SOA designs.

Chapter

7

# Learning XML-Centric Technology for SOA

The previous chapters show that where XML and SOA intersect, the object-oriented approaches to software development have an impact on scalability and performance. The FastSOA patterns use native XML technology for SOA and deliver 3 to 22 times faster performance.

This chapter covers the basics of the XQuery language, the scalability issues surrounding integration of XQuery into a Java application, the blunders I made while learning XQuery and native XML databases, and the safebets that will likely be in the XQuery specification in the near future and already exist in many XQuery implementations. By the end of this chapter, you will be able to write an XQuery yourself, or at least know where to look if you need additional help.

## 7.1 XML-Centric Options

After about the tenth time you write a program that takes in an XML parameter and outputs an XML parameter, you may begin to wonder if there is a better way. After all, every line of code you write will eventually need to be maintained. So why not use a declarative language to identify XML transformations and let the underlying engine figure out how to implement a function that meets your declared needs? This kind of thinking in the middleware space got started in the mid-1990s. The result is a cornucopia of new technologies, including XPath, XQuery, XML Stylesheet Language Transformations (XSLT,) and many others. For instance, Figure 7-1 shows that a combination of XQuery, XPath, and XSLT technology may be used to solve an XML problem.

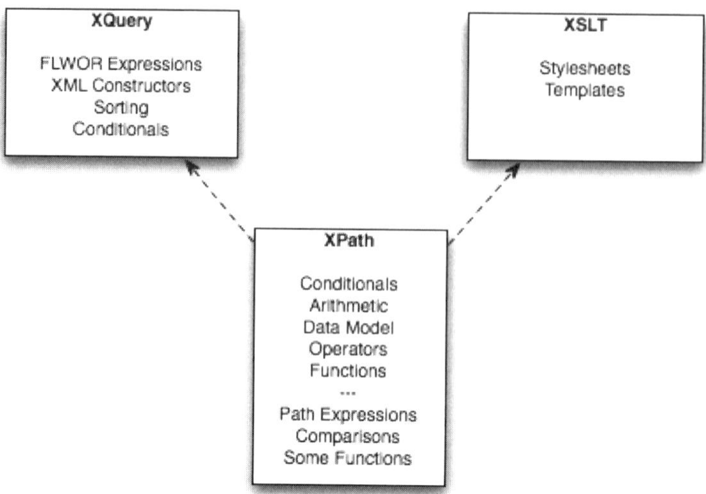


***Figure 7-1*** *From the developer's perspective, XQuery, XPath, and XSLT are XML-centric technologies that may be used in combination or individually.*

XPath 1.0 provided the basic syntax to parse through XML documents using path expressions, to provide simple comparison operators such as greater than and less than or equal, and to provide some functions such as return the parent node of the current selection. XPath 2.0 greatly expanded XPath capabilities by including a data model and type system, conditional execution with a path expression, and new arithmetic functions and a greatly expanded set of operators. Integration with XML schema also afforded it rich typing, which was absent in XPath 1.0.

While XPath is great at working with a single XML document, XQuery and XSLT are solutions made to work with multiple XML documents. For instance, FLWOR (an acronym of for-let-where-order by-return that is pronounced "flower") is a commonly used XQuery expression enabling you to locate nodes using XPath, construct and restructure XML, and sort and filter data in one or more XML documents.

Today, software architects and developers build transformational middleware using a combination of XQuery, XPath, and XSLT technology. However, in my experience, developers tend to cleave into two camps: XQuery fans and XSLT fans. I am an XQuery fan.

XQuery and XSLT have enough developer momentum behind them that both will coexist. In fact, working groups at the World Wide Web Consortium (W3C) are working on the most recent specifications for XQuery 1.0 and XSLT 2.0 in tandem.

Where XQuery and XSLT overlap is in the problems they solve: transformation of XML data, federation of XML collections, and advanced query of XML data. Developers will continue to see debates about the capabilities and virtues of each, including much myth and misunderstanding. For example, I often see the claim that XQuery's ability to query multiple, disparate sources in one pass gives it a distinct advantage over XSLT. In fact, XSLT 2.0 processors can have multiple nodes supplied as an input sequence. XSLT 1.0 has the document() function for accessing multiple sources within a single transformation, and XSLT 2.0 supports the new collection() function. I also often hear the claim that while XQuery syntax looks nicer, it lacks XSLT's template-style pattern matching. The vigorous debate behind XQuery and XLST means developers should expect improvements and challenges in both languages that would keep them close to one another in terms of function and capability.

My interest in XSLT started in 1999. The Software Development Forum, Java Special Interest Group (Java SIG) hosted a speaker on XSLT.[1] He brought 85 slides and had about 45 minutes to make a presentation. With all the questions he got from the attendees, he did not make it past slide 18. That about sums up my experience trying to learn XSLT. As a language, I am told by experts that XSLT is incredibly powerful, elegant, and sophisticated. XSLT just never set in for me. XQuery, on the other hand, was something that looks self-evident, packed with power, and offers lots of reasons to be liked.

### 7.1.1 Reasons to Like XQuery and Native XML Databases

Instead of going deep into XQuery and native XML database concepts, here are some simple reasons to like XQuery.

1 Details at http://www.sdforum.org.

1. **XQuery is a language.** It has iterators, branching, module libraries, variables, and many other things I would expect to find in Java, C#, JSP, ASP, and other languages. So I can write applications in XQuery, not just queries. SQL is terrific at describing queries, but you really need to wrap it with a programming language to make it useful on a day-to-day basis.
2. **The data model and type system are complete and make portability easy**. For instance, the XQuery data model specifies date types so you can be assured that any XQuery engine will have date functions for immediate use.
3. **XQuery is XPath integrated**. XQuery gives XPath expressions across collections of XML documents. XPath works very well when working on an individual XML document. With Xquery, applications use the same XPath syntax, but the paths work across collections of XML documents.
4. **XQuery naturally extends to map new data sources.** XQuery is easy to extend to map other data sources (other than just XML). For instance, many XQuery engines extend past the specification to allow calls to a Java method within a class, and that class might return to me data within a collection (such as a structured hashmap or a table). In these extensions, the XQuery receives the response to a method call as an XML document. The same situation is true for making a call to a Rich Site Syndication (RSS) feed for syndicated news, or making a call to a SOAP-based Web Service, or even to a REST-based Web Service. XQuery is naturally extended to support additional new data sources.
5. **XQuery works well for XML Web Services, SOA, and ESB applications.** These are XML applications. Many XQuery implementations already extend past the XQuery specification to provide support for Web Services. This seems very natural to me. For instance, MarkLogic lets me make SOAP calls from my XQuery. TigerLogic does so too and lets me query against JDBC sources using the same syntax as a query against a Web Service result.
6. **XQuery output can be XML, HTML, text, or anything else.** XQuery has no expectation for the output format of its return values. XQuery can just as easily output XML as it can output HTML.

7. **XQuery and native XML database technology solve my need for speed.** If anything, Web Services and Service-Oriented Architectures are turning out many new XML schemas and lots of complex XML data. Often, the XML tells my service details about time-to-live and replication information. XQuery and a native XML database make it much easier for me to implement data mitigation and aggregation services to facilitate performance improvements in the mid-tier.
8. **XQuery is a declarative rather than procedural programming environment.** In a declarative language you declare your intention for the data you want to work with and you let the language worry about the approach it needs to take to get that data. This gives the XQuery and native XML database an advantage in understanding and optimizing your application without requiring any extra effort on your part. If the XQuery implementer does a good job, then new versions of the XQuery implementation will improve performance of your application without requiring any changes to your declarative code.
9. **Nested "for" loops in XQuery are so easy!** If I wanted to do nested "for" loops in a SQL database, I would need to learn the programming language that comes along with that implementation.

## 7.2 XQuery in the SOA Stack: The Cookie Factory

The rest of this chapter will introduce you to XQuery, XPath, and native XML database technology through a set of examples built around a cookie factory. This cookie factory is like most manufacturers today. It receives orders from customers and orders ingredients for its products from suppliers. In the pre–Service-Oriented Architecture (SOA) days, the cookie factory IT staff may have bought a commercial software solution to run the business, hired engineers to write code to expose a Web browser interface for customers to place orders, and wrote code to work with the supplier's order system. These choices were slow and expensive; slow in that it took many engineering hours to switch suppliers or offer new products, and expensive from the cost of the commercial software licenses and engineers' salaries. In the days of SOA, hardly any business systems analyst recommends buying proprietary and commercial software to

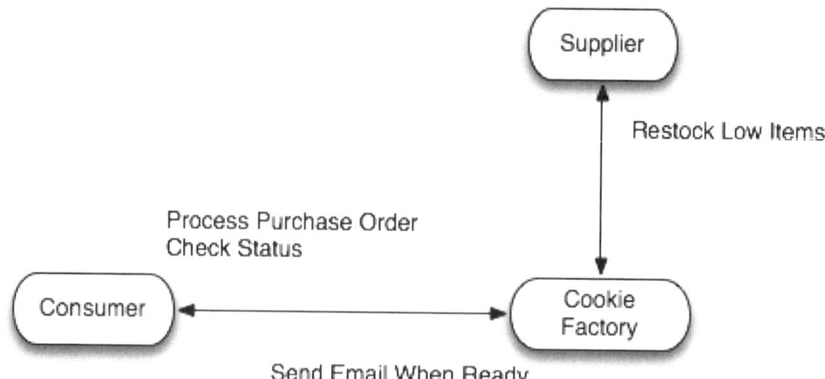


***Figure 7-2*** *The cookie factory provides services to receive orders from consumers, order ingredients from a supplier, and notify the consumers when their orders are ready to ship.*

build business integration solutions. Figure 7-2 shows the cookie factory after it adopted SOA.

The cookie factory provides standard Web Services interfaces for the following functions.

- **Process_Purchase_Order (PPO).** This is a service hosted by the cookie factory. Input to this service defines the number of dozen cookies wanted and the type of cookie. The service returns a purchase order (PO) number.
- **Check_Ready_Time (CRT).** This is a service hosted by the cookie factory. Input to this service is a PO number. The service returns the number of minutes until the order is ready for shipment or an out-of-stock notice that shows the reason for the delay.
- **Restock.** This is a service hosted by the supplier. The cookie factory makes a restock request when current inventory falls below the quantity that is needed to make 10 dozen cookies. Input to this service is the current inventory of one or more ingredients. The output is the new inventory levels at the cookie factory for the input ingredients.
- **Notification.** When a batch is finished, the cookie factory sends an email message to notify the consumer that the cookies are ready to ship.

The cookie factory service interface definitions give us a starting point to consider how to write the working code. There are many options to choose from, including programming language, XML parsing library, and application development environment. In my experience, these choices are driven by three factors:

1. The learning curve a software architect and developer takes to become proficient with the new tool, technology, and protocol.
2. The scalability and performance of the finished service.
3. The ease with which a new software developer maintains—fixes, patches, and corrects—the already-written software.

Writing the XQuery to implement the cookie factory service is easy once you have a working knowledge of XQuery itself. Next, I present the example data used in the cookie factory and show how to write the XQuery to implement the services.

## 7.3 The Data Used in the Cookie Factory Example

The cookie factory example requires two kinds of data persistence: a list of ingredients and their quantity in inventory, and a set of recipes to make cookies. The following shows the contents of ingredients.xml.

```
<?xml version="1.0" encoding="UTF-8"?>
<ingredients batchsize="12">
    <dry manager="gabriel">
        <flour amount="100" measure="lbs" stocketa="0"/>
        <salt amount="50" measure="lbs" stocketa="0"/>
        <bakingpowder amount="0" measure="lbs"
          stocketa="24"/>
        <sugar amount="250" measure="lbs" stocketa="0"/>
    </dry>
    <wet manager="emily">
        <water amount="100" measure="pints" stocketa="0"/>
        <vanilla amount="0" measure="pints" stocketa="48"/>
        <molasses amount="200" measure="pints"
          stocketa="0"/>
    </wet>
```

```
        <perishable manager="marlena">
            <egg amount="12" measure="dozen" stocketa="0"/>
            <milk amount="125" measure="pints" stocketa="0"/>
            <butter amount="55" measure="lbs" stocketa="0"/>
            <chocolatechips amount="220" measure="lbs"
              stocketa="0"/>
        </perishable>
    </ingredients>
```

The following shows the contents of directions.xml.

```
<?xml version="1.0" encoding="UTF-8"?>
<recipe>
    <cookie name="chocolate_chip">
        <quantity measure="dozen">500</quantity>
        <steps>
            <add ingredient="flour" quantity="5"/>
            <add ingredient="butter" quantity="3"/>
            <mix time="5" measure="minutes"/>
            <wait time="1" measure="minutes"/>
            <add ingredient="salt" quantity="3"/>
            <add ingredient="egg" quantity="4"/>
            <add ingredient="sugar" quantity="8"/>
            <mix time="1" measure="minutes"/>
            <wait time="1" measure="minutes"/>
            <add ingredient="vanilla" quantity="1"/>
            <add ingredient="bakingpowder" quantity="2"/>
            <add ingredient="chocolatechips"
              quantity="6"/>
            <mix time="1" measure="minutes"/>
            <wait time="1" measure="minutes"/>
            <bake time="7" measure="minutes"/>
            <cool time="3" measure="minutes"/>
        </steps>
    </cookie>
    <cookie name="ranger_cookie">
        <quantity measure="dozen">25</quantity>
        <steps>
            <add ingredient="flour" quantity="2"/>
            <add ingredient="butter" quantity="4"/>
            <mix time="5" measure="minutes"/>
```

```
                <wait time="1" measure="minutes"/>
                <add ingredient="salt" quantity="2"/>
                <add ingredient="egg" quantity="1"/>
                <add ingredient="sugar" quantity="4"/>
                <mix time="1" measure="minutes"/>
                <wait time="1" measure="minutes"/>
                <mix time="1" measure="minutes"/>
                <wait time="1" measure="minutes"/>
                <bake time="7" measure="minutes"/>
                <cool time="3" measure="minutes"/>
            </steps>
        </cookie>
    </recipe>
```

The data model in the above XML documents enables us to write XQuery code to answer the following questions.

- How many batches of cookies can I make with the current ingredients on hand?
- Do I have enough ingredients to make 10 dozen cookies?
- What is the next ingredient that I will run out of?
- How long will it take to make 10 dozen cookies?

For instance, the following XQuery answers the question, "Which of the wet ingredients is out of stock?"

```
(: Which of the wet ingredients is out of stock? :)
for $i in doc("ingredients.xml")/ingredients/wet/*
where $i/@amount=0
return $i
```

Execute this XQuery and receive the following results.

```
<vanilla amount="0" measure="pints" stocketa="48"/>
```

This is a FLWOR XQuery construct. It searches through the wet ingredients document looking for ingredients that have an amount attribute set to zero.

## 7.4 A Tour of XQuery

This section will teach you the basics of XQuery and native XML databases by showing the cookie factory services. The section begins by describing the naming and expression conventions. Then it shows how to form expressions, write queries (known as FLWOR expressions), and explain namespaces and the data model. You should end this chapter with a working knowledge of Xquery, enough to write the cookie factory. The resources section at the end of this chapter will give you a pointer to the books and on-line resources available to teach the finer points of XQuery and native XML databases.

### 7.4.1 Starting with the Basics

XQuery is a compact language that does not use XML itself to represent functions. Instead, XQuery looks like Java, C#, and other object-oriented languages.

XQuery does not use an end-of-line character such as Java's semicolons or Python's spacing characters. White space (tabs, spaces, returns) in an XQuery is not significant. White space is significant in quoted strings. And pretty much everything is case-sensitive in XQuery. This can make some XQuery look disturbingly complex.

```
let $x := 2 let $y := 3 return 10*$x+$y
```

The above example returns the value 23. This can introduce a problem later on where a new developer needs to quickly understand my code. Would you prefer to see the same code formatted as follows?

```
let $x := 2
let $y := 3
return 10*$x+$y
```

XQuery keyword, function, and operator names are case-sensitive and usually lowercase. All names in XQuery must be valid XML names and may include a namespace. XQuery uses parentheses to determine evaluation order, and many kinds of expressions have their own precedence.

```
( true() and false() ) or false() and true()
```

You express literal values in an XQuery directly by using single or double quotes surrounding a string. For example, the XQuery below is for a date type.

```
xs:date("2005-04-23")
```

XQuery defines variables in many places, including within a FLWOR expression, within a Let expression, within the prolog, and as the result of a function call.

Comments come with a smile. For instance, the following is a comment.

```
(: Hi, I am XQuery and I am here to help. :)
```

XQuery allows comments wherever it allows white space. XQuery allows XML comments, marked with <!-- and -->, in results data.

Comparison operators may be a little tricky to understand because of their support of sequences. XQuery provides comparison operators—eq, ne, lt, gt, le, ge in addition to <, >, and =.

```
doc("ingredients.xml")//@amount>10
```

The above XQuery returns true if any elements with an amount attribute have values greater than 10.

```
doc("ingredients.xml")//@amount gt 10
```

The same XQuery using gt returns true if there is only one amount attribute returned by the expression and the attribute value is greater than 10. If the XQuery returns more than one amount, XQuery raises an error.

XQuery provides conditional execution in if..then..else and typeswitch functions. If..then..else is a little different from most other programming languages in that the else clause is required. For instance, XQuery raises an error when parsing the following expression.

```
if ( doc("ingredients.xml")//@amount>10 )
then return "yes"
```

The correct expression includes an empty else clause as shown below.

```
if ( doc("ingredients.xml")//@amount>10 )
then "yes"
else ()
```

### 7.4.2 Structure of an XQuery

An XQuery has two parts: prolog and body. The prolog declares variables, identifies user-defined functions, and identifies namespaces. The prolog may also import schemas and functional modules. The body does the work of understanding the data and returns a value. For instance, the XQuery in Figure 7-3 returns an HTML-formatted list of ingredients and amounts. The list is alphabetically sorted by ingredient name and the value is half of what is actually in stock.

Prolog

```
declare namespace xqn = "http://www.xquerynow.com";

declare function xqn:half( $val as xs:double )
as xs:double
{
    let $half := $val div 2
    return $half
};
```

Body

```
<html><body>List of items:<br/><ul type="square">

{ for $ingredient in doc("ingredients.xml")/ingredients/dry/*
  order by name($ingredient)
  return <li>{ name( $ingredient ) },
 { xqn:half( number( $ingredient/@amount ) ) }</li>
}
</ul></body></html>
```

***Figure 7-3*** *An XQuery cleaves into two parts: The prolog defines namespaces and user-defined functions. The body defines the processing code.*

There are a number of XQuery concepts presented in Figure 7-3 that are worth commenting on now. The prolog declares a user-defined namespace and function, imports of external modules and schemas, default collation, and other default parameters. XQuery separates expressions in the prolog with a semicolon character. The body section, on the other hand, is a literal representation of the response plus any expressions needing to be computed, in which case curly brace ( { and } ) characters appear to escape the response. There is no formal declaration syntax for the prolog and body. XQuery magically deduces the difference from the lack of semicolon characters and the presence of curly braces. (To see the downside of this ambiguity, see Section 7.5.)

Don't worry for now about the syntax of the example given in Figure 7-3. We will cover that in detail in the coming sections of this chapter. The above XQuery emits the following results. (I added some spacing to the output to make it more readable.)

```
<html>
    <body>List of items:<br/>
        <ul type="square">
            <li>bakingpower, 0</li>
            <li>flour, 100</li>
            <li>salt, 50</li>
            <li>sugar, 250</li>
        </ul>
    </body>
</html>
```

Now let us dig into the basics of XQuery.

### 7.4.3 The Data Model: Nodes, Elements, and Sequences

XQuery started life as an XML query language, so it is reasonable to find the XQuery data model devoted to working with XML data. I will generalize the XQuery data into three categories, although there are more: nodes, atomic elements, and sequences.

#### *Nodes*

Nodes are XML elements. For instance, the following is a node from the directions.xml document described earlier in this chapter.

```
<quantity measure="dozen">500</quantity>
```

The node has a name—quantity—with a value of 500. The node has as attribute-named measure with a string value of "dozen." This is typical of a node minus other complexities such as custom datatypes defined with a DTD or XML Schema and namespace declarations. XQuery uses expressions to navigate nodes and identify attributes and names. The next section presents many examples of XPath functions to operate on these nodes.

Another typical node stores multiple values in a set of attributes but has no value itself.

```
<add ingredient="flour" quantity="5"/>
```

Before I move on to atomic elements I want to point out a key strength of XQuery and native XML databases over all other approaches to building XML and Service-Oriented Architecture (SOA) applications. A node may have child nodes, as follows.

```
<steps>
  <add ingredient="flour" quantity="5"/>
</steps>
```

I call the topmost node the document node, although technically it is an element node with no value itself but having child attribute nodes. XQuery and native XML database tools each have their own lingo to follow, since the XQuery Data Model does not define the database itself. For instance, Figure 7-4 shows the way Raining Data TigerLogic implements the inheritance model from a simple node all the way up to a database.

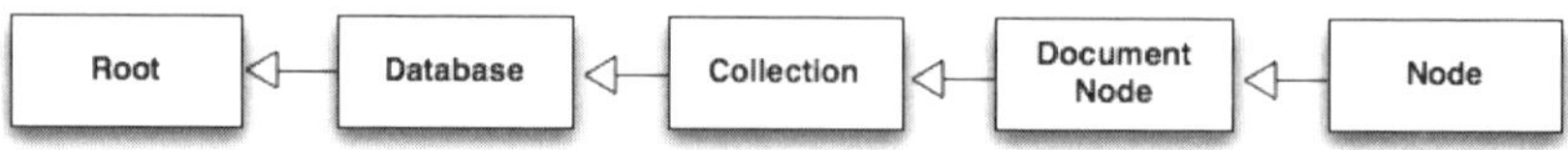


***Figure 7-4*** *XQuery nodes are especially powerful, since the parent of a node goes up and into collections and databases using a native XML database.*

The node model lets you use the same XQuery and path expressions to work with local node values and collection and database data sets. So you need to learn fewer expressions to do more, and the resulting code is easily maintained.

Figure 7-5 shows a more detailed view of the node definition in the context of the overall data model.

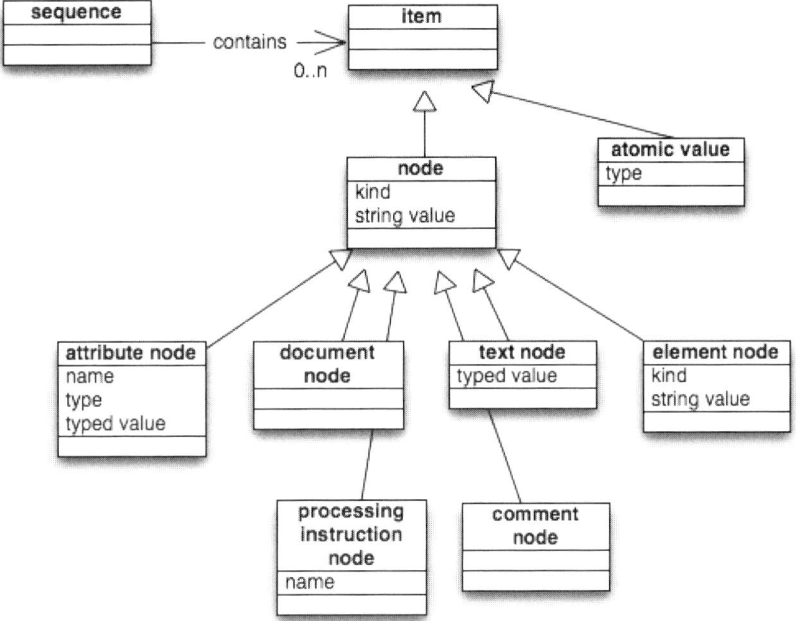


***Figure 7-5*** *A UML diagram of the XQUery data model*

As you can see, XQuery is defined in terms of an object oriented style data model, not in terms of XML text. Data going into an XQuery is an instance of the data model, and the same is true of the output from an XQuery. Every document is a tree of nodes, and the nodes themselves are document, element, attribute, text, processing instruction, and comment node types. (In my experience, I have rarely seen processing instruction and comment node types widely used.) Last, although nodes may contain the same name and values, each node is unique. (Of course, each node has a unique identity that it returns regardless of changes to its value or the values of its child nodes, if any.) So unless an implementation of the XQuery data model implements a node-level inheritance model, none is expected or implied.

### Atomic Elements

In addition to nodes, the XQuery data model provides for atomic items. These are individual data values with no association to a node. Atomic items use the XML Schema datatype definitions.[2] For instance, strings, Booleans, decimals, integers, floats, doubles, and

2 See http://www.w3.org/XML/Schema for details on XML Schema

date values come from XML Schema and are supported as first-class atomic items. The following shows some instances of atomic types.

```
xs:string
xs:integer
xs:double
```

When declaring variables, functions, and results data, an optional type phrase enables you to define the datatype. For instance, the following declares a user-defined function that only accepts decimal values and returns a double value.

```
declare function xqn:half( $val as xs:double )
as xs:double
```

Atomic elements are simple types that you may write into an XQuery to represent simple types directly. You can even write several simple types directly as literals in the XQuery language, including strings, integers, doubles, and decimals. For instance, the following may appear in an XQuery and represent atomic elements.

```
"This is a string"
315
1.382873
```

These values are immutable. For instance, the above string declaration will not let you change the value of a character within the string.

Many built-in XQuery functions return atomic values. For instance, the following automatically extracts the value of a node (sometimes called atomization).

```
substring( <amount>101</amount>, 1, 2)
```

### Sequences

The data model diagram in Figure 7-5 shows that an item is a single node or an atomic value. A series of items is known as a sequence. In XQuery, every value is a sequence, and there is no distinction between a single item and a sequence of items. Sequences may not contain other sequences; they may only contain nodes or atomic values.

XQuery expression returns a sequence of zero or more items. For instance, ingredients//dry returns a sequence of dry ingredients. Of course, ingredients//amount returns an empty sequence. There are ways to construct sequences manually, as shown in the following code segment.

```
(1, 2, 3)
(1 to 4)
()
```

XQuery expressions evaluate to sequences. The comma operator concatenates two values or sequences. For instance, the following is a sequence of three integer values.

```
1,2,3
```

A sequence containing a single value is the same as that value by itself. XQuery does not allow nesting sequences. For instance, the following XQuery returns the number of values in a sequence.

```
let $a := (1,2)
let $b := ($a, $b)
let $c := 5
let $d := ()
return (count($a), count($b), count($c), count($d) )
```

The above XQuery returns a sequence of (2,4,1,0) because $b is the same as (3,4,3,4).

I hope this makes sense to you, since the standard functions for working with nodes return sequences.

Some popular scripting languages—for instance, JSP, ASP, and PHP—enable you to embed expressions in scripts to generate HTML content directly. XQuery enables that too, plus XQuery lets you create XML and HTML forms inside of XQuery expressions.

```
let $xdoc := <flour amount="50"/>
```

The above code creates a new XML node. Node identifiers are immutable and XQuery defines no functions to alter the values of a node once created. Of course, you could replace a node with a new one.

Next, we will look at XQuery from an XPath perspective.

### 7.4.4 From XPath to XQuery

The XPath language is a non-XML syntax for addressing portions of an XML document. Developers saw XPath's advantages early on and treat it today like a small query language.

An XPath queries through a single document. As we see in Figure 7-6, XQuery and native XML databases extend the original idea to handle queries through multiple documents, with the documents residing in databases and collections. This section looks at XPath operations in a single document. The next section shows XPath applied to a collection of XML documents.

Developers use path expressions to traverse an input XML document and select elements, nodes, and attributes of interest. For instance, the following is a path expression to find the wet ingredients in the cookie factory example that are on order.

```
doc("ingredients.xml")/ingredients/wet/*[@stocketa>0]
```

A path expression is a series of location *steps* separated by slashes (/). A step is analogous to a SQL cursor. The step selects a set of nodes in relation to the current node. The selected nodes are used for the next step until you reach the end of the expression and the result is the remaining node. Figure 7-6 shows you how the previous example breaks down.

***Figure 7-6*** *XPath expressions in XQuery provide easy access to function calls, path definitions, and predicate queries.*

In the example, the expression begins with a function call (doc) that returns the ingredients.xml document. /ingredients consists of a single step that returns the <ingredients> node. The steps select the set of all ingredients elements that are children of the current node (the root of the document.)

The expression /ingredients/wet has two steps. The first step selects all children of the <ingredients> node and the second step selects all the <wet> elements of the ingredients node. The expression identifies all <wet> children of the parent of the current node, including the current node.

The example shows that path expressions may have up to three parts: an axis, a node test, and a predicate. The axis defines the direction to move in the document tree. In XQuery, the document tree has many similarities to a DOM document tree model. For instance, the child axis says to look at all child nodes. The parent axis looks at the parent node and the self axis says to look at the current node. XQuery gives you functions to use all the axes in a path expression.

A node test is an evaluation to determine which nodes along the axis are selected for the next step. For instance, in child::wet, child is the axis and wet is the node test. A child node satisfies the node test if it is an element with the name of wet. XQuery provides node tests that check the element, attribute, namespace name, and type (text, comment, processing instruction) of a node.

Finally, a predicate is an expression to filter nodes selected by the node test. Predicates are Boolean expressions. In the above example, the predicate [@stocketa>0] evaluates to true for all nodes that have an attribute named stocketa with a value greater than zero. A node for which the expression evaluates to true is included in the result set of the path expression.

Overall XQuery provides everything XPath supports. For instance, XQuery support of XPath includes the double slash (//) operator as a convenience to select all descendants of the current node as well as the current node itself.

XPath provides expressions to navigate relative to the current context. These are called axes. For example, the following path returns the child element of the in Web element.

```
doc("ingredients.xml")/ingredients/wet/child::item
```

XQuery provides many additional axis functions, including parent:: and descendant::.

### 7.4.5 Element Constructors

Every XQuery returns a sequence that may be an XML value, or an XML-like value. For instance, the following code shows various XQuery XML element constructors.

```
let $a := xs:integer( 10 )
return <xml><value>{$a}</value></xml>
```

The above XQuery returns an XML value.

```
<xml>
  <value>10</value>
</xml>
```

A similar XQuery constructs HTML code.

```
let $a := ( "frank", "jack", "lorette", "madeline" )

return
  <html>
  <body>
    <h1>My family:</h1>
    { for $i in $a
      return <p>{$i}</p>
    }
  </body>
</html>
```

The above XQuery returns HTML code.

```
<html>
    <body>
        <h1>My family:</h1>
        <p>frank</p>
        <p>jack</p>
        <p>lorette</p>
        <p>madeline</p>
    </body>
</html>
```

XQuery pretty much allows you to construct any structured output. The only problem you may encounter when constructing output is that XQuery applies strong typing and expects to output elements that have opening and closing tags.

XQuery is meant to be extensible. In the near future, expect to see alternative constructors.

### 7.4.6 FLWOR Expressions

FLWOR expressions provide a sophisticated and easy way to iterate over sequences in XQuery. In many ways, FLWOR looks like the SQL SELECT expression. So why didn't they call it select-let-order-where-return? Jason Hunter explained to me that the XQuery team did not like the idea of calling it the "slower" expression.

A FLWOR expression lets you loop over the elements of a sequence. For instance, the following XQuery finds the wet ingredients that are in stock.

```
(: Which wet ingredients are in stock? :)

for $i in doc("ingredients.xml")/ingredients/wet/*
let $amount := $i/@amount
where $amount>0
return $i
```

In the above example, the *for* expression returns a sequence of all the wet elements.

```
<water amount="100" measure="pints" stocketa="0"/>
<molasses amount="200" measure="pints" stocketa="0"/>
```

In a FLWOR, the *for* expression evaluates the expression following the *in* clause. The *for* expression creates a sequence (referred to using $i in the above example) with the evaluated values.

XQuery requires a FLWOR to have a *for* expression. Beyond that, FLWOR gives you a lot of options. For instance, suppose we want to create a list of all the ingredients that are out of stock.

```
(: Which ingredients are out-of-stock? :)

for $i in doc("ingredients.xml")/ingredients/*
  for $j in $i/*
    where $j/@amount=0
  return $j
```

The first *for* gets a sequence of all categories of ingredients—wet, dry, and perishable—and refers to the sequence in the $i variable. The second *for* iterates through all of the ingredients—flour, water, sugar, and so on—and the *where* clause filters out all the ingredients with amount attribute values that are not at zero.

Next, I will show you some FLWOR examples that answer the questions I presented for the cookie factory.

#### Do we have enough ingredients to make chocolate chip cookies?

In this FLWOR expression, we must join ingredients.xml and directions.xml together. We look at directions.xml to learn which ingredients are needed to make chocolate chip cookies. We look at ingredients.xml to learn if the ingredient is in stock, meaning if the amount is greater than zero.

```
(: Which ingredients are out of stock to make chocolate chip
cookies? :)

for $i in doc("directions.xml")/recipe/cookie
  where $i/@name="chocolate_chip"
      return for $j in $i/steps/add
        return for $k in
          doc("ingredients.xml")/ingredients/*
          for $l in $k/*
          where ( name($l) = string($j/@ingredient) )
            and ( $l/@amount=0 )
          return $l
```

This FLWOR expression uses a nested FLOWR expression to locate information in one document that is related to information in another document. The expression breaks down into two parts. The first part gets all of the ingredients needed to make a chocolate_chip cookie from the directions.xml document. The second part gets a list of all the ingredients that are in stock (in other words, the amount is greater than zero).

If you would like to see this in action, XQuery makes it easy to take this apart. For instance, we can process the following snippet of the above XQuery.

```
for $i in doc("directions.xml")/recipe/cookie
  where $i/@name="chocolate_chip"
         return for $j in $i/steps/add
    return $j
```

Processing this returns the following sequence.

```
<add ingredient="flour" quantity="5"/>
<add ingredient="butter" quantity="3"/>
<add ingredient="salt" quantity="3"/>
<add ingredient="egg" quantity="4"/>
<add ingredient="sugar" quantity="8"/>
<add ingredient="vanilla" quantity="1"/>
<add ingredient="bakingpowder" quantity="2"/>
<add ingredient="chocolatechips" quantity="6"/>
```

The above FLWOR expression iterates through the recipes for a recipe for chocolate_chip cookies. The second *for* clause returns a sequence with all the steps needed to make the cookies.

```
for $l in $k/*
  where ( name($l) = string($j/@ingredient) )
        and ( $l/@amount=0 )
  return $l
```

The above code is where the real work happens. The code matches the name of the ingredient ( name($l) ) to the ingredient from the directions ($j/@ingredient). The code returns a sequence of ingredients that are out of stock (amount = 0).

Don't worry about going crazy with FLWOR expressions. XQuery is declarative, so we can lean on the underlying XQuery implementation to optimize all these nested iterating loops to avoid performance problems. XQuery also provides user-defined functions (we'll get to these later in this chapter) to make complicated-looking expressions easier to understand.

### *How many ranger cookies can I make?*

The strategy I use is to normalize all of the ingredient amount values into the number of cookies I can make. Then I will find the ingredient that I have the least of. That will tell me how many ranger cookies I can make.

```
(: Calculate a sequence of all the ingredients for
   the given cookie of the number of batches possible
   to make given the existing inventory of each
   ingredient :)

let $a := for $i in doc("directions.xml")/recipe/cookie
  where $i/@name="ranger_cookie"
    return
      for $j in $i/steps/add

      let $amount :=
        for $k in doc("ingredients.xml")/ingredients/*
          for $l in $k/*
            where ( name($l) = string($j/@ingredient) )
        return xs:integer($l/@amount)

      let $batches := floor( $amount div
        xs:integer( $j/@quantity ) )

      return <quantity_on_hand
       name="{$j/@ingredient}">{$batches}
       </quantity_on_hand>

(: Pick the ingredient for which we have
   the least to make batches of cookies :)

let $b := for $m in $a
  where ( xs:integer( $m ) = min( $a ) )
  return $m

(: This is the maximum possible number of batches
   you can make given the existing inventory. :)
return $b
```

This XQuery divides into four parts. The first part looks through the directions.xml document and finds the steps to make a ranger_cookie.

```
let $a := for $i in doc("directions.xml")/recipe/cookie
  where $i/@name="ranger_cookie"
    return
      for $j in $i/steps/add
```

Then the XQuery looks at the ingredients.xml document for each ingredient called for in the recipe. The XQuery finds the amount of each ingredient that is in stock.

```
let $amount :=
        for $k in doc("ingredients.xml")/ingredients/*
          for $l in $k/*
            where ( name($l) = string($j/@ingredient) )
         return xs:integer($l/@amount)
```

The XQuery divides each ingredient by the amount needed for each batch by the amount in stock. This tells you how many batches you can produce with the current inventory of each ingredient.

```
let $batches := floor( $amount div
  xs:integer( $j/@quantity ) )
```

The XQuery constructs a sequence of elements named quantity_on_hand containing the number of batches you can produce.

```
return <quantity_on_hand
 name="{$j/@ingredient}">{$batches}
 </quantity_on_hand>
```

Next, the XQuery chooses the quantity_on_hand element with the smallest batch value.

```
let $b := for $m in $a
  where ( xs:integer( $m ) = min( $a ) )
  return $m
```

Finally, the XQuery returns the element with the smallest batch value.

```
return $b
```

By the way, it turns out that another way of asking the same question is, "What is the next ingredient that I will run out of?" And in the case of the recipe for ranger cookies, the answer is "eggs," after you make the next 12 batches of cookies.

#### *How long will it take to make chocolate chip cookies?*

For this question, the directions.xml document has all the data we need to find an answer.

```
let $a := for $i in doc("directions.xml")/recipe/cookie
  where $i/@name="chocolate_chip"
    return
      sum( $i/steps/*/@time )

return <time_to_make>{$a}</time_to_make>
```

The XQuery finds the chocolate_chip recipe from the directions.xml document. It then iterates through all the steps. When a step contains a time attribute, then its value is summed.

```
<time_to_make>20</time_to_make>
```

Pretty nifty, no?

### 7.4.7 Functions

XQuery provides two types of functions: built-in functions provided by the XQuery implementation and user-defined functions. The previous section showed FLWOR expressions using built-in functions, including sum(), min(), and the constructor function xs:integer(). Table 7-1 provides a handy list of functions inherited from XPath.

Each of the functions described in Table 7-1 takes in a value and returns a value of a set value type. For instance, we previously used

*Table 7-1 Nonexhaustive List of Handy XQuery and XPath Functions.*

| Function | Description |
|---|---|
| `boolean(item)` | Converts item into a Boolean |
| `ceiling(number)` | Returns the closest integer above number |
| `concat(s1, s2, ...)` | Concatenates strings |
| `contains( string, substring)` | True if string contains substring |
| `count(node-set)` | Returns the number of items in the item sequence. The items may be nodes, but they may also be atomic values. |
| `false()` | Returns false |
| `floor(number)` | Returns the closest integer below number |
| `id(idref)` | Returns the node with the 'ID' attribute equal to idref |
| `lang(language)` | Returns true if the context node has an xml:lang of language |
| `last()` | Returns the number of nodes matching the axis |
| `local-part(node)` | Returns the local part of the node's name |
| `name(node)` | Returns the node's name |
| `namespace(node)` | Returns the namespace URL of the node's name |
| `normalize-space(string)` | Normalizes whitespace |
| `number(item)` | Converts item to a number |
| `round(number)` | Rounds number to the nearest integer |
| `starts-with(string, head)` | True if string starts with head |
| `string(obj)` | Converts the object to a string |
| `string-length(string)` | Returns the string length of string |
| `substring-after(string, substring)` | Returns the substring of string after the matching substring |
| `substring-before(string, substring)` | Returns the substring of string before matching substring |
| `sum(node-set)` | Converts the node values of node-set to numbers and adds them |

***Table 7-1*** *Nonexhaustive List of Handy XQuery and XPath Functions.*

| Function | Description |
|---|---|
| `translate(string, from, to)` | Converts characters in a string, such as the 'tr' command |
| `true()` | Returns true |
| I maintain a list of XQuery and XPath functions at http://www.xquerynow.com/howto/thebasics/functions.html/. | |

the sum() function to return the double value of the total of a sequence of element attribute values.

The functions in Table 7-1 are built into XQuery in that they do not require an explicit namespace. Some namespaces are assumed by XQuery implementations. (See Section 7.4.9 for a list.) For instance, we can use true() to return a value of true rather than xs:true(). XQuery knows that these are equivalent. This is not true for the numeric constructors and other constructors. For instance, the following code shows a few of the constructors.

```
xs:decimal(string $srcval) => decimal
xs:integer(string $srcval) => integer
xs:Name(string $srcval) => Name
xs:QName(string $srcval) => QName
xs:boolean(string $srcval) => boolean
xs:duration(string $srcval) => duration
xs:dateTime(string $srcval) => dateTime
```

Each of these requires the xs namespace preamble to be recognized correctly by XQuery. For instance, xs:decimal( "183.28" ) takes the string "183.28" as an input and returns an xs:decimal value.

### *User-defined Functions*

XQuery could have been a quaint and ineffectual competitor to SQL if the XQuery Working Group did not add user-defined functions to the language specification. User-defined functions appear in the prolog section of an XQuery. The parameters and results may be primitive values, nodes, and sequences.

For instance, the following code implements a simple function that takes two values and returns the lesser of the two values.

```
declare function local:lesser(
      $a as xs:decimal?, $b as xs:decimal? ) as xs:decimal?
{
   if ( $a < $b )
   then $a
   else $b
};

local:lesser( 6,60 )
```

This XQuery uses a user-defined function called local:lesser. The namespace is local and the function name is lesser. The function takes two decimal parameters and returns a decimal value.

All XQuery expressions are available within a function declaration. I have seen user-defined functions that took 15 pages to print. Just remember to include the semicolon (;) to end a function.

### 7.4.8 Type Specification

XQuery is a strongly typed programming language, but it might not seem so from looking at the typical XQuery program. Similar to Java, C#, and other languages, XQuery uses a mix of static typing and dynamic typing. XQuery checks for static typing at compile time and dynamic typing at run time.

The types in XQuery are different from what you are probably familiar with in object-oriented programming. XQuery uses the XQuery data model to define datatypes using XML Schema notation.

```
if ( $myvalue instance of xs:integer )
then process-integer( $myvalue )
else ( )
```

The above code example evaluates the type of the $myvalue variable. If the value is an integer value, then the process-integer function operations on the myvalue value.

### 7.4.9 Namespaces

XQuery fully supports namespaces in function definitions and usage. Several namespaces are implicitly used by XQuery implementations. The following is a list of the namespaces that are by default already known.

- `xml = http://www.w3.org/XML/1998/namespace`
- `xs = http://www.w3.org/2001/XMLSchema`
- `xsi = http://www.w3.org/2001/XMLSchema-instance`
- `fn = http://www.w3.org/2006/11/xpath-functions`
- `local = http://www.w3.org/2005/11/xquery-local-functions`
- `err = http://www.w3.org/2005/xqt-errors`

For instance, in Section 7.4.7, I used the following function declaration.

```
declare function local:lesser(
      $a as xs:decimal?, $b as xs:decimal? ) as xs:decimal?
```

Customary namespace declarations can be used in element constructors, much as you would in XSLT.

```
<html xmlns="http://www.w3.org/1999/xhtml"
       xmlns:html="http://www.w3.org/1999/xhtml">
  <head>
    {
      let $title := "XQueryNow.com"
      return $title
    }
  </head>
</html>
```

XQuery supports another method that sets the namespace.

```
declare namespace html= "http://www.w3.org/1999/xhtml";

<html xmlns="http://www.w3.org/1999/xhtml">
  <head>
    {
      let $title := "XQueryNow.com"
      return $title
    }
  </head>
</html>
```

Usual rules about the nearest conflicting namespace declaration taking precedence apply. The above XQuery produces the following output.

```
<?xml version="1.0" encoding="UTF-8"?>
<html xmlns="http://www.w3.org/1999/xhtml">
   <head>
      <title>XQueryNow.com</title>
   </head>
</html>
```

### 7.4.10 Dates and Times

XQuery has dozens of functions to work with dates and times. For instance, the following XQuery returns the current time.

```
fn:current-dateTime()
```

That is all. Unlike Java, there are no Gregorian chants involved.

## 7.5 My First XQuery Blunders

XQuery is not an elegant language. I am used to the precision of Java and Python. Java makes you go through the effort of explicitly defining and typing all the objects used.

```
import com.pushtotest.tool.Lingo;
Lingo myobj = new Lingo();
```

There is nothing ambiguous about the above Java code. You know which Lingo object you are using (if there is more than one) and exactly when it is instantiated.

Python uses explicit spacing to denote functions, subfunctions, and clauses of code.

```
myobj = Lingo()
if myobj.lastResult() == "good":
    print "The result was good"
        if myobj.getResultCode() == 27:
            print "Result code is 27"
```

```
else:
    print "The result was not good"
```

Python makes very clear—almost compulsively so—the flow of a program. Compare that to XQuery.

```
for $i in doc("directions.xml")/recipe where $i/
@name="chocolate_chip" return for $j in $i/steps/add return
for $k in doc("ingredients.xml")/ingredients/* for $l in $k/*
where ( name($l) = string($j/@ingredient) ) and ( $l/
@amount=0 ) return $l
```

So it should be of no great surprise to you when learning XQuery that you are in for some pretty good blunders. Consider the following blunders I made when learning XQuery.

### 7.5.1 Blunder 1: Declarative, Modal, Dynamic All at Once

If you come from a Java, C, C++, C# or other procedural programming background, then XQuery is going to require some adjustment in your thinking. XQuery is a declarative language. Sometimes you just need to lose control, sit back in your comfy chair, and hope that XQuery does the right thing. Doing so for me was not that easy and led to some of my first XQuery blunders.

```
if ( $a = 1 ) then return <value>$a</value>
```

When I ran this the first time, I expected to see the number 1 (in an XML <value> tag) printed to the console of my XQuery engine. Instead I got a syntax error. XQuery requires *if* functions to include an *else* clause. So I tried again.

```
if ( $a = 1 ) then return <value>$a</value> else return
<value>$b</value>
```

Running this *if* results in an error too. The *else* clause is there but the nature of a function in XQuery is that it returns a result. So putting the return function in an *if* function is invalid.

```
if ( $a = 1 ) then <value>$a</value> else <value>$b</value>
```

I thought, "I'm going to get it right this time! Right?" Well, yes and no. The output I found was as follows:

```
<value>$a</value>
```

What I was looking for in the output was the value of the $a variable, not a string literal of $a. Let's try again.

```
if ( $a = 1 ) then <value>{$a}</value> else <value>{$b}</
value>
```

In the above code I used the { and } characters to tell XQuery to evaluate an expression. In this case the expression is to return the value of the $a variable.

```
<value>1</value>
```

That's it! That is the result I was looking for! The experience told me three things to expect when learning XQuery:

1. XQuery is declarative as opposed to procedural. I can't tell XQuery how to process a program at the same level that I can a Java and Python program. Sometimes I will be frustrated, and when that happens, I need to "take a chill pill."[3]
2. XQuery is modal and dynamic even within a single expression. For instance, the if..then..else expression always returns a result and the *then* and *else* clause values are dynamically typed at run time. So <mynode/> returns an XML element, 1 returns an integer, and mynode returns a string. XQuery figures the type out for you dynamically at run time unless you specify the type in a declaration. XQuery 1.0 supports XML Schema[4] simple types (such as string, integer, dateTime, etc.), types from imported schemas (such as USAddress), and XML document structure types (such as document, element, attribute, node, processing instruction, comment, etc.). Last, to insert an expression into a *then* and *else* clause requires the use of { and } characters.

---

3 "You need to take a chill pill, Dad" is advice from my 11-year-old daughter, Madeline.

4 See http://www.w3.org/TR/xmlschema-2.

3. XQuery does not support many of the debugging tricks and techniques I have grown accustomed to using in Java and Python. For instance, there is no print expression that I can insert into an XQuery to identify state while an XQuery runs. In Xquery, I am not writing procedural scripts—I am declaring an XQuery. Some XQuery implementations include fn:trace().

### 7.5.2 Blunder 2: The Generic Error and Debugging

Consider a second blunder in the following XQuery.

```
let $mydoc := <frank><birthdate>1961-04-23</birthdate></
frank>

let $birth := $mydoc/frank/birthdate

let $diff := fn:get-minutes-from-dayTimeDuration(
  xs:dateTime( fn:current-dateTime() )
  - xs:dateTime( $cachedurl/timein ) )

return $diff
```

The above XQuery is meant to return the number of minutes that I have lived. It fails. Why? Because the path expression to find my birthdate in the $mydoc document is incorrect. The $birth variable contains an empty sequence. Unfortunately, the XQuery engine I originally ran this on simply replied:

```
[0000] Unknown general error.
```

This shows me two additional things about XQuery:

1. XQuery is so new that when debugging an XQuery, I need to include the possibility that the error I am seeing is actually a bug in the XQuery implementation. As a result, I now keep 4 XQuery engines installed on my development machine to run side-by-side comparisons when I bump into problems.
2. XQuery implementations do not by default show me their intermediate code or optimizer's execution plan for debug-

ging. And very few XQuery implementations include a debugger to do step-through and variable value inspection.

### 7.5.3 Blunder 3: Semicolons in the Query Prolog

Consider the following function definition in the query prolog.

```
define function greetings()
{
  <Hello/>
}
greetings()
```

Everywhere else in an XQuery expressions end themselves. In the prolog all declarations end with a semicolon. The semicolon is missing from the above function definition. The correct form is as follows:

```
define function greetings()
{
  <Hello/>
};
greetings()
```

### 7.5.4 Blunder 4: XML versus XML Documents

XML parsers normally output an XML declaration when they save XML content to a file. You've likely seen this file header.

```
<?xml version='1.0'?>
<billofsale>
<amount>500</amount>
</billofsale>
```

So imagine you are in the context of a Java application that receives a String containing the contents of an XML file, including the XML declaration.

```
String xmldoc = "<?xml version=/"1.0/"?>
<billofsale><amount>500</amount></billofsale>";
```

To insert this document into a database using an XQuery and an XML database, you might write the following.

```
tig:insert-document("mydocument", "<?xml
version='1.0'?><billofsale>
<amount>500</amount></billofsale>" )
```

The above example uses the TigerLogic[5] syntax that is similar to most other XQuery extensions to support native XML database.

This will throw an XQuery error, as the xmldoc includes the XML declaration. The declaration works fine for an XML file, but it is not a valid XML in an XQuery. Why?

The XQuery operates on and produces XDM instances, not serialized XML documents. The XQuery/XSLT serializer might be implemented and then be used to produce serialized XML documents, but the XQuery/XPath Data Model (XDM) does not include the XML prefix for the very obvious reason that it deals solely with serialized XML and not with abstract (parsed) XML.

Think of the situation from the XQuery parser's perspective. The XML declaration looks syntactically on par with:

```
let $b := "<?xml version="1.0"?>" "<billofsale> ..."
```

That causes the error. Some of the XQuery engines provide a workaround to this problem, including the following.

- Saxon provides an extension function, saxon:parse(), that runs the XML file—including the XML declaration—through its parser.[6]
- MarkLogic provides an extension function, xdmp:unquote(), that parses an XML file and returns an XML document.[7]
- TigerLogic provides a Java API to evaluate XQuery expressions that takes an optional stream and parses the stream into an XML document. For example:[8]

5 See http://www.rainingdata.com/products/tl/index.html.
6 See http://www.saxonica.com.
7 See http://www.marklogic.com.
8 See http://www.rainingdata.com/products/tl/index.html.

```
String myxml =
  '<?xml vesion=\'1.0\'?><test>MyString</test>';
InputStream stream =
  new ByteArrayInputStream( myxml.getBytes() );
ResultSet rs = statement.execute(
' insert document $1 into 'tig:///Database/Collection/
1368134769D'', stream );
stream.close();
```

### 7.5.5 Blunder 5: Don't Think Procedurally

At one point I wanted to see if I could calculate the time it takes to make a cookie by totaling up the time for each step from the directions.xml document. I used the following XQuery.

```
let $totaltime := 0
for $i in doc("directions.xml")
let $totaltime := $totaltime + $i/@time
return <total>{$totaltime}</total>
```

That won't work! I got the following error message.

```
The attribute axis starting at a document-node() node will
never select anything.
```

Instead, try this:

```
sum( doc("directions.xml")//@time )
```

The result will be as follows:

```
20.0
```

### 7.5.6 Blunder 6: Sometimes You Need to Be Explicit

I wanted to return a list of ingredients and their amounts presented in HTML format and ordered alphabetically by ingredient name. I tried this XQuery.

```
<html><body>List of items:<br/><ul type="square">
```

```
{for $ingredient in
  doc("ingredients.xml")/ingredients/dry/*
  order by name($ingredient)
  return
    <li>{name( $ingredient )}, {$ingredient/@amount}</li>
}
</ul></body></html>
```

This returns an error:

```
E Attribute nodes must be created before the children of an
element node
```

The $ingredient/@amount expression of the return value returns the value of the attribute for the element. For instance, the XQuery returns the <flour> element with an amount attribute equal to the value of 100.

```
<flour amount="100" … />
```

XQuery interprets the return expression as: Find the name of the first dry ingredient, append a comma to it, then find the amount attribute, and append the whole mess to the <li> element. That does not make any sense and XQuery throws the error.

I tried a second approach to this problem as follows:

```
<html><body>List of items:<br/><ul type="square">

{ for $ingredient in doc("ingredients.xml")/ingredients/dry/*
  order by name($ingredient)
  return <li>{ $ingredient/@amount }</li>
}
</ul></body></html>
```

XQuery interpreted this return expression as: Find the amount attribute and add it as an attribute to the <li> element>. This is not what I want but it is valid XQuery so I get the following result.

```
<html>
    <body>List of items:<br/>
```

```
        <ul type="square">
            <li amount="0"/>
            <li amount="100"/>
            <li amount="50"/>
            <li amount="250"/>
        </ul>
    </body>
</html>
```

Pretty good! Huh! XQuery adds the amount attribute to the <li> tag. I tried a third approach to this XQuery as follows:

```
<html><body>List of items:<br/><ul type="square">

{ for $ingredient in doc("ingredients.xml")/ingredients/dry/*
  order by name($ingredient)
  return <li>{ name( $ingredient ) },
    { number( $ingredient/@amount ) }</li>
}
</ul></body></html>
```

This XQuery gives the following result.

```
<html>
    <body>List of items:<br/>
        <ul type="square">
            <li>bakingpower, 0</li>
            <li>flour, 100</li>
            <li>salt, 50</li>
            <li>sugar, 250</li>
        </ul>
    </body>
</html>
```

This is what I was after. The return result delivers an HTML list with the name of the ingredient and the value of the amount attribute.

### 7.5.7 Blunder 7: Value versus General Comparisons

XQuery 1.0 provides two mechanisms for comparing data: value comparisons and general comparisons.[9] The first thing I noticed was the confusing naming conventions: both compare values. Other than preferring to write "=" instead of "eq," why would I use one over the other?

General comparisons use the operators common to modern programming languages (=, !=, <, >, <=, >=), but they are in reality different from the languages you already know. Value comparisons use operators that are nearer and dearer to the hearts of the FORTRAN programmers out there (eq, ne, lt, gt, le, ge) but work the same way comparison operators work in more traditional languages.

XML is pretty flexible, and a lot of people take full advantage of that flexibility. Elements can be optional, repeating, and recursive, and often a query author may not be able to easily ensure they're only comparing something to a single node. Consider the following query against the XMP sample data found in the W3C's XML Query Use Cases document.[10]

```
for $i in doc( 'bib.xml' )/book
where $i/author/first = 'Norman Cohen'
    return $i
```

The document in question contains four books, some of which contain a single author, but one contains multiple authors and another has no author at all. As the query author, I don't know this, so I need the flexibility of a general comparison to accomplish the task at hand. The general comparison works so that the comparison is true if any of the authors found match 'Norman Cohen'. If a given book has no authors, then the comparison is simply false. Conversely, if I had used the eq value comparison, I would have gotten an error from my query, since value comparisons cannot compare against multiple values.

Flexibility is nice, but it doesn't come for free. Let's consider the literal interpretation of a general comparison in Java:

9 XQuery has three comparisons if you count node comparisons.
10 See http://www.w3.org/TR/xquery-use-cases/#xmp-data

```
for( int i = 0 ; i < left.length ; ++i )
    {
        for( int j = 0 ; j < right.length ; ++j )
        {
            if( value_compare( left[ i ], right[ j ] ) )
            {
                return true;
            }
        }
    }
return false;
```

Now imagine that every single time you needed to compare two values in your Java program you had to do that! Obviously, in general (no pun intended), this is not the most efficient way to perform a comparison.

This is a worst-case example of a general comparison. The reality is that, XQuery being a declarative language, most XQuery processors will have internal optimizers that will mitigate a lot of the bloat that can happen with a worst-case general comparison. For instance, given our original query, since we know the right-hand side consists of a single atomic value, 'Norman Cohen', it can easily get away with removal of the inner loop.

Nonetheless, often the explicit code is better overall than implicit optimization, and for this and a few other reasons to follow we have value comparisons. Value comparisons compare just two atomic values, a single left- and right-hand side. They are much less flexible but generally more efficient. The cost is in flexibility: If you happen to point one at a sequence of more than one value, get ready for your query to bomb, so use value comparisons wisely.

Value comparisons are one area where a little extra knowledge about your XQuery processor may be helpful. For instance, SQL comparisons are more like value comparisons than general comparisons, and therefore XQuery leveraged over a number of relational databases can be seriously affected by your choice of processor. Database query engines employ custom algorithms to perform joins, such as hash-join, merge-sort join, and index-based joins, and the type of comparison you employ has a direct impact. In some cases, the choice of a value comparison over a general comparison can directly affect the ability of the processor to perform a hash-join, or use an index, which can have a huge impact on query performance. To illustrate, consider the XMP sample data once more in the following query.[11]

```
for $i in doc( 'bib.xml' )//book
  for $j in doc( 'reviews.xml' )//entry
  where $i/title eq $j/title
  return $i
```

In this query we are performing a join, and since I know that in this particular data model both <book> and <entry> contain exactly one title element, I've chosen to use a value comparison. On the one hand, I know that it is at worst as efficient as a general comparison and at best much better, and it will most likely lead to a much more efficient query when the query processor optimizes my join query.

Aside from these examples involved in the implicit optimization for a particular XQuery optimizer, generally it is good practice in XQuery to be very explicit about what you do know about your data, so use value comparisons wisely, but use them only when you're sure you can. No one wants an error instead of a query result, so the less you know about your data the more you may want to gravitate to general comparisons. Choose your tool wisely, and, remember, if neither is precise enough for you, there are always quantified expressions.[12] But those are another story altogether.

## 7.6 The Unfinished Parts of XQuery

XQuery 1.0 is a remarkable accomplishment. The specification delivers a functional language that is a whole lot more useful than many other 1.0 specifications. However, there are missing parts of the specification that many XQuery implementations are delivering in advance of the specification. You should expect the following additions to the XQuery standard.

### 7.6.1 Federated Queries: SOAP, JDBC, and Java Data Sources

The XQuery 1.0 specification does not include a mechanism to extend XQuery to new data sources. The doc() function lets you identify the file name path to an XML document. Many XQuery imple-

11 See http://www.w3.org/TR/xquery-use-cases/#xmp-data.

12 See http://www.w3.org/TR/xquery/#id-quantified-expressions.

mentations have extended the doc() function to accept a path to data stored in a database. The terminology for the database diverges from XQuery implementation to implementation. However, they all so far provide for a database to contain a group of XML documents known as a *collection;* and, each collection has a *root node*. This is illustrated in Figure 7-7.

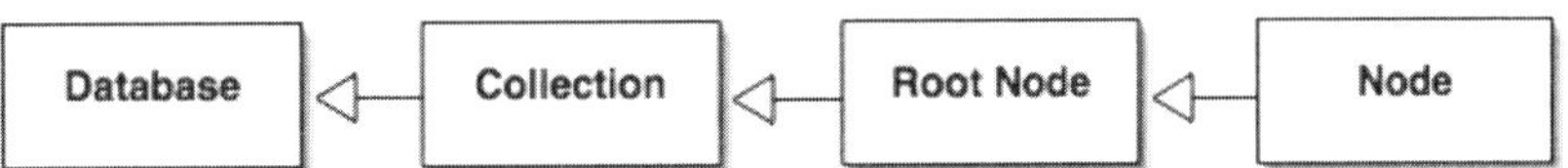


***Figure 7-7*** *XQuery nodes are especially powerful, since the parent of a node goes up and into collections and databases using a native XML database.*

The following shows several native XML data persistence functions that come with the TigerLogic XQuery engine. TigerLogic delivers an XQuery implementation and a native XML database. This illustrates what many other XQuery engines implement too.

```
tig:create-database( 'automobiles', () )

let $config := ()
return
     tig:create-collection( 'automobiles', 'foreign-auto',
     'Automobile-stuff', ( ), $config )

insert document

  for $i in doc( "file:///c:/auto/cars.xml" )
    where $i/model = 'BMW' or
    substring( $i/model, 0, 8 ) = 'Mercedes'
    return
      <german-car>{ $i }</german-car>

into "tig:///mydatabase/foreign-auto"

let $a := collection('tig://mydatabase/foreign-auto' )
```

The above code creates a new database named automobiles and a collection named foreign-auto. The insert document expression finds BMW or Mercedes autos from the cars.xml document and inserts these entries into the foreign-auto collection.

Raining Data, the publisher of TigerLogic, implemented its own create/update/delete extensions (commonly referred to as CRUD functions) to the XQuery 1.0 specification. Most of the XQuery implementations (MarkLogic, Oracle, Ipedo, etc.) today have their own nonstandard commands while they wait for the W3C XQuery Working Group to finish the Update specification. Adopting a current CRUD extension to XQuery is a "safe bet" to make today, because it is likely that the software publisher putting forward an XQuery implementation with its extensions will also offer a migration path to the XQuery Update specification when it is ready.

### *SOAP Web Services Data Source*

SOAP-based Web Services interfaces to a service are XML-based message protocols. Many XQuery engines have extended the doc() function to enable an XQuery to make a call to a Web Service. The XQuery works with the service response in native XML form. For instance, the following XQuery makes a SOAP call to a service using TigerLogic.

```
import service namespace sw=
'http://www.WeatherReport.com/WebServices/
WeatherReport.asmx?WSDL'
operation GetWeatherReport
port WeatherReportHttpGet;

sw:GetWeatherReport('Cleveland')
```

In the above Xquery, the prolog section declares a SOAP service that is described using the Web Service Definition Language (WSDL) The sw:GetWeatherReport then sends a request to the service to retrieve the weather report for Cleveland. The weather report returns an XML response document that is easily searched using XPath expressions.

Most XQuery implementations today are already extending their implementation to support Web Services requests. I fully expect we will all get together and twist Jim Melton's arm long enough for him to agree that this function will become part of XQuery in some form sometime in the near future. If it does not become part of the specification itself, it will be reasonable for users to expect it as part of any XQuery implementation.

### JDBC Relational Data Source

Most of the world's data is stored in relational database tables that are accessible through SQL expressions. SQL queries return a rowset, which may be transformed into XML data and operated upon from an XQuery. Several XQuery implementations have adapters that allow an XQuery to issue a SQL expression. For instance, the following shows TigerLogic executing a SQL expression.

```
declare namespace cfn='SQLServerDataSource';
cfn:execute-select( (),
      'the-bobs',
      'SELECT * FROM EMPLOYEES WHERE FIRSTNAME = Bob' )
```

The example above executes a query to select employee information for employees with first name of Bob. No schema URI is given, so the results use default mapping (are flat). The root-node name is used to generate the root node of the flat XML.

### Java Data Source

So far we have seen XQuery extended to support native XML database persistence, Web Services, and relational databases. It's like eating potato chips! It's hard to stop after just a few. One more extension to XQuery we will cover shows how Java functions may become XQuery data sources. I would bet that XQuery in some way will eventually support the Java data source too.

The following is specific to TigerLogic and possible in the code base of Java-based XQuery implementations. (It just takes a little creativity.) For instance, using TigerLogic follow these steps.

1. Write a Java class. The class must be static and be part of a package of your choosing. Compile the class and put it into a JAR package.
2. Write a function descriptor XML file to identify the class and method.
3. Register the Java functions you want to use with TigerLogic using the tig:register-java-functions function.
4. Verify that the Java functions are registered correctly by listing them using the tig:list-java-functions function.
5. To unregister (drop) the registered Java functions, use the tig:drop-java-functions function.

The following instance shows this in practical terms. I begin by creating a Java program.

```
package test.rdta.java;

public class TestPrimitive {
    // zero argument methods
    public static float zeroArgFloat()
    {
        return (float)3.40282351234567890123456789012345678 90E33 ;
    }
    ...
    // one argument methods
    public static float oneArgFloat(float f)
    {
        return f ;
    }
    public static void main (String args[])
    {
        System.out.println( TestPrimitive.zeroArgFloat() );
    }
}
```

Compile this program and package it into a JAR file. In this example the JAR file is testprimitive.jar. Create a function descriptor XML file. In this example, we use myFunctionDescriptor.xml.

```
<function-descriptor id="jf_primitive"
targetNamespace="http://www.rainingdata.com/TigerLogic/
namespaces/javafunc" author="Bob Smith">
<classpath url="file:///C:/javafunc/javaPrograms/classes/
testprimitive.jar"/>
 <function package='test.rdta.java' class='TestPrimitive'
name='oneArgFloat'
bound-name='JavaFunc_TestOneArgFloat'>
  <java return='float' mode='primitive'>
    <arg type="float" mode="primitive"/>
  </java>
 </function>"
</function-descriptor>
```

Next, I register the Java function in an XQuery:

```
tig:register-java-functions( "jf_primitive",
doc(file:///C:/javafunc/myFunctionDescritor.xml)  )
```

With the function registered, my XQuery is ready to use the Java function.

```
declare namespace jf ="http://www.rainingdata.com/TigerLogic/
namespaces/javafunc";
jf:JavaFunc_TestOneArgFloat(xs:float("3.4028E20"))
```

Here we call a Java function using the defined alias name with the XML Schema float datatype (which is mapped to Java float datatype) that the called Java function required. The result of this XQuery is a Java float value returned as an XML Schema float value.

## 7.7 Where to Find Answers to XQuery Questions

Many of my blunders were solved by one of the sources of XQuery information listed in Table 7.20.

***Table 7-2*** *Sources of XQuery Information, Help, and Assistance*

| Source | Description |
|---|---|
| www.xquerynow.com | A free on-line community site providing free tips, techniques, how-to articles, and tools to rapidly learn how to be proficient with XQuery and native XML database technology. |
| www.xquery.com | Jason Hunter's site for XQuery fans to share ideas and ask each other questions on an email list hosted by the service. talk@xquery.com is an email list where many XQuery engine implementers answer technical questions about XQuery. |
| www.w3c.com | The official source of the XQuery, XPath, XSLT, and other specifications. (The same people that brought you the Web.) |

*Table 7-2 Sources of XQuery Information, Help, and Assistance*

| Source | Description |
|---|---|
| www.w3.org/TR/xquery-requirements | The XQuery specification document defines the goals and requirements for the XQuery data model and query language. |
| www.w3.org/TR/xquery | The XQuery 1.0 specification document defines the language grammar. Pretty geeky stuff here. |
| www.w3.org/TR/xquery-use-cases | A document showing several dozen XQuery scripts. Good stuff if you are a learn-by-example kind of person. |
| www.w3.org/TR/xpath-data-model | Defines the XQuery 1.0 data model. |
| www.w3.org/TR/xquery-semantics | Defines the XPath 2.0 and XQuery 1.0 language. |
| www.w3.org/TR/xmlquery-full-text-use-cases | Examples to show full-text search can be performed using XQuery and XPath. |
| www.w3.org/TR/xpath-functions | A list of functions and operators required by XPath 2.0, XQuery 1.0, and XSLT 2.0. |
| www.w3.org/TR/xquery-full-text-requirements | An extension to XPath/XQuery languages, full-text search facilitates searching tokenized text. This document defines this extension to XPath and XQuery languages. |
| www.w3.org/TR/xpath20 | The XPath 2.0 specification document. |
| www.gnu.org/software/qexo/XQ-Gen-XML.html | Quexo is an XQuery implementation that compiles XQuery programs on the fly directly to Java bytecodes. Distributed under a free open-source license. Bundled into TestMaker. A terrific tool to experiment with and learn XQuery. |

## 7.8 Summary

This chapter covered the basics of the XQuery language, the scalability issues surrounding integration of XQuery into a Java application, the blunders I made while learning XQuery and native XML databases, and the safe bets of new features that will likely be in the XQuery specification in the near future and already exist in many XQuery implementations.

The next chapter moves the discussion of XML technology into the future of SOA. XML is a great medium for describing service interfaces, messages exchanged between services, and service dependencies (sometimes called governance.) Chapter 8 discusses these and the resulting impact on scalability and performance.

# Chapter 8

# Getting SOA-Ready

*XML* is very important to the information technology industry, because it gives software developers, architects, and operations managers an easy and efficient way to model data in a way that expresses metadata—data about the data. Before XML, most distributed systems treated data and services separately. With XML, service interfaces become more easily understandable, since the interface definition is self-describing XML. And the data in the message that moves through the service interface expresses meaning semantically in the message. Data and services merge with XML. Consequently, the IT industry is using SOA techniques to turn the newly available XML data into business value through reusable components that implement business policies and use composite data service software. This chapter shows how your business or organization benefits from putting data, metadata, and policies to work, and gives you a methodology and checklist to make certain your organization is SOA-ready.

## 8.1 Composite Data Services

Composite applications are a key reason for enterprise interest and support for SOA. Stitching together existing software components into new applications rapidly means an enterprise or organization can deliver business value quickly and inexpensively. Figure 8-1 illustrates a composite application I wrote that takes driving directions from a mapping service on the Web and combines it with Krispy Kreme's store locator service. This composite application ensures I will never be far from a delicious and refreshing donut as I travel to a business meeting.

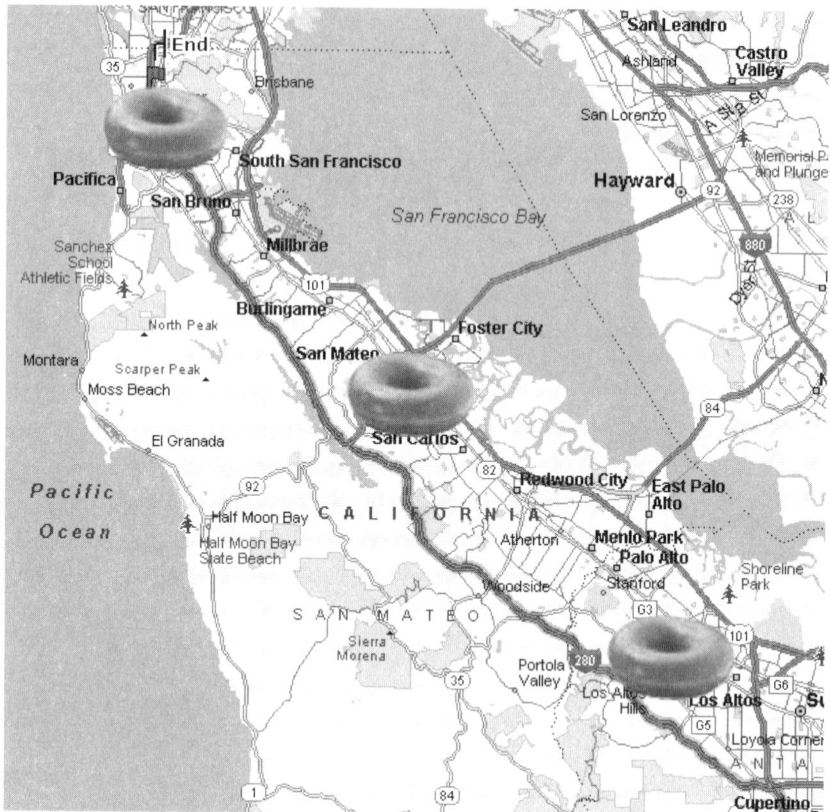


*Figure 8-1 Integrating a map-rendering service with the donut shop locating service into a composite application.*

While the above application is a good example of a mashup it also shows how composite applications are powerful and deliver business value, composite applications introduce two key problems for every business and organization:

- Maintaining composite applications requires deliberate and long-term effort. For instance, what happens nine months from now when the donut locator service changes message schemas? Additionally, my composite application uses Java code to know the order in which to call the services, and any new developer maintaining the code will need to learn my code.

- Performance and scalability depend on the response times of the underlying services. For instance, each use of my composite application depends on responses from the mapping and donut locator services. The slower these services respond, the slower my composite application performs.

Table 8-1 shows the choices a software developer needs to make to be successful with composite applications.

***Table 8-1*** *Developer Decision Task Areas to Build SOA Composite Applications*

| **Task** | **Function** |
|---|---|
| Class/object definition | Classes encapsulate data and provide methods to operate on the data. For instance, in the donut-mapping example, I implement a class for the driving directions and a class for the donut shop locations with methods to glue the two together into a map. |
| Language and platform | A choice of programming language impacts how rapidly a developer is able to build the application. For instance, Java has no query language and it has a collection architecture for mapping data objects. XML, on the other hand, is strong at defining data mapping and has a relatively new query language (XQuery). |
| Workflow container | A workflow container provides services for the developer to search for the most appropriate service and the container determines the order in which to call the services. For instance, in my composite application I need to call the donut locator service first and then the mapping service. |

***Table 8-1** Developer Decision Task Areas to Build SOA Composite Applications (continued)*

| Task | Function |
|---|---|
| Taxonomy and registry | A registry abstracts the service endpoints to make it possible for the composite application to choose the best available service at run time. For instance, I should be able to use the same donut-mapping application in Australia and dynamically find a better mapping service for the Australian road system without changing the code by using a registry and taxonomy. |
| Data access services | Data access services provide a standard interface for the composite application to store, retrieve, and update enterprise data, databases, message queues, Web services, and data persistence stores. The data access services also provide mid-tier policy and service data persistence using the FastSOA mid-tier cache architecture presented in Chapter 5. |

Making these choices now means that my business will save many hours of potentially difficult software maintenance over time, that my composite application is reusable by other developers in the organization, and that the composite application is much less susceptible to service outages and downtime as the underlying services, platforms, and datacenters change. And change is inevitable.

The reuse of composite applications is key to long-term SOA scalability. For instance, a colleague at work took my donut-mapping service and added it to her coffee shop locating service. Each time she operates her service, a set of resources (servers, network bandwidth, memory, and processors) executes the coffee shop location service and that, in turn, operates my donut-mapping service. My service uses additional resources and causes the servers hosting the mapping and donut locator services to use their resources. In reality, the locations of the donut shops rarely change and the maps of the region rarely change.

Yet, each reuse of the composite application causes server resources to be applied to answer essentially the same question: Where are the donuts and coffee? In scalability terms this is an n + 1 data access scalability problem; each reuse of my service causes an equal number more of resources to be used.

Composite Data Services (CDS) is a pattern for software components that are callable through a standard service interface and encapsulate the data, methods, workflow, taxonomy, and data access for a composite application.

CDS is a pattern that may be implemented using any of today's available technology (Java, .NET, relational database, native XML technology, and others). The key to a successful CDS approach is to make certain your tools and technology choices are complete. CDS development uses commercial or open-source tool sets in the following categories:

- Class/object definition
- Language and platform
- Workflow
- Taxonomy and registry
- Data access and caching

In the next sections, we'll examine the CDS architecture and the tool sets to build them.

### 8.1.1 Class/Object Definition

Object-oriented design patterns encapsulate data and provide methods to operate on the data. For instance, in the donut-mapping example I define an object for the driving directions and an object for the donut shop locations with methods to glue the two objects together into a map. Objects make code reuse easy and reduce bugs.

In an SOA environment, objects are the only place to implement the business logic of a service. Developers are often tempted to put business logic into the other parts of CDS architecture—for instance, in the workflow or registry functions. Processors are inexpensive, and subsequently it may seem that every device running in a datacenter has a scripting, macro, or other programming capability. I strongly caution you against implementing business logic anywhere but in an object. By doing so, you prevent developers from having the benefits of an integrated development environment, including source code control, debugger, versioning, test frameworks, and code module reuse among team members.

An object and its methods are the entry point to a CDS component. Figure 8-2 illustrates a user operating a CDS by requesting the validateAddress method through a REST request. (REST uses HTTP protocols and XML payloads to access objects and methods.) In addition to a user, CDS requests come from services, composite applications, and processes.

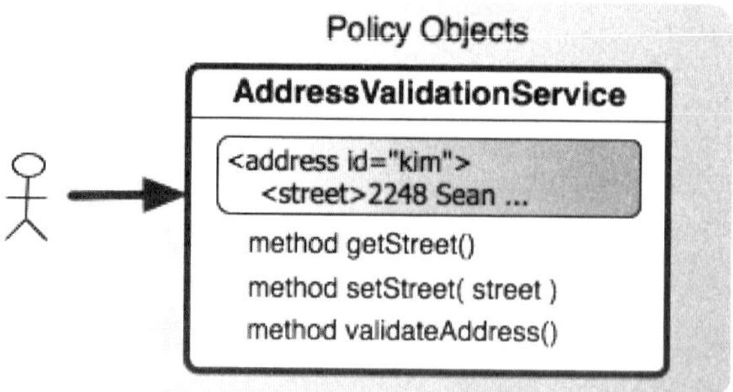


***Figure 8-2*** *A software object encapsulates the address information and exposes methods to operate on the data, including the validateAddress method.*

The operating environment that runs a CDS component takes care of the object life cycle for the CDS object, including instantiating CDS objects, receiving the request to the method through a communication protocol (SOAP, REST, AJAX, JMS message), operating the object during its life cycle, and cleaning up after it is no longer needed.

Next, we will see how the choice of language and platform makes a difference to CDS performance and scalability and to the developer's productivity.

### 8.1.2 Language and Platform

When working in SOA projects that primarily use XML data, the performance and developer productivity gains presented in Chapter 4 move many developers to choose native XML technology approaches. For instance, consider that Java has no query language. Java was never meant to do what XML does well—model data in parent-child structures and provide a query language.

Java did not have a standard way to model collections of data for the first five years of its life. Java objects were supposed to hold their data, and some objects might hold other objects. Until the Java collections architecture emerged, there was no official way to map the relationship between collections of objects.

XML, on the other hand, began by defining a data model and the way to express relationships between the entities. XML does well at modeling parent-child structures and recent extensions (XML Schema, XSD include files, and namespaces) make XML a good choice for collections of data in document-oriented formats. Ironically, until the XML Query language (XQuery) there was no native XML programming language to do anything with the data expressed in XML formats. Consider the differences in data models presented in Figure 8-3.

```
<address id="kim">
  <street>2248 Sean Drive</street>
  <city>Campbell</city>
  <state>California</state>
</address>
```

```
public class address
{
  String id = "kim";
  String street = "2248 Sean Drive";
  String city = "Campbell";
  String state = "California";
  ...
}
```

***Figure 8-3*** *The same address is represented in XML (on the left) and a Java object (on the right.) When looking at the <street> value you know this is a street. When looking at the Java street object you only know that this is a string. Since all the other fields are strings in the Java example, a street may as well be a city.*

The average software developer is left with a big question: Since Java does not support XML natively, the XQuery programming language is so new, this book says developers get a 22 times performance and scalability improvement when using native XML technology, developers are building composite applications and composite views of data from data sources that change, and developers want to let other developers reuse their work, then what is the safest and most efficient choice to make?

In reality, there is a compromise technology architecture that fuses data and services into reusable CDS components. For instance, Java supports a proposed programming interface that lets Java objects work with XML data natively through the XQuery API for Java (XQJ).[1]

Figure 8-2 illustrates the data and methods available in the AddressValidationService object. There is no reason to write an entire address verification capability into the validateAddress function if some other service already provides address validation.

---

1 For details, see http://www.jcp.org/en/jsr/detail?id=225.

Next, we look at how the validateAddress function operates a workflow process to validate the address.

### 8.1.3 Workflow Container

Any time a method operates a complex, multistep process, it is better to use a process workflow engine over hard-coding the flow in an object. Workflow engines are very good at maintaining state, especially for long-lived transactions; they are scalable since they process tasks in an asynchronous pattern; and they handle transactions well in that they can back out of a change in the event of an exception.

For instance, the CDS AddressValidateService object needs to validate addresses for people living close by and people who live within the rest of the country. The business saves expenses and increases profit if it uses a less expensive address validation service for people living close by. The workflow for this example implements three services:

- Service 1 checks a back-end database system to see if the address is for a customer who lives within 50 miles of the business.
- Service 2 validates local addresses using a local directory from a local communications provider.
- Service 3 validates distant addresses by using a more expensive national directory service.

Figure 8-4 illustrates a call to the validateAddress method initiating a workflow.

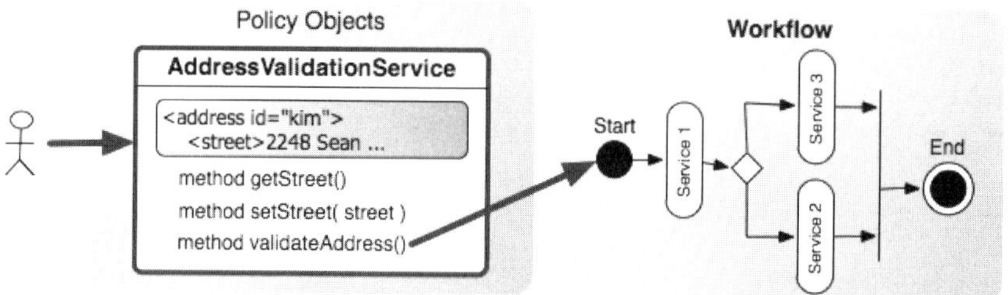


*Figure 8-4 Accessing the validateAddress method initiates a workflow.*

When the user of the AddressValidationService object invokes the validateAddress method, the workflow uses Service 1 to determine if the address is within 50 miles of the business. If it is, then the workflow branches to Service 2 to use the less expensive local directory service; otherwise, the workflow uses Service 3 from a national directory service. The end of the flow answers the validateAddress() method with a true/false answer. True if the address is valid and false otherwise.

Once a software developer writes the object and workflow, these are now available for reuse. For instance, if the object and workflow were created in the United States, ideally the same object and workflow would be reusable in Switzerland. To work with the Swiss address system, Service 1 needs to be changed slightly to work with Swiss address paths to the XML data, and Services 2 and 3 need new service endpoints for the Swiss directory services.

Combining objects and workflow engines in a CDS delivers easier software maintenance and reusable software components. Next, we will add the ability to enable Services 2 and 3 to find the directory services automatically.

### 8.1.4 Taxonomy and Registry

Java is a tower of abstraction. The average software developer's code goes through 10 or more layers of abstraction before commanding the hardware of the underlying computer. Abstraction has its benefits, including greater flexibility as the underlying systems change. In a CDS environment, a service registry implements an abstraction of service endpoints. Taxonomy gives a CDS an abstract and flexible way to identify the most appropriate registered service.

A registry is a database of service endpoints organized by taxonomy. The service endpoints identify XML messages as input in a request and provide an expected response in an XML message. Often these input and output messages are defined in a Web Services Description Language (WSDL) document, but not always. Many developers believe that the SOAP protocols for exchanging documents or making remote procedure calls between systems is the wrong design and, further, that WSDL will never be good enough to truly describe the exchange. These "restifarians" are also lovers of XML and interoperability, but they believe Representational State Transfer (REST) is a better way of building distributed systems. REST asychronously transfers state from one object to another. In one application, REST uses a Web page to describe a service interface with the expectation that a developer will read the Web page and write code to make meaningful requests and analyze the responses. CDS bridges this gap.

Figure 8-5 shows a service in a CDS component workflow performing a taxonomical search to find the appropriate service endpoint to call to resolve an address validation request.

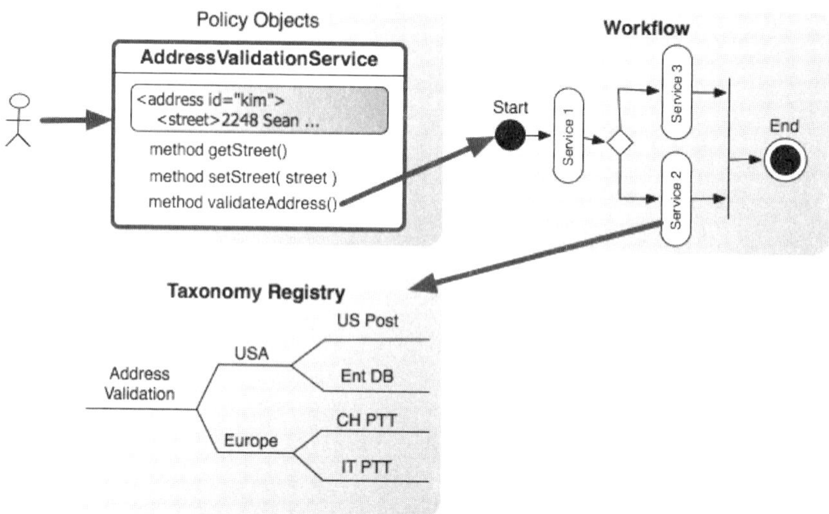


***Figure 8-5*** *Service 2 in the workflow uses a service to validate an address. Service 2 searches the taxonomy to determine the appropriate service.*

The business logic created for the AddressValidationService CDS is smart enough to search the taxonomy to find the correct external address validation service. In the example illustrated in Figure 8-5, the CDS performs a taxonomical search of address validation services by choosing between USA and European address validation services. Since this CDS operates on U.S. addresses, it then chooses between using the U.S. Post Office directory service and an Enterprise Database (Ent DB) service.

A UDDI registry may service the CDS taxonomy searching capability; however, this is not very likely. UDDI protocol adoption is a failure by contrast to the relative success of SOAP and WSDL. The ontologists of the world—taxonomy builders—never adopted UDDI. More importantly, the idea of UDDI is backward from how taxonomy is created in the real world. UDDI expects a set of centralized registries to be used by the data-categorizing experts of the world. Experts at categorizing services are at the edge of the network and not in the center. An informal poll of UDDI registry products I conducted in 2006 shows that the average number of service end points for each organizing a UDDI registry is 15. CDS reflects this reality by building taxonomy into the CDS itself.

CDS expects taxonomy to be represented in XML and stored in a database within the CDS itself. The objects and services in the CDS know how to search taxonomy within the CDS to determine the location of service end points. As the number of CDS components within an organization grows, a centralized registry may be beneficial. When that happens, the centralized registry uses publish and subscribe techniques for the CDS components to share their taxonomies with the registry.

Next let's look at how the CDS accesses data and provides mid-tier service and data caching for CDS acceleration.

### 8.1.5 Data Access Services

A CDS component accesses and persists data for services through a data access tier.

In the example from the above sections, the data access tier provides the directory data the CDS needs for the validateAddress() method to return a response. For instance, once the workflow uses

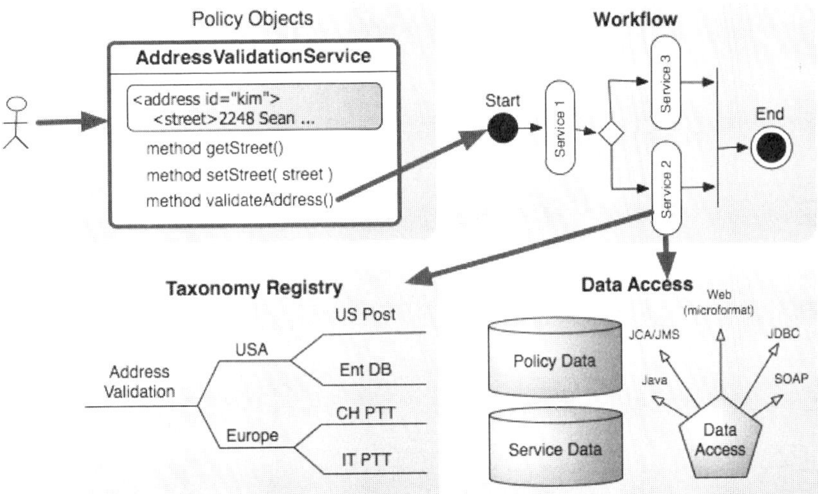


***Figure 8-6*** *The data access layer enables the process to send the address to the service over a SOAP request and cache the results in a mid-tier service data cache.*

the taxonomy to find the correct service, a data access layer enables the process to send the address to the service over a SOAP request. At this stage, mid-tier caching accelerates data access by caching response data and policy data, such as the results of the search through the taxonomy. (See Figure 8.6.)

The data access tier provides a common interface for databases and services holding data needed for the CDS to provide a response to requests. A CDS component needs three types of data access providers:

- **Federated Data sources.** The data access tier provides a service interface for databases (both relational and native XML,) SOAP-based Web Services, REST and XML-RPC services, message queues, service buses, business integration services, and direct access to other CDS components and objects.
- **Service cache.** The service cache is to persist the cached message payloads. For instance, the service database holds a SOAP message in XML form, an HTML Web page, text from a short message, and binary from a JPEG or GIF image. Identical requests are then served from the cache as long as the cached data is still valid.
- **Policy cache.** The policy cache holds units of business logic that look into the service database contents and make decisions on servicing requests with data from the service database or passing through the request to the application tier. For instance, a policy that receives a SOAP request validates security information in the SOAP header to validate that a user may receive previously cached response data. In another instance a policy checks the time-to-live value from a stock market price quote to see if it can respond to a request from the stock value stored in the service database.

The advantage to using the FastSOA mid-tier service cache pattern in a CDS is in its ability to store any general type of data, and its strength in quickly matching services with sets of complex parameters to efficiently determine when a service request can be serviced from the cache. Responses from the cache accelerate the CDS response.

Chapter 4 presented a variety of ways to leverage data access services to provide a standard interface to store, retrieve, and update enterprise data, databases, Web services, and data persistence stores.

In the above sections, I showed an example business project where the CDS delivered a compact, concise, and efficient architecture to answer address validation service requests. The CDS component building architecture used objects, workflow, taxonomy, and data access technology. The CDS component is self-contained, accessible through standard protocols, easily maintained, and completely reusable.

Commercial and open-source tools, libraries, and frameworks are available to build CDS components. (Later in this chapter, we'll look at a method for evaluating these tools.) While you could adopt parts of the CDS architecture presented in the above sections and discard others, I recommend you formalize your service building around the CDS architecture. Figure 8-7 shows the entire CDS architecture as a container to bring these concepts together.

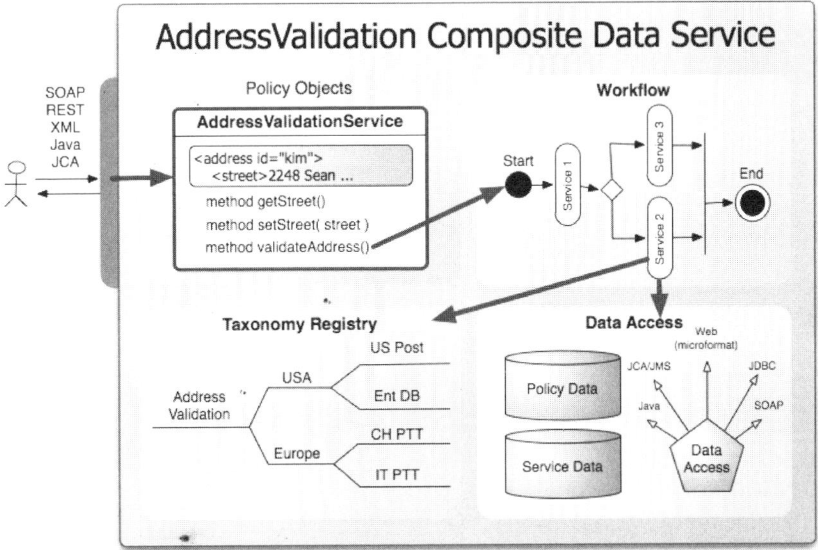


*Figure 8-7 The Composite Data Service (CDS) component architecture.*

Enterprise information system executives are in love with SOA for its promise to provide inexpensive and rapid development of composite applications. A composite application reduces the overall cost of information system development and operations by providing an easy and efficient way to reuse data and services. The CDS component architecture puts all of policy objects, workflow, taxonomy, and data access objects for a single CDS component into a single container. Adopting the CDS architecture provides a service interface means for an enterprise to stitch together CDS components as needed—reusing them over and over again. Figure 8-8 shows a CDS component providing a browser interface with two main user interface elements served from a single CDS.

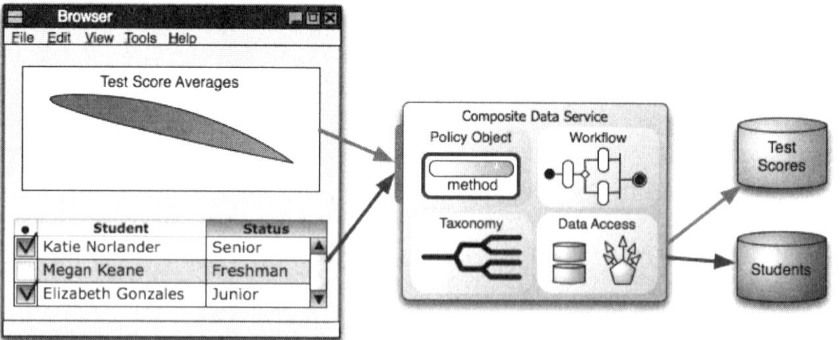


***Figure 8-8*** *A Web interface for two services (test scores and students) served by a single Composite Data Service.*

The CDS component architecture would not be possible without data and metadata being available through standard service interfaces and in a common data model. Prior to XML adoption, how would we represent taxonomy in a way that a CDS component could use? The next section shows how XML makes a huge difference in creating metadata and its benefit to an enterprise, organization, or institution.

## 8.2 Creating Business Value with Metadata

XML is very important to information technology, because it gives the world a way to model data in a way that expresses data about the data. XML helped the world achieve a critical mass of data and metadata to help businesses realize value from their information systems. Before we achieved this critical mass, corporate information systems were purely a cost of doing business—an expense. We built these systems for mundane things such as sending invoices to customers. After reaching a critical mass of data and metadata, the company information system became a profit center, where the flow of information delivers business value. For instance, a customer portal for customers of a business providing financial and investment information increases the number of customer stock purchases for the investment firm hosting the portal. Component Data Services (CDS) was not possible until we could combined policies, data, and metadata.

Policies are components of business logic automated by metadata that can take action on data. The action may be a transformation, notification, persistence for later use, or federation with other data to create new views of data. Business logic is a process that furthers the missions of a business or organization.

In the 1980s and 1990s, businesses hired software developers to implement metadata-driven policies within their organization (behind their firewall), but these systems could only operate on what the organization knew internally—inventory levels, buying habits, payment records—and the resulting code could not be reused, even among departments within the same organization, because the code was hard-coded for one set of data. The widespread availability of data and metadata makes policies, written as CDS components, possible. What are *policies*? Let me try a metaphor.

Policies are verbs, data is the noun, and metadata is an adjective.[2]

Place an order for popular windshield wipers.

| verb | adverb | noun |
|---|---|---|
| policy | metadata | data |

***Figure 8-9*** *Defining policies, data, and metadata through a linguistic metaphor*

Until the widespread availability of data and metadata, businesses and organizations could not write an entire sentence! (See Figure 8.9).

Several organizations already understand the power of metadata-driven policies and have created their own. Consider these examples: Microformats, United States Department of Defense Discovery Metadata Standard (DDMS), and Electronic Business XML (ebXML) Business Object Documents (BODs).

2 I use this metaphor in honor of my late aunt, Betsy Hilbert, a long-time member of the Modern Linguistic Association and Chair of the English Department of Miami Dade University.

### 8.2.1 Microformats

Microformats provide data about the data in a Web page.[3] Currently a research project among a group of Web thought leaders, much excitement is driving microformats activity at the World Wide Web Consortium.[4] It is a safe bet that we will see microformats and a query language such as XQuery emerge as a leading way to turn the content of the Web into a queriable database.

For instance, my biography page on the XQueryNow.com site lists my next birthday encoded in the Microformat iCalendar format.[5] Figure 8-10 contrasts a VCalendar format to iCalendar. The iCalendar format is valid Web page content that is decorated with metadata giving a program (such as a CDS) the information it needs to operate on a birthdate. Microformats turn Web content into the world's largest queriable database.

```
BEGIN:VCALENDAR
PRODID:-//XYZproduct//EN
VERSION:2.0
BEGIN:VEVENT
URL:http://www.xquerynow.com/AboutUs/bio.html
DTSTART:20070423
DTEND:20070423
SUMMARY:Frank's Birthday
LOCATION:Campbell\, California\, USA
END:VEVENT
END:VCALENDAR
```

```
<span class="vevent">
 <a class="url" href="http://www.xquerynow.com/AboutUs/bio.html">
  <span class="summary">Frank's Birthday</span>:
  <abbr class="dtstart" title="2007-04-23">April 23</abbr>-
  <abbr class="dtend" title="2007-04-23">1</abbr>,
 at the <span class="location">Campbell, California, USA</span>
 </a>
</span>
```

appears as:

Frank's Birthday: **April 23- 1**, at the Campbell, California, USA

***Figure 8-10*** *Announcing Frank Cohen's birthday on the left in VCalendar format and on the right using a Microformat iCalendar format.*

The microformat hCalendar is a simple, open, distributed calendaring and event format, based on the iCalendar standard (RFC 2445), suitable for embedding in HTML (and XHTML), Atom, RSS, and arbitrary XML. However, hCalendar is one of several open microformat standards. Many of the microformats are seen as enablers for collaborative commerce. For instance, microformats deliver metadata and queriable formats for the following.

- **Companies**—contact information, organization, reputation, relationships, products, services

3 See http://microformats.org/about
4 See http://www.w3c.org.
5 See http://www.xquerynow.com/AboutUs/bio.html.

- **People**—relationships, product recommendations, contact information
- **Products**—information, specials, inventories, contents, manuals
- **Dates**—events, conferences, tradeshows, meetings
- **News**—articles, product reviews, sales specials

Each of the microformats provides metadata for data delivered through Web content. The metadata is in XML form and ideal for consumption and transformation in a set of CDS components.

Next, we'll see how the U.S. Depart of Defense (DoD) plans to deliver value through the use of metadata.

### 8.2.2 Discovery Metadata

The U.S. Department of Defense (DoD) is building its own Internet—called the Global Information Grid (GIG)—to provide information sharing and to make its operations more efficient and support joint missions. One of the GIG-related efforts delivers a set of standards and services to support Network-centric Computing Environments (NCES).[6] NCES provides a standard way to publish and discover content on the GIG.

The DoD faces the huge challenge of changing attitudes among many data owners to make the GIG work. The U.S. Congress's investigation into the failure to defend the country from the terrorist acts of September 11, 2001, found that a key factor was the lack of information sharing among U.S. federal departments and organizations. The often Byzantine-like and convoluted world of departmental and organizational charters, missions, and management seems to enforce a "my data is mine" attitude. The DoD NCES effort seeks to allow communities of interest (COI) to form, where participants can publish their data using a metadata registry and discover data from other groups of information through metadata queries. Figure 8-11 illustrates the design.

The Department of Defense Discovery Metadata Standard (DDMS) defines discovery metadata elements for resources posted to community and organizational shared spaces.[7] *Discovery* is the abil-

6 See http://www.disa.mil/nces/ne3.html.
7 See http://www.afei.org/news/ddms.pdf.

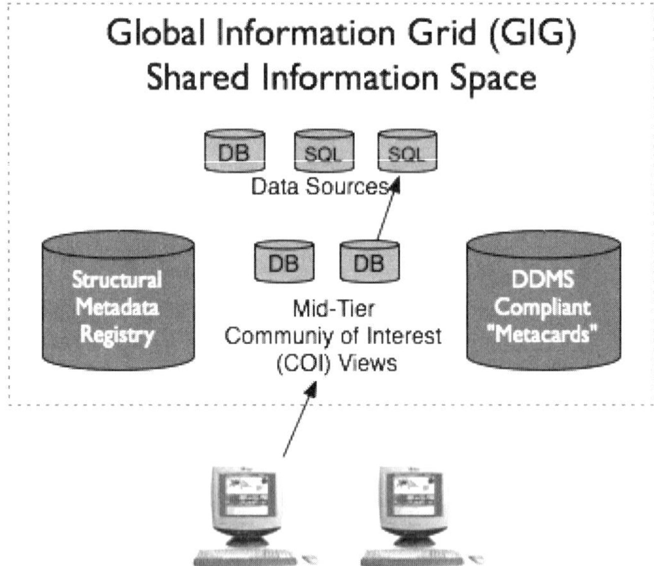


*Figure 8-11 Metadata enables data creators to publish their data to known and unanticipated data consumers and for consumers to discover data that interests them.*

ity to locate data assets through a consistent and flexible search. The DDMS specifies a set of information fields that are to be used to describe any data or service asset that is made known to the enterprise. DDMS establishes a standard for defining and publishing metadata across DoD disciplines, domains, and data formats.

To a CDS component, the DDMS looks like wonderful taxonomy to discover and aggregate data. Any department that wants to make known data and functions it maintains has taxonomy to add its metadata to the overall discovery mechanism. DDMS becomes a giant repository of metadata in the same way that Google is a searchable metadata repository of the Web. CDS components are important to DDMS by making data, metadata, and functions manageable and reusable.

Next, I discuss the third example of a business and organization using metadata to deliver value.

## 8.2.3 Business Object Documents

The Open Applications Group Integration Specification (OAGIS) is an effort to provide a canonical business language for information integration.[8] It delivers the metadata definitions for messages commonly exchanged between a business or organization and customers, vendors, and partners, as well as for identifying business processes (scenarios) that allow businesses and applications to communicate.

OAGIS defines approximately 150 common business messages and is built on the Universal Business Language (UBL)[9] specification in the electronic business using XML (ebXML)[10] schemas. UBL 1.0 defines eight standard documents anyone would recognize: order, order response, order response simple, order change, order cancellation, dispatch advice, receipt advice, and invoice. UBL maps to commonly used paper documents and to the Electronic Data Interchange (EDI) standard formats.[11]

Businesses and organizations are making their own vertical applications of the OAGIS metadata. For instance, General Motors and other automotive industry enterprises support the Software Technology in Automotive Retailing (STAR) effort to standardize messages between automotive parts dealerships and parts manufacturers in the STAR Business Object Document (BOD) standard.[12] STAR BODs are a vertical industry application of OAGIS and UBL.

Chapters 4 and 5 showed the performance impact of choosing a metadata format such as the STAR BODs in an enterprise information system. For instance, a Get Purchase Order (GPO) BOD to order a windshield wiper is a 7,500-byte XML request message. The same GPO BOD to order an entire GM Suburban truck is a 10-megabyte XML request message.

BODs are an ideal medium for CDS components. They are XML and easily managed, transformed, and processed using CDS components. Plus, the CDS policy and service cache provides an easy means to accelerate BOD processing performance and scalability.

The above examples (microformats, Discovery Metadata, and Business Object Documents) are indications that a huge amount of metadata is already available to your business and organization. The widespread adoption of XML for data and metadata drives the value available to businesses and organizations through the adoption of CDS components. With a CDS component, the business logic auto-

---

8 See http://www-128.ibm.com/developerworks/xml/library/x-oagis/.
9 See http://www.oasis-open.org/committees/tc_home.php?wg_abbrev=ubl.
10 See http://www.ebxml.org/geninfo.htm.
11 See http://www.anu.edu.au/people/Roger.Clarke/EC/EDIIntro.html.
12 See http://xml.coverpages.org/star.html.

mated by metadata takes action on data without software developer intervention or an administrator's intervention.

With the widespread adoption of XML data and metadata, it should be no surprise to you that SOA developers, architects, and IT managers are challenged to select appropriate tools and technology to adopt XML and avoid a huge performance, scalability, and developer productivity impact on their datacenter. The next two sections of this chapter present a way of looking at SOA tools and technologies to determine which are appropriate for your business and organization.

## 8.3 Enterprise Options to Build Business Logic

A survey of CIOs, architects, and developers attending the 2006 Gartner conference on application integration and Web Services showed widespread agreement that there will never be a time when a composite application will be entirely built using drag-and-drop graphical design tools.[13] Put another way, survey respondents believe there will always be code to write in SOA applications.

If our future does not include building composite applications in some graphic tool, where should we put the code? Here are some popular choices.

- **Enterprise data tier**. This is the land of large-scale back-end database systems and the heart of any data silo. While the relational database vendor community supports the SQL query language, few have a reason to provide SQL interoperability, and most provide their own procedural language. Additionally, these database programming languages make it possible to expose procedural interfaces to operate functions that deliver data and services. Plus, many of these programming languages have the ability to make service requests to other systems to retrieve data and operate functions not implemented solely in the database. Anyone with a strong data management background will likely think that running code in the database is a good thing. Keep in mind that running SOA code in a database may be a very expensive proposition, as the commercial database vendors charge software license fees based on the number of CPUs.

13 See http://www.gartner.com/events.

Also, the available pool of software developers with skills to build and maintain SOA code that runs in the database tier may be small.

- **Middle tier using an application server**. An application server operates a Web application, enterprise application, and service in a threaded, clustered, and manageable container in the middle tier of an SOA environment. The application server provides value-added services, including session management, failover among a cluster of application servers, logging, debugging, and management services. Included tools take SOA definition files (WSDL, XML, and others) and creates proxy programs to receive and respond to service requests. On the plus side for application servers is the wide availability of software developers with application server experience—literally millions of developers in locations all around the globe. The downside is similar to databases in that commercial application servers are sold on a per-CPU software license and object-oriented (Java and .NET) application servers are typically inefficient at handling XML-oriented applications.
- **Middle tier with CDS components**. This is an application server of a different sort. This application server is specific to SOA, XML, and CDS components. It sits in the middle tier, provides responses to service requests, and operates entirely in the native data format of the request (XML, images, binary files, Web content). The CDS components deliver data transformation, service acceleration through data and service caching, and federation of data across multiple data sources. CDS components provide business logic in objects, a workflow automation container, queriable taxonomy, and data access objects, including a policy cache and service cache. Due to the excellent performance and scalability of XML persistence engines, the total cost of ownership (TCO) to operate a CDS application server is less than operating SOA code in the database and application server tiers.
- **Presentation tier.** Building SOA code in the presentation tier makes the service consumer really, really fat. At some point you may ask why the consumer needs to talk to an application server and not to the enterprise data tier itself? For instance, DreamFactory sells a fat-client creation utility

based on the original Apple HyperCard idea that fully supports Web Service and several SOA protocols.[14]

- **Software as a service tier.** The software industry continues to experiment in various means to shift from traditional boxed solutions to solutions delivered on demand and hosted on a service provider's datacenter. SOA applications are often good candidates for deployment through Software As Service (SAS) techniques. In the SAS environment, you implement SOA services using macro and scripting languages built in to the SAS applications, and the service provider manages the operating environment.
- **XML accelerator**. XML accelerators are appliances that provide SOA and Web Services processing capabilities that offload common tasks (security encryption, message schema validation, message transformation) from application and database servers. Simple SOA features are possibly implemented in XML accelerators. However, the relatively few developers with such experience and the lack of data persistence in XML accelerators seem to make this a long shot.
- **Web tier**. Web servers universally ship with a selection of scripting languages with support for SOA and Web Services protocols. For instance, the Apache Web server comes with a JavaScript interpreter that is easily configurable to respond to REST-style requests such as AJAX and RSS.

Each of these is a viable place to write and operate SOA code. However, the common thread to all of them is the need to provide a full programming environment with protocol support and a persistence engine to be successful in SOA environments.

The above list is not exhaustive of all the choices available. Every week developers argue for their new and interesting ideas and discussion on the most appropriate place for an enterprise or organization to build SOA business logic. Unfortunately, this discussion is also driving a CIO fatigue disorder I call LazySOA.

## 8.4 LazySOA and Being Ready for SOA

Sometimes SOA may look like a moving target. Each week I read about new SOA inventions, new opinions of governance and implementation techniques, and announcements of new SOA tools. I have

14 See http://www.dreamfactory.com.

to be honest in saying that SOA sometimes looks more like a nervous disorder than a technology or governance for information systems. While speaking with an information systems executive for a large manufacturing institution, I saw the LazySOA effect:

```
"I get the Composite Data Services idea but don't I just
really need a registry, an XML accelerator, a service bus, and
a federated data integrator? And then I'm done with SOA?
Right?"
```

The question is an indicator to me that CIOs are searching for a list of tools, appliances, and skills that make their business ready for SOA. This bears investigation. In the sections that follow I present a list of tools that should be on your list with an explanation of each for your datacenter to be SOA-ready.

- Service Registry
- XML Accelerator
- Enterprise Service Bus
- Data Access Service and Components
- Deployment and Monitoring
- Composite Data Service Container

### 8.4.1 Service Registry

A registry is a database of services with a query mechanism for consumers to discover services and retrieve a service endpoint to which the consumer can bind to make a request of the service. A service discovery registry mechanism is important, because it is a dynamic mechanism that enables the discovery and utilization of services during execution time. This enables savings in operational dollars by reducing integration costs and enabling composite applications. Registry products offer the following basic features.

1. Publishing and discovering services and the metadata for services
2. Creating and enforcing policies
3. Facilitating consumer/provider contracts and consumption agreements

4. Dynamically make changes to business services without disrupting consuming applications
5. Manage service life cycles as service interface schemas change and evolve over time

Sometimes you may hear the term *registry/repository*. Registries are designed for service publishing and discovery. The early registries deliver a registry database schema and package of software objects for publishing services in the database and running queries for discovery. The schema in these registry products runs on a relational database that you provide. The second generation of registry products bundles its own database to store registry information. Registry products that have their own data persistence engine offer users the ability to store additional SOA artifacts and metadata in the registry persistence engine. The registry becomes an Information Object Repository (IOR) for SOA artifacts, such as WSDL documents; WS-Policy documents; Business Process Workflow documents; and other endpoint descriptors, such as JMS, Java endpoints, JCA interfaces, and JMS queues.

Of course, you would do well to ask yourself which data and metadata are appropriately stored in a registry? Perhaps usage statistics or simple registry entry transformations make sense. Another possibility is a publish/subscribe mechanism to enable users to subscribe to receive notifications when a user adds a new service to the registry. Another possibility is user and group permissions for the registry. For instance, the registry could persist information on which group of users may publish services to the registry. However, this begs the question of whether a registry should also be an LDAP-style directory of users, groups, and privileges. These issues put me squarely on the fence when it comes to determining an appropriate SOA artifact to store in a registry persistence engine.

Registry/repository products are continuing down their product road maps and shortly will provide interfaces for UDDI and ebXML registries (with transformation and cross registration possible between the two), service policy validation, and taxonomy/catalog builder capabilities.

Last, you might ask yourself why your company needs a registry if you only have 25 or fewer services? Perhaps a Web page listing the available services with the Web page content marked up in a registry microformat would be better. Additionally, I recommend you question the registry provider for the performance and scalability characteristics of its bundled persistence engine. This will make a difference when your business starts storing thousands of service descriptions. Chapters 4 and 5 gave my methodology for testing persistence engines for scalability and performance.

A good second step to become ready for SOA is to evaluate an XML accelerator.

### 8.4.2 XML Accelerator

Network acceleration has been around for a while. The theory goes that moving often requested data closer to the consumer accelerates performance. That works satisfactorily when the data is easy to identify—such as static Web pages—but tends not to work for XML-based messages.

XML accelerators understand the context of the XML messages moving through their routers, which makes them different from network accelerators. XML acceleration appliances improve performance from three perspectives:

1. XML accelerators offload the effort to decode security protocols from an application server. For instance, an incoming SOAP request over HTTPS protocols using WS-Security protocols requires two steps of decoding before the business logic of an application server can make sense of the request: decrypting the SSL package that encodes the SOAP request and decoding the portions of the SOAP payload according to the WS-Security–defined headers in the SOAP request message. Of course, the response SOAP message will have to go through the same security encoding before it returns to the consumer.
2. Validate the request. Using XML Schema or DTDs, the XML accelerator appliance checks that the XML message conforms to a message format supported by the service that handles the incoming request. Validation may also be linked to routing functions, where the XML accelerator routes an incoming XML request using an older XML message schema to a legacy service dedicated to supporting the older schema.
3. Transform the message to a different schema. This is handy for information systems that have progressed their request message schema but still want to support consumers using

the older schema. The transformation is limited in that the accelerator appliance has no database and no way to communicate with datasource providers to do more than simple transformations.

4. Change the routing of the request. By looking at the headers of a message, the accelerator changes the destination URL for the message.

XML accelerator appliances benefit a business by moving the cost of operating a service from a Java application server to the appliance box. XML accelerator appliances provide acceleration by applying dedicated hardware resources to the appliance's tasks. Commercial Java application servers are commanding fees from $25,000 to $50,000 per CPU. Moving security protocol decoding, message validation, transformation, and simple routing into a $10,000 XML accelerator appliance saves an enterprise from buying Java application server licenses. Plus, the XML accelerator is concise and limited in its scope of operations and does not require any programming and little administrative overhead.

Calling these appliances "accelerators" is somewhat rhetorical. It is akin to calling something FastSOA—faster than what? XML accelerators add their own overhead. Inside the accelerator, a processor parses the XML message to decode the contents from a security protocol, validate the message, or do a transformation into a new message schema. The accelerator then repackages the XML message as an XML request and forwards it on to the application server for processing. That parsing and repackaging does not help the code in the application server to get a jump on the contents of the message—the application server has to go through its own second parsing of the message.

Additionally, the majority of Web Services and SOA applications I have seen use synchronous—blocking—requests. The consumer keeps the socket open until it receives a response. This puts the XML accelerator in the middle, acting as a network router at the socket and packet level of the exchange. This adds more overhead to the exchange and makes the accelerator appliance another potential point of failure in your network. A rhetoric-free name for these appliances is XML security gateway appliances, but that is not as sexy and compelling as XML accelerator.

XML accelerators deliver valuable benefits to make an enterprise and organization ready for SOA. The next section shows the benefits of an Enterprise Service Bus (ESB).

### 8.4.3 Enterprise Service Bus (ESB)

Enterprise Service Bus (ESB) tools become important as enterprises begin to realize the benefits of composite applications in SOA. Enterprises build Web and XML applications that rapidly bind to one or more services in a Web infrastructure using open standard protocols over routed networks to transmit data defined in industry-accepted schemas. Usually, an enterprise or organization's initial SOA applications access data and functions from a defined set of servers at statically defined addresses, and over time the applications access data and functions dynamically from the most appropriate service provider available.

From a system administrator, executive information systems technology management, software development and quality assurance perspective, SOA requires a new set of skills and expertise to deliver service excellence. The old methodology depends heavily on hand-coded installation scripts, manually applied operating system patches, and procedural component tests. This methodology is not flexible, reliable, and agile enough for enterprises to succeed in an SOA environment.

An ESB tool automates SOA application provisioning through automated installation, configuration, and updating of servers in your datacenter. An ESB also provides service-to-service communication and service lifecycle management.

ESB is different from a CDS container in that that CDS is a runtime environment that provides objects, taxonomy, data persistence, and data access in reusable software components. The ESB at runtime connects and mediates sending messages between services—including CDS components—within the ESB architecture and connects and mediates all communications and interactions between services. These services are natively hosted services—executed entirely within the ESB environment—and connected business services, such as Web services and enterprise data services hosted by application servers, wrappers, or adapters. (See Figure 8-12.

An ESB provides service life-cycle management functions to transition from development configuration to deployment and production environments. The ESB normally provides modeling and configuration tools to support each phase of the ESB life-cycle across a distributed environment. For instance, an ESB allows for service, process, and resource file migration between development, test, and production systems. Administrators use the ESB to identify deploy-

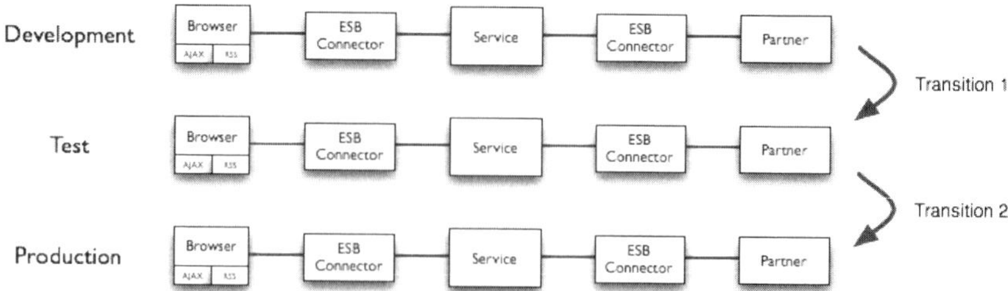


***Figure 8-12*** *ESB tools manage communication within a service and also provide automation to transition from development to test to production environments.*

ment policies, and the ESB works with a monitoring service to confirm successful deployments against a set of unit/functional tests. ESB tools normally also include a visual tool to map processes, data mapping, and relationships between applications.

ESB tools needs to be evaluated in two areas: provisioning and deployment automation and service-to-service communication.

### *Evaluating Provisioning and Deployment Automation*

The enterprises and organizations I have helped with ESB evaluations tend to be driven by the following forces.

1. New services change frequently to address changing customer, supplier, and partner needs.
2. Capacity planning decisions change frequently to ensure optimal infrastructure utilization rates and to eliminate performance bottlenecks.
3. Systems and applications change frequently as a business adds new system components to the datacenter.
4. Personnel changes require system provisioning changes, including operating system and directory account provisioning and password changes.

In response to these forces, many enterprises and organizations use a set of configuration utilities to manage change. These configuration utilities include management consoles, installer utilities, scripting utilities, software updating services, application optimization, and load-balancing solutions. The problems using configuration utilities include the following.

- System administrators and engineers require proprietary or custom scripting language knowledge. Companies sometimes change engineers and system administrators like toner cartridges, and this personnel turnover means lost knowledge and problems managing change over time.
- Configuration utilities are often error prone to use and may introduce security issues. For example, some configuration utilities require granting administrator (root) access to a system technician.
- Configuration utilities normally have no business intelligence to know how to change datacenter configuration to optimize underutilized equipment.
- Configuration utilities are not normally compatible with other configuration utilities. In SOA environments, enterprise application functions are provisioned as orchestrations of a series of individual services within one datacenter. For instance, the configuration utility that establishes a database service must be compatible with the configuration utility that installs a JDBC connector to access the database and the utility that establishes the EJB that holds the business logic to access the database.
- Using disparate and multiple configuration utilities in a datacenter does not provide an overall view of changes in a datacenter to management.
- A configuration utility provides no mechanism to check a change and deployment plan prior to actually making the change to the datacenter.
- Configuration utilities are themselves software. Changes to their functionality or the scripts that drive them need to be captured for use by team members who will join your project later, and versions of their functionality or scripts must be archived to explain changes to the subsequent engineer who provides on-going maintenance support.

All of the above issues drive enterprise operations and system administrators to consider ESB tools as a deployment solution. I recommend you evaluate an ESB against the above list of forces and issues. Then consider if the ESB tool is appropriate to your situation. Consider if the ESB tools you are considering will meet these types of deployments.

- One-to-many situations, where a single change must be frequently and rapidly made to a large number of systems. For instance, consider the scenario where a system administrator needs to update a file on a group of servers in a datacenter.
- One-to-one situations, where a single change must be repeatedly made to one target environment. For instance, consider a scenario where the system administrator needs to install a CDS component onto a group of servers in a datacenter.
- Orchestration situations, where multiple steps must be accomplished for each change in a multitier and multiple-system environment. For instance, consider a scenario wherein a systems administrator needs to provision a service at several levels of service integration, including a Web server, application server, and a Web application to a group of servers in a datacenter.

### *Evaluating Service-to-Service Communication Capabilities*

ESB tools provide service-to-service communication capabilities that need to be evaluated like any other software component: performance, scalability, function, and developer productivity. Chapters 3, 4, and 5 provided a framework and test methodology for performance and scalability. Beyond that, your evaluation of communication capabilities needs to cover the function of the connector and how easy the components are to use. ESB applications normally are object-oriented, XML-based, distributed environments to deliver composite applications, and your organization will need people with these skills. The communication components need to provide an extensible framework and environment that at a minimum delivers the following features.

- Common framework to add communication components to services using the native protocols of the target services
- Maintains an audit log of components in use and deployments over time
- Compares the current state of target services with their expected state

- Simulates a change—for instance, adoption of a new message schema or service interface—to identify configuration problems
- Notifies system administrators of problems and actions

The next step to become ready for SOA is to evaluate data access services, including data integration services and components for data access.

### 8.4.4 Data Access Service and Components

Data access services provide a common interface and software components to create data and service interoperability between systems. With data persistence features close at hand, data access products may also provide data mitigation and aggregation. Data access cleaves into two parts: federated data integrators and data access connectors.

#### *Federated Data Integrators*

A federated data integrator queries multiple data sources and presents the data to its consumer in a single combined view. The integrator requires the following components to be successful for an enterprise:

- Support multiple protocols (for instance, SOAP, REST)
- High-speed persistence engine to maintain the view
- Transformation or scripting language to implement pattern matching and schema transformations

A subset of data federation is Master Data Management (MDM). Businesses use MDM to provide and maintain a federated view and synchronization of an organization's core business entities. For instance, a business with operations in several locations or across several products usually has data scattered across a range of application systems in a variety of different formats. The types of master data vary by industry and organization, but examples include customers, suppliers, products, employees, and finances.

MDM data federation is important to a business because it does not require owners of data silos to comply with your requests to modify the silos or move the data from the silo into a data warehouse. Instead, MDM provides an easier way to create composite views of data from each silo system. More importantly, MDM allows data updates across silos. For instance, customers participating in multiple business units update their address information in one business unit and the MDM federated data integrator updates all of the silos.

An evaluation method for federated data integrator tools includes a feature/function checklist, scalability and performance testing, and the ultimate question, "Do I trust the technology and vendor to hold my data?" Additionally, I recommend you meet the consulting and system integrator businesses that use and recommend the federated data integrator tools. These will be the people you will turn to when things go wrong over time.

Many federated integrator tools comes with specialized connectors to a variety of datasources. The next section shows how to evaluate data access connectors from companies that specialize in data access connectors.

### Data Access Connectors

The typical business or organization has a datacenter supporting multiple generations of applications. Instead of redeveloping these applications, it usually makes more economic and strategic sense to reuse the existing assets. Providing XML-based interfaces to these assets is often achievable using a data access connector. With the connector in place, the existing asset may be used from a composite application and CDS.

Evaluating data access connectors for your business or organization comes down to two issues: Does the connector support the specific protocol and dialect of my existing application, and does the connector provide the performance and scalability to a level that meets my service-level agreements?

Many data access connector vendors also include service life-cycle management and assurance functions. Some vendors even provide data persistence in support of their connector management. In these instances, keep in mind the bigger picture and ask if these value-added services really add value.

The next step to become ready for SOA is to evaluate business process management and monitoring tools.

### 8.4.5 Deployment and Monitoring

Service monitoring and quality assurance tools come under the general topic Business Activity Monitoring (BAM). BAM applies operational business intelligence and application integration technologies to automated processes to continually refine them based on feedback that comes directly from knowledge of operational events. At least, that's the theory.

The problem with managing SOA quality is that you need to operate the service to know that it is functional and meets your service-level agreements (SLAs). I am reminded of sitting next to a telephone waiting for a girlfriend to call. Uncertain if the phone is working, checking the phone for a dial tone will give her a busy signal. Monitoring and assuring quality in SOA environments is like that; until you use a service, you just don't know if it works!

In addition to auditing business processes (and business process management systems) and sending event-driven alerts that trigger process adjustments, BAM solutions also can be used to alert individuals to changes in the business that may require action. Executives often use BAM to provide data points against which to measure operation manager performance and for strategic planning.

BAM solutions deliver the following benefits to a business or organization:

- Reduce the risk of service outages
- Improve the speed and confidence of service delivery to users
- Provide a quality of service–level guarantee to partners and users
- Plan accurately for service capacity needs
- Outline a schedule and estimated costs to successfully deliver against service-level agreements

While there are many off-the-shelf service monitor tools available, the big downside is that they usually do not deliver the exact knowledge you need. The problem comes from a gap between the monitor's ability to test a service and building the business logic so the monitor understands the context of the service. The PushToTest test methodology I presented in Chapter 6 is built around intelligent test agents that implement the behavior of archetypal users. The service monitor periodically operates the service using a test agent in the same way a real user would. The monitor then sounds alarms, summarizes reports, and presents a live dashboard.

Evaluate service monitor and quality assurance tools against the following criteria to ensure the tool will meet your business or organization's needs.

- Operates in a distributed architecture, where a central console coordinates multiple tests from multiple locations on your network.
- Periodic functional (unit) health check.
- Development environment to build and maintain intelligent test agents using click-and-drag or scripting programming techniques.
- User-selectable criteria for alerts, including issues such as long service response, number of servers down, number of failed requests in the last minute, and more.
- Status definition based on ranges of values for each monitor.
- Define a set of actions to trigger depending on the state of a server. For instance, if a service responds too slowly, the monitor waits 10 minutes before sending a service problem notification.
- Monitor system is enabled to receive external events to trigger an alert and notification.
- Provide multiple states for each service under observation. For instance, allow a service to go into "maintenance mode" without having to manually turn off the monitor.

The final step to become ready for SOA is to evaluate development and operating environments for CDS components.

### 8.4.6 Composite Data Service Container

Building, operating, and maintaining CDS components requires a platform that includes object development functions, workflow operations, taxonomy building, data persistence, and data access functions. Evaluating and selecting a CDS container requires investigation of scalability and performance characteristics, developer productivity (to demonstrate the container's ease of use), and maintainability (effort to upgrade and patch the system for bugs and performance improvements).

Evaluate CDS containers against the following:

- **Business service interaction**—determines the set of products, protocols, and service protocols the CDS container supports. For instance, if your container needs to provide data access to IBM CICS legacy systems, make certain a CICS data access component is available and compatible with the CDS container.
- **Object development environment**—enables software developers to build software objects that encapsulate CDS data and provides methods to operate on the data. Software developers will expect an integrated development environment and debugging tools to facilitate building CDS component objects and life-cycle management.
- **Registry and taxonomy construction**—enables CDS registration and discovery through standard service interfaces. Check for support of UDDI version 3 registry and ebXML registry/repository features.
- **Data access**—provides efficient and effective access to data across the enterprise. Check for performance and scalability using the PushToTest method presented in Chapter 6.
- **Security management services**—provide user and group provisioning and roles-based access management. Check for compatibility with your corporate security service.

Is that all there is to be ready for SOA?

### 8.4.7 SOA-Ready

This section began with a CIO asking what he needs to do to ready his enterprise for SOA. The previous sections deliver tools, components, and technology for an enterprise data center to be ready to robustly support SOA composite applications, mid-tier service acceleration through caching, and application/component reuse. Figure 8-13 brings these components together into a concise, ready for SOA architecture.

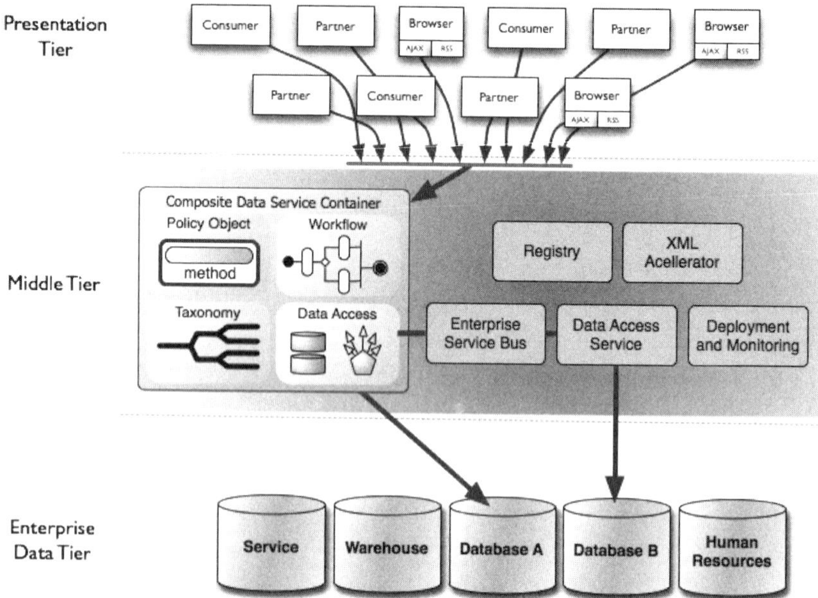


***Figure 8-13*** *Middle tier SOA components—service registry, accelerator, Enterprise Service Bus (ESB,) and data integrator—help an enterprise and organization achieve SOA agility, but they are not the only components needed to be successful.*

Figure 8-13 shows one way these middle-tier SOA tools function together. In other instances, the tiers work together differently. For instance, there is no reason why an XML accelerator could not do security decryption work for a CDS component. Also, adding these devices to a datacenter may help SOA deployments but it does not guarantee SOA governance, as the data services are normally open protocol and service enabled, so applications may find multiple paths to work around your mid-tier appliances and access the data service directly.

The ready for SOA architecture presented in Figure 8-13 reduces the amount of processing that happens in expensive Java application server licenses, mitigates single points of contention problems, and delivers a flexibility not achievable with traditional software development patterns and methods. Being ready for SOA delivers SOA acceleration (intelligent, policy-driven caching using native XML data persistence and policies written in XQuery), data federation (a single URL to receive composite application data from a variety of data sources), and security policy operations (routing, tracking, and auditing systems by keeping track of messages).

Next, I describe my method for evaluating SOA tools for scalability, performance, and developer productivity.

## 8.5 How to Evaluate SOA Tools

The PushToTest methodology I presented in Chapter 6 tests a service for scalability and performance. In my work with large and small companies that need to understand the scalability and performance of services in their own environment, experience shows me the need for a second methodology to truly understand SOA tools, technology, and techniques. I call this second methodology the "Kit."

My company—PushToTest—provides performance and developer productivity "kits" to BEA, Raining Data, Sun, GM, IBM, and others. The kits implement a set of real-world use cases using a variety of commonly used techniques and software libraries (both commercial and open-source.) We measure the resulting software implementations for scalability, performance, and developer productivity. The kit delivers to software developers immediately usable reference software code and best practices and a total cost of ownership (TCO) analysis to business managers. Companies engaging

***Table 8-2*** *Publicly Available SOA Performance Kits*

| Kit Name | Location |
|---|---|
| Raining Data FastSOA Performance Kit | http://www.rainingdata.com/products/soa/soatestkit/index2.html |
| BEA SOA Performance and Developer Productivity Kit | http://www.bea.com/framework.jsp?CNT=fea00025.htm&FP=/content/news_events/features_news/features |
| The SOAP Encoding Performance Kit featuring IBM WebSphere | http://www.pushtotest.com/Downloads/kits/webspherekit.html |
| Web Services Performance and Developer Knowledge Kit | http://www.pushtotest.com/Downloads/kits/origperfkit.html |

PushToTest to build a kit have the option to use the performance and scalability knowledge internally or to bundle it with the release of the kit. Either way, software developers on their internal engineering team benefit from having an independent group use their product in ways the everyday developer would, and the wider software developer community benefits from having an immediate view into working code and best practices to provide the tool's benefits.

Most of the time, it is in the best interest of the software vendor to release the kit under an open-source license. Table 8-2 gives a list of publicly available kits that are available to you.

In summary, the evaluation method to understand scalability, performance, and developer productivity in SOA environments depends on the following criteria.

1. **Governance**—architecture, tools and platform choices, deployment (registry), cvs/subversion control, reports on usage and quality of service delivered
2. **Performance**—tools, libraries, hardware, network routing
3. **Scalability**—datacenters, grids, blades, network load balancing
4. **Developer productivity**—learning curve, comparative lines of code, ease of maintenance

Armed with the methodology, tools, and techniques, your business or organization will evaluate SOA tools to be ready for SOA.

### 8.5.1 Delivering Business Value with SOA

In the world today, the Web is making a change from a set of static Web pages to a rich database of data encoded in a set of microformats. A 2006 survey of attendees to Gartner's Application Integration and Web Services conference showed that a third of the survey respondents already have AJAX in their datacenter. The XML future is already here. If the Web was disruptive like a bomb blast, then XML is a nuclear explosion!

How will we handle this rich new world of data? Will the world's software developers, architects, and operations managers realize the potential business value of harnessing this data into actionable knowledge? Or will XML become some giant noise producer?

The scalability, performance, and developer productivity made possible with CDS components makes a huge impact on the world. Figure 8-14 illustrates a world whose information services needs are served by a grid of CDS components.

This journey into the future has already taught us many important qualities that are needed to be successful in an SOA world.

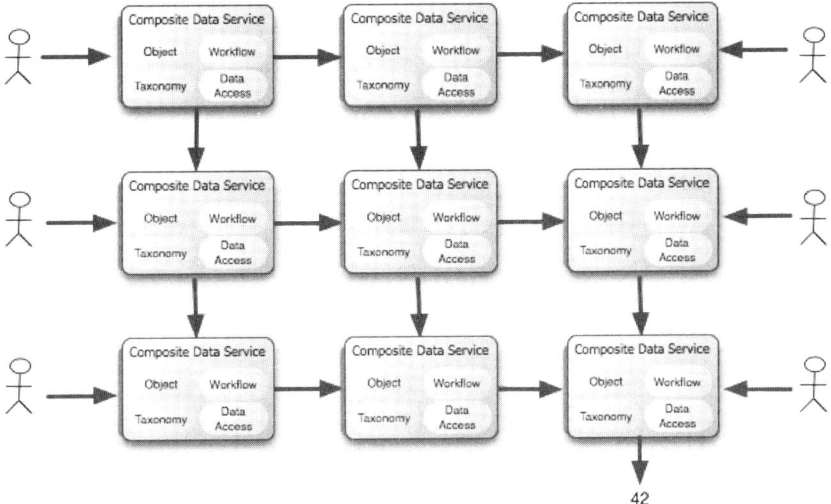


***Figure 8-14*** *Microformats and CDS turn the Web into the world's largest scalable database. The knowledge contained in this database delivers business value through policies.*

1. Accept that there is no gatekeeper on XML schemas. Every atom may have its own XML schema. Any data persistence engine needs to support native XML persistence with the full flexibility of the XML data model.
2. Build data and service objects in one. Object-oriented design patterns applied using native XML technology deliver the scalability, performance, and flexibility needed for SOA success.
3. Given the choice of objects, relational data models, and XML tools, choose XML when the SOA application primarily uses XML.
4. Evaluate SOA tools (ESB, XML accelerator, persistence, etc.) on their ability to handle your data and be flexible to change.

XML has changed our world. The systems we build enable better communication than ever before. Will we use this new technology to usher in a new era of communication and understanding? To create a better world, we now have the capability, and the responsibility to work together and solve the world's problems as we voyage on spaceship Earth.

# Glossary

A key to understanding the concepts presented in this book is my belief that good, robust, successful, and scalable software comes from many practices and backgrounds. This glossary is composed of terms from the World Wide Web consortium glossary[1] and terms I frequently use. I maintain and publish a glossary of terms. Please send your contributions to fcohen@rainingdata.com.

**access**

To interact with a system entity in order to manipulate, use, gain knowledge of, and/or obtain a representation of some or all of a system entity's resources.

**access control**

Protection of resources against unauthorized access; a process by which use of resources is regulated according to a security policy and is permitted by only authorized system entities according to that policy.

1 http://www.w3.org/TR/ws-gloss/

**access control information**

Any information used for access control purposes, including contextual information.

Contextual information might include source IP address, encryption strength, the type of operation being requested, time of day, etc. Portions of access control information may be specific to the request itself, some may be associated with the connection via which the request is transmitted, and others (for example, time of day) may be "environmental."

**access rights (privileges)**

A description of the type of authorized interactions a subject can have with a resource. Examples include read, write, execute, add, modify, and delete.

**actor**

A person or organization that may be the owner of agents that either seek to use Web services or provide Web services.

A physical or conceptual entity that can perform actions. For instance, people; companies; machines; running software. An actor can take on (or implement) one or more roles. An actor at one level of abstraction may be viewed as a role at a lower level of abstraction.

**agent**

An agent is a program acting on behalf of a person or organization. As a piece of software, an agent may implement the methods of a JUnit TestCase class to operate a system and test its ability to function.

**anonymity**

The quality or state of being anonymous, which is the condition of having a name or identity that is unknown or concealed.

**architecture**

The software architecture of a program or computing system is the structure or structures of the system. This structure includes software components, the externally visible properties of those components, the relationships among them and the constraints on their use.

A software architecture is an abstraction of the run-time elements of a software system during some phase of its operation. A system may be composed of many levels of abstraction and many phases of operation, each with its own software architecture.

**artifact**

A piece of digital information. An artifact may be any size, and may be composed of other artifacts. Examples of artifacts: a message; a URI; an XML document; a PNG image; a bit stream.

**asynchronous**

An interaction is said to be asynchronous when the associated messages are chronologically and procedurally decoupled. For example, in a request-response interaction, the client agent can process the response at some indeterminate point in the future when its existence is discovered. Mechanisms to do this include polling, notification by receipt of another message, etc.

**attribute**

A distinct characteristic of an object. An object's attributes are said to describe the object. Objects' attributes are often specified in terms of their physical traits, such as size, shape, weight, and color, etc., for real-world objects. Objects in cyberspace might have attributes describing size, type of encoding, network address, etc.

**audit guard**

An audit guard is a mechanism used on behalf of an owner that monitors actions and agents to verify the satisfaction of obligations.

**authentication**

Authentication is the process of verifying that a potential partner in a conversation is capable of representing a person or organization.

**authorization**

The process of determining, by evaluating applicable access control information, whether a subject is allowed to have the specified types of access to a particular resource. Usually, authorization is in the context of authentication. Once a subject is authenticated, it may be authorized to perform different types of access.

**binding**

An association between an interface, a concrete protocol and a data format. A binding specifies the protocol and data format to be used in transmitting messages defined by the associated interface.

The mapping of an interface and its associated operations to a particular concrete message format and transmission protocol.

**capability**

A capability is a named piece of functionality (or feature) that is declared as supported or requested by an agent.

**choreography**

A choreography defines the sequence and conditions under which multiple cooperating independent agents exchange messages in order to perform a task to achieve a goal state.

Web Services Choreography concerns the interactions of services with their users. Any user of a Web service, automated or otherwise, is a client of that service. These users may, in turn, be other Web Services, applications or human beings. Transactions among Web Services and their clients must clearly be well defined at the time of their execution, and may consist of multiple separate interactions whose composition constitutes a complete transaction. This composition, its message protocols, interfaces, sequencing, and associated logic, is considered to be a choreography.

**component**

A component is a software object, meant to interact with other components, encapsulating certain functionality or a set of functionalities. A component has a clearly defined interface and conforms to a prescribed behavior common to all components within an architecture.

A component is an abstract unit of software instructions and internal state that provides a transformation of data via its interface.

A component is a unit of architecture with defined boundaries.

**confidentiality**

Assuring information will be kept secret, with access limited to appropriate persons.

**Composable**

Applications in SOAs are created by composing pre-existing, well-tested services from multiple providers.

**configuration**

A collection of properties that may be changed. A property may influence the behavior of an entity.

**connection**

A transport layer virtual circuit established between two programs for the purpose of communication.

**control**

To cause a desired change in state. Management systems may control the life cycle of manageable Web services or information flow such as messages.

**conversation**

A Web service conversation involves maintaining some state during an interaction that involves multiple messages and/or participants.

**credentials**

Data that is transferred to establish a claimed principal identity.

**delivery policy**

A delivery policy is a policy that constrains the methods by which messages are delivered by the message transport.

**digital signature**

A value computed with a cryptographic algorithm and appended to a data object in such a way that any recipient of the data can use the signature to verify the data's origin and integrity.

**discovery**

The act of locating a machine-processable description of a Web service-related resource that may have been previously unknown and that meets certain functional criteria. It involves matching a set of functional and other criteria with a set of resource descriptions. The goal is to find an appropriate Web service-related resource.

**discovery service**

A discovery service is a service that enables agents to retrieve Web services-related resource description.

**Discoverable and Dynamic Services**

Adjectives to describe the design-time techniques to identify the location and function of a service. For instance, services are bound at runtime, rather than compile time.

**diversely owned**

SOA applications may be composed of services which are owned and operated by outside organizations. Diverse ownership implies that the published service interface will be treated as a blackbox from the standpoint of the programmers since they cannot penetrate the interface and modify code and behavior behind it.

**document**

Any data that can be represented in a digital form.

**Electronic Data Interchange (EDI)**

The automated exchange of any predefined and structured data for business among information systems of two or more organizations.

**domain**

A domain is an identified set of agents and/or resources that is subject to the constraints of one of more policies.

**Enterprise Application Integration (EAI)**

Centralized approach to application development that requires a central database of record.

**encryption**

Cryptographic transformation of data (called "plaintext") into a form (called "ciphertext") that conceals the data's original meaning to prevent it from being known or used. If the transformation is reversible, the corresponding reversal process is called "decryption," which is a transformation that restores encrypted data to its original state.

**end point**

An association between a binding and a network address, specified by a URI, that may be used to communicate with an instance of a service. An end point indicates a specific location for accessing a service using a specific protocol and data format.

**gateway**

An agent that terminates a message on an inbound interface with the intent of presenting it through an outbound interface as a new message. Unlike a proxy, a gateway receives messages as if it were the final receiver for the message. Due to possible mismatches between the inbound and outbound interfaces, a message may be modified and may have some or all of its meaning lost during the conversion process. For example, an HTTP PUT has no equivalent in SMTP.

Note: a gateway may or may not be a SOAP node; however a gateway is never a SOAP intermediary, since gateways terminate messages and SOAP intermediaries relay them instead. Being a gateway is typically a permanent role, whilst being a SOAP intermediary is message specific.

**identifier**

An identifier is an unambiguous name for a resource.

**initial SOAP sender**

The SOAP sender that originates a SOAP message at the starting point of a SOAP message path.

**integrity**

Assuring information will not be accidentally or maliciously altered or destroyed.

**Interoperable**

Standards ensure that services from differing organizations can use each other's services.

**locationally transparent**

SOA applications are constructed in such a way that the overall system is unaware of, or at least ambivalent to the location of various services.

**loosely coupled**

SOAs are composed of multiple services connected in such a way as to be resilient in the face of network failures and latency. This loose coupling gives SOA applications a distinctly different architecture than programs that are distributed, but still connected synchronously and in ways that make the overall system brittle.

**manageable service**

A Web service becomes a manageable service with additional semantics, policy statements, and monitoring and control (or management) capabilities (exposed via a management interface) all for the purpose of managing the service.

**management**

The utilization of the management capabilities by the management system in order to perform monitoring of values, tracking of states and control of entities in order to produce and maintain a stable operational environment.

**management capability**

Capabilities that a Web service has for the purposes of controlling or monitoring the service, and that can be exposed to a management system for the sole purpose of managing the service.

**management interface**

Interface through which the management capabilities of a service are exposed.

**management policy**

Policy associated with a Web service solely for the purpose of describing the management obligations and permissions for the service.

**management semantics**

The management semantics of a service augment the semantics of a service with management-specific semantics. These management semantics form the contract between the provider entity and the requester entity that expresses the effects and requirements pertaining to the management and management policies for a service.

**message**

A message is the basic unit of data sent from one Web services agent to another in the context of Web services.

The basic unit of communication between a Web service and a requester: data to be communicated to or from a Web service as a single logical transmission.

**message correlation**

Message correlation is the association of a message with a context. Message correlation ensures that the requester agent can match the reply with the request, especially when multiple replies may be possible.

**message exchange pattern (MEP)**

A Message Exchanage Pattern (MEP) is a template, devoid of application semantics, that describes a generic pattern for the exchange of messages between agents. It describes the relationships (e.g., temporal, causal, sequential, etc.) of multiple messages exchanged in conformance with the pattern, as well as the normal and abnormal termination of any message exchange conforming to the pattern.

**message receiver**

A message receiver is an agent that receives a message.

**message reliability**

Message reliability is the degree of certainty that a message will be delivered and that sender and receiver will both have the same understanding of the delivery status.

**message sender**

A message sender is the agent that transmits a message.

**message transport**

A message transport is a mechanism that may be used by agents to deliver messages.

**network-addressable**

Networks are central to the idea of services that are discoverable and interoperable. This allows applications to be composed that run on different machines.

**non-repudiation**

Method by which the sender of data is provided with proof of delivery and the recipient is assured of the sender's identity, so that neither can later deny having processed the data.

**obligation**

An obligation is a kind of policy that prescribes actions and/or states of an agent and/or resource.

**operation**

A set of messages related to a single Web service action.

**orchestration**

An orchestration defines the sequence and conditions in which one Web service invokes other Web services in order to realize some useful function. I.e., an orchestration is the pattern of interactions that a Web service agent must follow in order to achieve its goal.

**permission**

A permission is a kind of policy that prescribes the allowed actions and states of an agent and/or resource.

**permission guard**

A permission guard is a mechanism deployed on behalf of an owner to enforce permission policies.

**person or organization**

A person or organization may be the owner of agents that provide or request Web services.

**policy**

A policy is a constraint on the behavior of agents or person or organization.

**policy guard**

A policy guard is a mechanism that enforces one or more policies. It is deployed on behalf of an owner.

**principal**

A system entity whose identity can be authenticated.

**privacy policy**

A set of rules and practices that specify or regulate how a person or organization collects, processes (uses) and discloses another party's personal data as a result of an interaction.

**provider agent**

An agent that is capable of and empowered to perform the actions associated with a service on behalf of its owner — the provider entity.

**provider entity**

The person or organization that is providing a Web service.

**protocol**

A set of formal rules describing how to transmit data, especially across a network. Low level protocols define the electrical and physical standards to be observed, bit- and byte-ordering and the transmission and error detection and correction of the bit stream. High level protocols deal with the data formatting, including the syntax of messages, the terminal to computer dialogue, character sets, sequencing of messages etc.

**proxy**

An agent that relays a message between a requester agent and a provider agent, appearing to the Web service to be the requester.

**quality of service**

Quality of Service is an obligation accepted and advertised by a provider entity to service consumers.

**reference architecture**

A reference architecture is the generalized architecture of several end systems that share one or more common domains. The reference architecture defines the infrastructure common to the end systems and the interfaces of components that will be included in the end systems. The reference architecture is then instantiated to create a software architecture of a specific system. The definition of the reference architecture facilitates deriving and extending new software architectures for classes of systems. A reference architecture, therefore, plays a dual role with regard to specific target software architectures. First, it generalizes and extracts common functions and configurations. Second, it provides a base for instantiating target systems that use that common base more reliably and cost effectively.

**registry**

Authoritative, centrally controlled store of information.

**requester agent**

A software agent that wishes to interact with a provider agent in order to request that a task be performed on behalf of its owner — the requester entity.

**requester entity**

The person or organization that wishes to use a provider entity's Web service.

**safe**

Property of an interaction which does not have any significance of taking an action other than retrieval of information.

**security administration**

Configuring, securing and/or deploying of systems or applications enabling a security domain.

**security architecture**

A plan and set of principles for an administrative domain and its security domains that describe the security services that a system is required to provide to meet the needs of its users, the system elements required to implement the services, and the performance levels required in the elements to deal with the threat environment. A complete security architecture for a system addresses administrative security, communication security, computer security, emanations security, personnel security, and physical security, and prescribes security policies for each. A complete security architecture needs to deal with both intentional, intelligent threats and accidental threats. A security architecture should explicitly evolve over time as an integral part of its administrative domain's evolution.

**security auditing**

A service that reliably and securely records security-related events producing an audit trail enabling the reconstruction and examination of a sequence of events. Security events could include authentication events, policy enforcement decisions, and others. The resulting audit trail may be used to detect attacks, confirm compliance with policy, deter abuse, or other purposes.

**security domain**

An environment or context that is defined by security models and a security architecture, including a set of resources and set of system entities that are authorized to access the resources. One or more security domains may reside in a single administrative domain. The traits defining a given security domain typically evolve over time.

**security mechanism**

A process (or a device incorporating such a process) that can be used in a system to implement a security service that is provided by or within the system.

**security model**

A schematic description of a set of entities and relationships by which a specified set of security services are provided by or within a system.

**security policy**

A set of rules and practices that specify or regulate how a system or organization provides security services to protect resources. Security policies are components of security architectures. Significant portions of security policies are implemented via security services, using security policy expressions.

**security policy expression**

A mapping of principal identities and/or attributes thereof with allowable actions. Security policy expressions are often essentially access control lists.

**security service**

A processing or communication service that is provided by a system to give a specific kind of protection to resources, where said resources may reside with said system or reside with other systems, for example, an authentication service or a PKI-based document attribution and authentication service. A security service is a superset of AAA services. Security services typically implement portions of security policies and are implemented via security mechanisms.

**self-healing**

When applications are created by composing dynamically discovered components that are owned by multiple organizations, the ability of the system to rediscover and bind to working services when services fail is critical.

**service**

A service is an abstract resource that represents a capability of performing tasks that form a coherent functionality from the point of view of providers entities and requesters entities. To be used, a service must be realized by a concrete provider agent.

**service description**

A service description is a set of documents that describe the interface to and semantics of a service.

**service interface**

A service interface is the abstract boundary that a service exposes. It defines the types of messages and the message exchange patterns that are involved in interacting with the service, together with any conditions implied by those messages.

**service intermediary**

A service intermediary is a Web service whose main role is to transform messages in a value-added way. (From a messaging point of view, an intermediary processes messages en route from one agent to another.) Specifically, we say that a service intermediary is a service whose outgoing messages are equivalent to its incoming messages in some application-defined sense.

**service role**

An abstract set of tasks that is identified to be relevant by a person or organization offering a service. Service roles are also associated with particular aspects of messages exchanged with a service.

**service semantics**

The semantics of a service is the behavior expected when interacting with the service. The semantics expresses a contract (not necessarily a legal contract) between the provider entity and the requester entity. It expresses the effect of invoking the service. A service semantics may be formally described in a machine readable form, identified but not formally defined, or informally defined via an out of band agreement between the provider and the requester entity.

**service-oriented architecture**

A set of components which can be invoked, and whose interface descriptions can be published and discovered.

**session**

A lasting interaction between system entities, often involving a user, typified by the maintenance of some state of the interaction for the duration of the interaction.

Such an interaction may not be limited to a single connection between the system entities.

**SOAP (Simple Object Access Protocol)**

The formal set of conventions governing the format and processing rules of a SOAP message. These conventions include the interactions among SOAP nodes generating and accepting SOAP messages for the purpose of exchanging information along a SOAP message path.

**SOAP application**

A software entity that produces, consumes or otherwise acts upon SOAP messages in a manner conforming to the SOAP processing model.

**SOAP binding**

The formal set of rules for carrying a SOAP message within or on top of another protocol (underlying protocol) for the purpose of exchange. Examples of SOAP bindings include carrying a SOAP message within an HTTP entity-body, or over a TCP stream.

**SOAP body**

A collection of zero or more element information items targeted at an ultimate SOAP receiver in the SOAP message path.

**SOAP envelope**

The outermost element information item of a SOAP message.

**SOAP fault**

A SOAP element information item which contains fault information generated by a SOAP node.

**SOAP feature**

An extension of the SOAP messaging framework typically associated with the exchange of messages between communicating SOAP nodes. Examples of features include "reliability," "security," "correlation," "routing," and the concept of message exchange patterns.

**SOAP header**

A collection of zero or more SOAP header blocks each of which might be targeted at any SOAP receiver within the SOAP message path.

**SOAP header block**

An element information item used to delimit data that logically constitutes a single computational unit within the SOAP header. The type of a SOAP header block is identified by the fully qualified name of the header block element information item.

**SOAP intermediary**

A SOAP intermediary is both a SOAP receiver and a SOAP sender and is targetable from within a SOAP message. It processes the SOAP header blocks targeted at it and acts to forward a SOAP message towards an ultimate SOAP receiver.

**SOAP message**

The basic unit of communication between SOAP nodes.

**SOAP message exchange pattern (MEP)**

A template for the exchange of SOAP messages between SOAP nodes enabled by one or more underlying SOAP protocol bindings. A SOAP MEP is an example of a SOAP feature.

**SOAP message path**

The set of SOAP nodes through which a single SOAP message passes. This includes the initial SOAP sender, zero or more SOAP intermediaries, and an ultimate SOAP receiver.

**SOAP node**

The embodiment of the processing logic necessary to transmit, receive, process and/or relay a SOAP message, according to the set of conventions defined by this recommendation. A SOAP node is responsible for enforcing the rules that govern the exchange of SOAP messages. It accesses the services provided by the underlying protocols through one or more SOAP bindings.

**SOAP receiver**

A SOAP node that accepts a SOAP message.

**SOAP role**

A SOAP node's expected function in processing a message. A SOAP node can act in multiple roles.

**SOAP sender**

A SOAP node that transmits a SOAP message.

**state**

A set of attributes representing the properties of a component at some point in time.

**synchronous**

An interaction is said to be synchronous when the participating agents must be available to receive and process the associated messages from the time the interaction is initiated until all messages are actually received or some failure condition is determined. The exact meaning of "available to receive the message" depends on the characteristics of the participating agents (including the transfer protocol it uses); it may, but does not necessarily, imply tight time synchronization, blocking a thread, etc.

**system entity**

An active element of a computer/network system. For example, an automated process or set of processes, a subsystem, a person or group of persons that incorporates a distinct set of functionality.

**transaction**

Transaction is a feature of the architecture that supports the coordination of results or operations on state in a multi-step interaction. The fundamental characteristic of a transaction is the ability to join multiple actions into the same unit of work, such that the actions either succeed or fail as a unit.

**ultimate SOAP receiver**

The SOAP receiver that is a final destination of a SOAP message. It is responsible for processing the contents of the SOAP body and any SOAP header blocks targeted at it. In some circumstances, a SOAP message might not reach an ultimate SOAP receiver, for example because of a problem at a SOAP intermediary. An ultimate SOAP receiver cannot also be a SOAP intermediary for the same SOAP message.

**usage auditing**

Service that reliably and securely records usage-related events producing an audit trail enabling the reconstruction and examination of a sequence of events. Usage events could include resource allocation events and resource freeing events.

**Web service**

There are many things that might be called "Web services" in the world at large. However, for the purpose of this Working Group and this architecture, and without prejudice toward other definitions, we will use the following definition:

A Web service is a software system designed to support interoperable machine-to-machine interaction over a network. It has an interface described in a machine-processable format (specifically WSDL). Other systems interact with the Web service in a manner prescribed by its description using SOAP-messages, typically conveyed using HTTP with an XML serialization in conjunction with other Web-related standards.

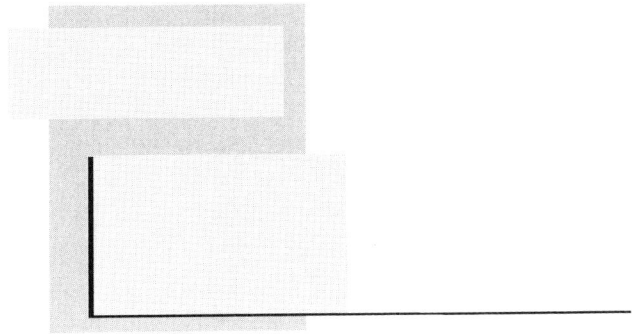

# Resources

Here are resources, services, documentation, and other sources of knowledge available to you.

The XQuery specification

http://www.w3.org/XML/Query

An introduction to XQuery

http://www-106.ibm.com/developerworks/xml/library/x-xquery.html

The XPath 2.0 specification separately from XQuery

http://www.w3.org/TR/xpath20/

A community of software architects and developers that share XQuery tips, techniques, and news

http://www.xquerynow.com

Groups working to extend the SQL standard for XML operations:

The SQLX Group (http://www.swlx.org),

INCITS H2 group (http://www.incits.org/tc_home/h2.htm),

ISO/IEC JTC1/SC32/WG3's (http://metadata-standards.org)

XQEngine is an open-source Java component for querying XML documents

http://www.fatdog.com/

XQuery Normalizer and Static Analyzer (XQNSTA) is a Java API and GUI for normalizing and computing the static type of XQuery expressions

http://www.alphaworks.ibm.com/tech/xqnsta

Free open-source test tool, TestMaker, now includes an XQuery engine for parsing Web Service responses

http://www.pushtotest.com

TigerLogic is a commercial XML database and XQuery engine

http://www.tigerlogic.com

MarkLogic is a commercial content management system using XQuery

http://xqzone.marklogic.com/

Xperanto searches XML documents, flat files, and spreadsheets

http://www.almaden.ibm.com/software/dm/Xperanto/index.shtml

JSR 225- The XQuery API for Java

http://www.jcp.org/en/jsr/detail?id=225

XQuery Test Suite is a proposed test suite for XQuery from IBM and Microsoft.

http://xw2k.sdct.itl.nist.gov/BRADY/xmlquery/testSuite/NIST/files/readme.html

The XSLT specification is a standard for transforming data.

http://www.w3.org/Style/XSL

Free open-source test tool, TestMaker, now includes an XQuery engine for parsing Web Service responses

http://www.pushtotest.com

TigerLogic is a commercial XML database and XQuery engine

http://www.rainingdata.com/products/tl

### *Articles on SOA performance and scalability testing.*

The "FastSOA Performance Kit," http://www.xquerynow.com/library/fastsoa provides a methodology, test platform, and results analysis technique to evaluate SOA performance and scalability.

Web Services Performance Benchmark study is available from the PushToTest Web site for free.

http://www.pushtotest.com/Downloads/kits/soakit.html

Java Testing and Design: From Unit Tests to Automated Web Tests
http://thebook.pushtotest.com

*Performance Testing SOAP Applications* article at
http://www-128.ibm.com/developerworks/webservices/library/ws-testsoap/

*Discover SOAP encoding's impact on Web service performance* article at
http://www-128.ibm.com/developerworks/webservices/library/ws-soapenc/

### *Articles on XQuery.*

*Debunking XQuery Myths and Misunderstandings* article at
http://www-128.ibm.com/developerworks/xml/library/x-xqmyth.html

Introduction to XQuery
http://www-106.ibm.com/developerworks/xml/library/x-xquery.html

### *Articles on native XML databases*

Ronald Bourret's XML Database Guide is at
http://www.rpbourret.com/xml/XMLDatabaseProds.htm

Simple Object Access Protocol specification at
http://www.w3.org/TR/2003/REC-soap12-part0-20030624

Web Services Description Language specification at
http://www.w3.org/TR/wsdl

Apache Axis project for an open-source SOAP stack at
http://ws.apache.org/axis

Streaming XML Parsers (StAX) at
http://dev2dev.bea.com/xml/stax.html (StAX)

XML Binding Compiler at
http://java.sun.com/developer/technicalArticles/WebServices/jaxb

Document Object Model (DOM) description at
http://www.webopedia.com/TERM/D/DOM.html

Kawa/Qexo is an open-source XQuery engine
http://www.gnu.org/software/kawa/

# Index

## Q



## R



## S

## U



## V



## W